ART AT AUCTION 1975–76

The Birth of Christ and the Annunciation to the Shepherds
A miniature by the Dresden Master from a Flemish Book of Hours with 84 large miniatures, [Ghent or Bruges, *circa* 1510]
London £370,000($666,000). 5.VII.76

ART AT AUCTION

The Year at Sotheby Parke Bernet

1975–76

Two hundred and forty-second season

RIZZOLI INTERNATIONAL · SOTHEBY PARKE BERNET

© Sotheby Parke Bernet Publications Ltd, 1976

First published 1976 jointly by
Sotheby Parke Bernet Publications Ltd
81 Adams Drive, Totowa, New Jersey 07512
and
Rizzoli International Publications Inc
712 Fifth Avenue, New York, N.Y. 10019
Library of Congress Catalog Card Number 76-14702

Edited by Anne Jackson
assisted by Joan Sarll (UK) and Barbara Evans (USA)

Production by Peter Ling
Layouts by Martin Ashley

All rights reserved, including the right to reproduce this book,
or portions thereof, in any form

ISBN: 0 85667 030 8

Printed in Great Britain by Jolly & Barber Ltd, Rugby, Warwickshire
Bound in Great Britain by W & J Mackay Ltd, Chatham, Kent

Endpaper illustration:
A view of the interior of the Lutheran Church, Amsterdam, where the
Geus van den Heuvel sale took place, from a contemporary engraving

Contents

9	*Amsterdam: three centuries of collecting* by Willem A. van Geffen
19	Old Master Paintings
36	Old Master Drawings
48	*William Alexander and Lord MacCartney's Embassy to China* by Dudley Snelgrove
55	English Paintings and Drawings
64	*Rosa Bonheur and Sir Edwin Landseer: a study in mutual admiration* by Jeremy Maas
86	European Paintings
98	Topographical Paintings
100	South African Paintings
104	Canadian Paintings
106	*The Sale of the Geraldine Rockefeller Dodge Collection* by Jerry E. Patterson
122	American Paintings and Sculpture
128	Impressionist and Modern Paintings, Drawings and Sculpture
146	*Diaghilev in Monte Carlo* by Julian Barran
166	Contemporary Art
175	Prints
189	Manuscripts and Printed Books
194	*An unrecorded Flemish Book of Hours* by Christopher de Hamel
200	*The Botanical Library formed by the late Arpad Plesch* by Wilfrid Blunt
235	Works of Art
252	Icons
256	Russian Works of Art
260	Objects of Vertu
268	*Baths, Baroque and Bavaria* by T. H. Clarke
276	Portrait Miniatures
279	Silver and Pewter
292	*'Thou Sheer, Immaculate and Silver Fountain'* by John Culme

An eighteenth-century German *nécessaire de voyage* in silver-gilt and Meissen, Augsburg, 1749-51
Monte Carlo Fr550,000(£65,476:$117,857). 24.VI.76
From the collection of Iya, Lady Abdy

Contents *continued*

- 303 Arms, Armour and Militaria
- 307 Coins and Medals
- 311 Antiquities, Indian, Tibetan and Tribal Art
- 323 Islamic Works of Art
- 326 *Islamic Week Sale of Carpets* by Donald King
- 343 Chinese Ceramics and Works of Art
- 365 Japanese Ceramics and Works of Art
- 377 European Ceramics
- 378 *The Milton Milestone Collection of early Wedgwood* by Bruce Tattersall
- 404 *Oriental Ceramics and English studio pottery* by Ian Bennett
- 409 Furniture, Decorations and Textiles
- 438 *Victorian stained glass and decorative design* by Martin Harrison
- 443 Clocks, Watches and Scientific Instruments
- 451 Musical Instruments
- 455 Art Nouveau and Art Deco
- 459 Jewellery
- 473 Glass and Paperweights
- 479 Wine Sales
- 481 Photographs
- 483 Collectors' Sales
- 486 Index

Note:
The prices given throughout this book are the hammer prices, exclusive of any buyer's premium or sales tax which may have been applicable in any of the salerooms.

Due to the fluctuation in exchange rates during the season the conversion between different currencies has been calculated at two average rates. While providing an adequate guide the sterling or dollar equivalents in brackets after the actual sale prices do not necessarily conform with the exact exchange rate applying on the date of sale.

The following average rates in relation to the pound sterling have been used throughout:

	1975 (September-December)	1976 (January-July)
US Dollars	2	1.8
Canadian Dollars	2	1.8
French Francs	9	8.4
Swiss Francs	5.5	4.5
Dutch Gilders	5.4	4.9
Italian Lire	1500	1500
South African Rand	1.55	1.55

Amsterdam: three centuries of collecting

Willem A. van Geffen

On 26 and 27 April 1976, under the chalk-white, domed ceiling of the Round Lutheran Church on an Amsterdam canal, one of Holland's last great private collections was auctioned: the Bas de Geus van den Heuvel collection. By the time Sotheby Mak van Waay's managing director, Jan Pieter Glerum, standing under the eighteenth-century 12-metre high church organ, had brought the hammer down for the last time around midnight, 379 paintings, watercolours and etchings had changed hands for the total amount of Fl14,400,000: an all time auction record for the Low Countries.

The Geus van den Heuvel collection contained a choice selection of the greatest names from over three centuries of Dutch painting. Among them were seventeenth-century artists such as Adriaen van Ostade, Salomon van Ruysdael, Jan Steen, Albert Cuyp and Willem van de Velde, the younger. The eighteenth century was well represented by Isaac Ouwater and Jan de Beijer; the Romantic school by Hermanus and B. C. Koekkoek, Schelfhout and Springer; the Hague school and the Amsterdam Impressionists by Jongkind, Isaäc Israëls, Jacob and Willem Maris.

The highest price fetched was Fl660,000 for a peasant scene by Adriaen van Ostade. In 1656, two years after van Ostade painted this work a contemporary, colleague and Amsterdam collector, no less a person than Rembrandt Harmenzoon van Rijn, was declared insolvent. His possessions had to be put up for auction. When catalogued, approximately seventy-five paintings and many portfolios of drawings by Rembrandt and works by such artists as Anthony van Dyck, Rubens, Adriaen Brouwer, Hercules Seghers and Simon de Vlieger, as well as a collection of arms, jewellery, Venetian glass and valuable fabrics were estimated at Fl17,400. The actual sale, however, which today would be the dream of any auction house in the world, then totalled only Fl5,000. In 1976, by comparison, a small etching by Rembrandt (a self-portrait of 1638 measuring only 13.5cm by 10.5cm) alone fetched Fl29,000 at the Geus van den Heuvel auction.

Not surprisingly there have been strong links between the great Amsterdam collectors and the city's auction houses since the seventeenth century. In 1647, one year before the end of the Eighty Years' War between the Netherlands and Spain, Amsterdam's burgomasters commissioned Philip Vingboons, masterbuilder, to construct the Oude-Zyds Heerenlogement (literally, gentlemen's lodgings) on the Grimburgwal. This stately hall with its impressive lines took over the function of the Princenhof on the Oude-Zyds Voor-Burchwal, accommodating important visitors to

PIETER PIETERSZ. BRUEGHEL
The inn of St Michel
On panel, signed and dated 1619, 19¾in by 26in
Fl280,000(£57,143: $102,857)

JAN JANSZ. VAN DER HEYDEN
A view in a Dutch town
On panel, signed with monogram, 13¾in by 15¼in
Fl316,000(£64,490: $116,082)

AMSTERDAM: THREE CENTURIES OF COLLECTING 11

ADRIAEN JANSZ. VAN OSTADE
The interior of an inn
On panel, signed and dated 1654, 17½in by 14¾in
Fl660,000(£134,694:$242,449)

The paintings illustrated on these two pages are from the collection of the late Bas de Geus van den Heuvel sold in Amsterdam on 26 April 1976

the city of Amsterdam. Here the city council received its guests, among whom were Tsar Peter the Great and William of Orange, later King of England, in a beautifully-decorated state room in the 'Logement'. In this room were displayed valuables, textiles and jewellery which had been put up for auction, as was already the custom in other town inns. Clearly, when influential names were lacking on the guest-list, the Heerenlogement was used for other activities. The auctions, however, were not held within the building but in its courtyard. Outside, all the year round, bonds, houses and other properties were auctioned and sold by order of the authorities. Much later the Heerenlogement was to be used solely for auctioneering, but in the seventeenth century its dual role of guest-house and saleroom was symbolic of a time when art dealing and the auction world were not yet separate entities.

Though art dealers were officially part of the same guild as booksellers and printers its members did not monopolise the trade. Jewellers, florists, brewers, bakers and butchers also busied themselves with art dealing. As the market-place was often, literally, the only place where the artist could acquaint the general public with his work, the sale of works of art originally took place in the open air. In this respect Amsterdam was in good company: Antwerp held its Friday market and Paris its Foire de St Germain which lasted for two months each year until 1786, offering a great range of paintings and prints. In Amsterdam the city councillors leased the right to hold sales to the highest bidder and the St Lucas Guild, that of the painters, watched over the auctions. No public auction was permitted without the presence of the warden of the Guild and sale catalogues were checked by the Guild's officials. This supervision was essential as signatures were widely faked in the seventeenth century. If an artist fell out of fashion his name or monogram was often replaced without scruple by that of another more popular. No qualms were felt about identifying the work of a pupil or even a copy with the master's name. As many seventeenth-century 'regents'[1] preferred to collect the works of Italian painters rather than those of their compatriots Dutch masters frequently came under the hammer (or 'rod', as was used at that time) as Italian.

However, if the signatures were not always to be trusted, in other respects the auction house was bound by the strictest rules. In seventeenth-century Amsterdam there were about eighty conditions of sale. Buyers were forbidden to call each other names, to insult or injure one another, or to damage articles which had been sold. The fine for such behaviour was Fl3. It was, furthermore, strictly forbidden for dealers to form rings to influence a sale and for this offenders risked a fine of Fl10.

Some painters were also dealers and collectors, and many of the dealers formed their own collections. The well-known regent (patrician) families were foremost among the collectors of works of art, but often after the death of the senior members, the family collection ended up in the saleroom. In seventeenth- and eighteenth-century sale catalogues the names of such patrician families as the van Marselis, the Witsens, the Valckeniers, the Rendorps and the Six frequently appear. In 1704, at the death of Pieter Six of the influential cloth-dyeing, regent and burgomaster family, a great many of his pictures were auctioned. Half a century earlier another member of the Six family, the thirty-five year old Jan Six (sixteen times burgomaster of Amsterdam) had tried to save Rembrandt from bankruptcy by lending him an amount of Fl1,082.

[1] A regent was an influential citizen, often head of a charitable organisation such as an almshouse.

AMSTERDAM: THREE CENTURIES OF COLLECTING 13

Some early art dealing taking place in the courtyard of Amsterdam's first auction house, the Oude-Zyds Heerenlogement, as depicted in an eighteenth-century engraving

14 AMSTERDAM: THREE CENTURIES OF COLLECTING

A pair of Dutch parcel-gilt tazzas, maker's mark *VDH*, attributed to Abraham van den Hecken, Amsterdam, *circa* 1600, diameter 7¾in
Amsterdam Fl152,000(£31,020:$55,836). 24.II.76
From the collection of the Lutheran Church, Amsterdam

Private possessions brought to the saleroom sometimes numbered a hundred or more paintings at a time, although the value of the individual works varied widely. In April 1728, for instance, 106 pictures, the complete collection of the Amsterdam gold and silversmith, Anthony Grill, were offered for sale by auction. In 1720, eight years before his death, Anthony Grill and his wife, Elizabeth, had given the Lutheran Church a pair of silver-gilt tazzas attributed to the Flemish-German goldsmith, Abraham van den Hecken. More than two and a half centuries later these reappeared among the possessions of the Lutheran Church and on 24 February 1976 were sold at Sotheby Mak van Waay.

No seventeenth- or eighteenth-century Amsterdam auction can compare with that of the complete collection of the amateur artist and collector, Gerrit Braamkamp, whose accumulation of no less than 316 pictures in his fine house 'Swedenryck' on the Heerengracht, attracted the pilgrimage of many foreign art lovers. Taking place on 31 July 1771 and comprising works by virtually all the great Dutch seventeenth-century masters, it fetched in total the then unheard-of sum of Fl252,833. One buyer who was particularly unlucky with her purchases was the Russian Empress. She had ordered the *Lying-in Room* by Gerard Dou and the *Ox-driver* by Paulus Potter, among other works, to be bought on her behalf for the Hermitage, but the ship that transported the newly acquired treasures to St Petersburg sank.

Many Dutch works of art disappeared abroad in the late seventeenth and especially in the eighteenth centuries, when the number of auctions greatly increased. Not only the Russian, but also the English, French, Polish and German courts eagerly took advantage of the large number of Dutch paintings on offer. Hundreds of masterpieces (often assembled by Amsterdam collectors) found their way into foreign collections. One of the numerous small German princes, Wilhelm VIII of Hesse-Kassel, acquired several collections through the Dutch painter-dealer, Philip van Dyk. When the latter died in 1753, his estate of 163 Old Masters also went abroad.

Royal families not only collected works of art but sold them at auction as well. In 1713, the collection of William III, King of England, who had died eleven years previously was put up for sale and realised Fl43,875. At the end of the Seven Years' War, in May 1765, the Elector of Saxony attracted much attention by auctioning his collection of 155 paintings in Amsterdam. It made a total of Fl54,000; a Leonardo da Vinci reaching Fl3,000, but Dutch masters obtaining only very modest prices.

Towards the end of the eighteenth century, when the effects of the French Revolution were being felt throughout Europe, the auctions held in Amsterdam turned over much larger sums of money than in the preceding decades. French domination, however, subsequently ruined the market, as the Dutch adopted French culture at an alarming rate, and the value of their own works of art fell accordingly. This can best be illustrated in that an English clockmaker was able to exchange his timepieces at the rate of one per painting, for the works of the seventeenth-century artist, Albert Cuyp, in the latter's own birthplace, Dordrecht.

The first nineteenth-century Jan Six (1756-1827), son of a regent, not wishing to stay in Amsterdam while it was governed by the French, went into voluntary exile at his country estate in Hillegom, taking with him the treasured portraits of his family, among which was the world-celebrated portrait by Rembrandt of the former Jan Six. Yet another Jan Six married Lucretia Johanna van Winter, daughter of the great Dutch collector, who died in 1815. Half the famous van Winter collection became added to that of the Six; the other half, including two Rembrandts, was finally sold to the Rothschilds, creating the basis of one of their earliest collections.

In 1839, when the first steam engine rumbled through the polders between Amsterdam and Haarlem, Simon Jacob Mak van Waay stood in top-boots in his Dordrecht garden selling shrubs and canaries at his first auction! Subsequently, a greater awareness of the value of antiques led to the first modest spring and autumn antique auctions.

While the Romantic artist Andreas Schelfhout was paid by having his clients cover his winter scenes with golden ten-guilder pieces, the Netherlands were rapidly selling off their heritage. Occasionally big auctions attracted particular attention as in 1848, when in the uncertain climate of western Europe, the Netherland's King William I

ROELANT JACOBSZ. SAVERIJ
A peasant wedding
On panel, signed and dated 1615,
18½in by 12in
Amsterdam Fl340,000
(£69,387:$124,897). 26.III.76
This painting and the one facing
are from the collection of the late
Bas de Geus van den Heuvel

rid himself of part of his collection. On that occasion, the London dealer, Mawson, shipped the most expensive of the King's Rubens (Fl 18,000) across the channel, together with an Anthony van Dyck which made an auction record of Fl63,600. Mawson also obtained Rembrandt's portrait of Jan Pellicorn for Fl30,200 and Hobbema's *Watermill* for Fl27,000. A self-portrait by Rembrandt found favour in an English buyer's eyes at Fl3,750.

The year 1885 saw the birth in Amsterdam of two aspiring collectors. They were never to meet but each was to make history in the collecting and auctioneering world. Their names were Willem J. R. Dreesman and Bas de Geus van den Heuvel. The first was the son of Anton C. R. Dreesman, founder of the chain of department stores 'Vroom and Dreesman' and at the same time the founder of a collection of clocks and paintings. Willem Dreesman developed his father's hobby and became a serious collector. He started a brilliant collection of silver and porcelain at his home in the Johannes Vermeerstreet and translated his love of Amsterdam into a magnificent collection of paintings, clocks and silver depicting typically local subjects or bearing makers' marks or signatures which related to the city.

Bas de Geus van den Heuvel's fortune was totally different. In the early 1930s, the brothers Bas and Klaas sold their building contractors' business and decided to enjoy life and their money. Bas was reminded by his brother of his earlier frequent visits to the Rijksmuseum and followed his advice not only to look at paintings, but to *buy* them as well. The world of sand and cement quickly made way for a new world of auction rooms and art galleries.

At that time Europe was suffering from the effects of financial depression and so little money was available for art that the auction house, Frederik Muller, in Amsterdam was giving away a second Romantic master to anyone who purchased a first. For a few thousand guilders it was also possible to buy a reasonable seventeenth-century work. In 1932 Mak van Waay sold an Isaäc Israëls for Fl575 and the Amsterdam

JOHAN BARTHOLD
JONGKIND
A river landscape near Overschie
Signed and dated 1866,
13in by 48¾in
Amsterdam Fl155,000
(£75,950:$136,710).
27.III.76

Impressionist, Breitner, was barely managing to achieve a hundred guilders for his best canvasses. In the same year Bas de Geus van den Heuvel bought *A peasant wedding* by Roèlant Saverij at Muller's for Fl3,000 which, at the recent sale of his collection, achieved the astonishing sum of Fl340,000. In November 1940, at the same auctioneers, he acquired a beautiful canal scene by the eighteenth-century painter Isaac Ouwater for Fl400 (at the recent sale it fetched Fl210,000). This canvas (see illustration p. 86) was one of the earliest and the most important among his collection of views of the city of Amsterdam, and he was to wait another twenty years before managing to acquire his second and third Ouwaters from the Dreesman collection.

Willem Dreesman died in 1955 and his heirs (seven children in all) were not able to sell his collection to the city of Amsterdam, even for a price far below its true market value. The city had just completed several major purchases from the collection of the art dealer-collector, Regnault, and claimed that it had no further funds available. Dreesman's children decided to put the collection up for auction. To their astonishment, the city then bought a number of the works for a sum exceeding that which they had been asked to pay for the entire collection.

Bas de Geus van den Heuvel followed the Dreesman example. During his lifetime he determined that his whole collection should be auctioned after his death: 'I do not believe in creating a private museum that attracts perhaps a few dozen visitors a year, neither do I believe in a donation to a state or city museum. They might hang ten per cent of my collection and spirit the rest away into a cellar. I have enjoyed my pictures. Now let others have their turn.'

The catalogue of the collection was prepared and printed in the early '60s in the deepest secrecy. The printer knew the client only as 'Mr X' and the whole edition was hidden in a safe in 1963. Mr X survived his catalogue by thirteen years and the art dealing world then prepared itself for the greatest battle in the history of Amsterdam auctioneering.

The interior of the Lutheran Church, Amsterdam, where the collection of the late Bas de Geus van den Heuvel was auctioned

The auction-tournament lasted two days and surpassed the boldest expectations. On the first evening the first seventy lots exceeded Fl6,000,000, one and a half million more than the estimated total for the seventeenth-century works. The whole yield for this category, plus a small group of eighteenth-century works, was no less than Fl8,000,000. On the second day, many international auction records were broken as a torrent of unbelievable prices astonished the 800 or 900 hopeful buyers from seven countries: the Netherlands, Belgium, England, France, Germany, Switzerland and the United States of America. The highest price for an Amsterdam Impressionist was achieved by a view of the city by George Hendrik Breitner (illustrated p. 96). An Isaäc Israëls, *Girls sorting coffee*, bought in 1958 by Bas de Geus van den Heuvel from the Regnault collection for the record price at that time of Fl24,000, went for Fl155,000 (illustrated p. 97). A Jongkind of skaters on the River Merwede near Dordrecht, dated 1870, was bid up to Fl140,000; a second Jongkind, *A river landscape near Overschie*, to Fl155,000. A Jacob Maris of two windmills exceeded both at Fl160,000 (illustrated p. 97).

Possibly the greatest irony of this memorable sale was that the two works by Ouwater, which Bas de Geus van den Heuvel had purchased at the sale of Willem Dreesman's collection in 1960, were bought back by one of Dreesman's sons. Thus the circle had been completed.

Paintings, Drawings and Sculpture

19   OLD MASTER PAINTINGS
36   OLD MASTER DRAWINGS
55   ENGLISH PAINTINGS, DRAWINGS AND SCULPTURE
86   EUROPEAN PAINTINGS
98   TOPOGRAPHICAL PAINTINGS
100 SOUTH AFRICAN PAINTINGS
104 CANADIAN PAINTINGS
122 AMERICAN PAINTINGS AND SCULPTURE
128 IMPRESSIONIST PAINTINGS, DRAWINGS AND SCULPTURE
166 CONTEMPORARY ART

BARTOLOMMEO DI FRUOSINO
The Crucifixion
On panel, 11¼in by 18½in
New York $40,000(£22,222). 22.I.76

20 OLD MASTER PAINTINGS

PELLEGRINO DA MARIANO
Madonna and Child
On panel, 30in by 19¾in
Florence L10,000,000(£6,666:$13,332). 18.XII.75

MASTER OF THE MAGDALEN LEGEND
Portrait of a man
On panel, 15½in by 11in
New York $26,000(£14,444). 16.VI.76

MARIOTTO ALBERTINELLI and GIULIANO BUGIARDINI
The Virgin and Child with saints
On panel, 38¼in by 37¼in
London £20,000($36,000). 7.VII.76

FRANCO-FLEMISH SCHOOL, FIFTEENTH CENTURY
The Virgin and Child with saints and a donor
On panel, 17½in by 12¾in
London £6,200($11,160). 7.VII.76
From the collection of Mrs H. Pazofsky

TIZIANO VECELLIO called TITIAN
Portrait of a gentleman
48in by 38¼in
London £72,000($129,600). 24.III.76

OLD MASTER PAINTINGS 23

ADRIAEN YSENBRANT
St Barbara and St Mary Magdalen
The wings of a triptych, on panel, 33in by 11½in each
New York $100,000(£55,555). 22.I.76
From the collection of the late Harriet Jonas

HENDRIK AVERCAMP
A winter scene
On panel, signed in monogram, 16¼in by 23½in
London £25,000($45,000). 7.VII.76

JAN BRUEGHEL THE ELDER
A river landscape
On metal, 12¾in by 16in
London £73,000($146,000).
10.XII.75
From the collection of the late
Isidore Ostrer

DAVID TENIERS THE YOUNGER
Peasants playing bowls outside an inn
On panel, signed, 10¾in by 14½in
London £23,000($41,400). 7.VII.76

NS BOL
story of Venus and
onis
uache on paper laid
vn on panel, signed
dated 1589, 8in by 10in
v York $39,000(£19,500).
II.75
m the collection of the late
Charles E. Dunlap

FRANS POST
A view in Brazil with the ruined cathedral of Olinda
On panel, signed, 17$\frac{1}{4}$in by 23$\frac{1}{4}$in
London £75,000($135,000). 10.XII.76

FRANS VAN MIERIS THE ELDER
A lady feeding a parrot
On panel, 8⅞in by 6⅞in
New York $155,000(£77,500). 4.XII.75
From the collection of the late Mrs Charles E. Dunlap

28 OLD MASTER PAINTINGS

JACOBUS LINTHORST
A flower piece
Signed and dated 1793, 40¼in by 34in
London £24,000($43,200). 7.VII.75

PIETER CLAESZ
Still life with a crab
On panel, signed in
monogram and dated
1651, 19¾in by 26¾in
London £15,000($30,000)
10.XII.75

FRANCOIS-HUBERT DROUAIS
A boy with a portfolio
Signed *Drouais le fils 1760*, 23½in by 19¼in
New York $52,500(£26,250). 4.XII.75
From the collection of the late Mrs Charles E. Dunlap

30 OLD MASTER PAINTINGS

GIOVANNI DOMENICO TIEPOLO
The Tiepolo family
Inscribed on the back of the stretcher *Ritratti della Famiglia Tiepolo col Ritratto del pittore Pietro Longhi/Venezia*, 25in by 36½in
London £100,000($180,000). 24.III.76
From the collection of Eva, Countess of Rosebery

GIOVANNI DOMENICO TIEPOLO
The Coronation of the Virgin
39¼in by 29½in
London £80,000($144,000). 24.III.76
From the collection of Eva, Countess of Rosebery

32 OLD MASTER PAINTINGS

FRANCESCO ZUCCARELLI, RA
Peasants and cattle in a landscape
46in by 52in
London £19,500($35,100).
7.VII.76

HENDRIK VAN LINT called STUDIO
A classical landscape with Venus and Apollo
17¾in by 28¼in
London £6,500($11,700). 7.VII.76
From the collection of V. T. Schaerer

OLD MASTER PAINTINGS 33

LUCA CARLEVARIS
Venice: the Piazzetta
37½in by 58in
London £18,500($37,000).
10.XII.75

GIOVANNI PAOLO PANINI
A caprice of Roman monuments
Signed and dated 1735, 49in by 70¼in
London £18,000($32,400). 7.VII.76

34 OLD MASTER PAINTINGS

FRANCESCO GUARDI
Above: *Venice: San Giorgio Maggiore*
Below: *Venice: The Dogana and Santa Maria della Salute*
A pair, each 13in by 19in
London £125,000($225,000). 7.VII.76

MICHELE MARIESCHI
Venice: Santa Maria della Salute
One of a pair, each 22in by 33in
London £28,000($50,400). 7.VII.76

HENDRIK VAN LINT called STUDIO
Rome: the Piazza del Popolo
One of a pair, signed and dated 1750, $18\frac{1}{4}$in by $28\frac{3}{4}$in
London £29,000($52,200). 24.III.76

36 OLD MASTER DRAWINGS

ANDREA MANTEGNA
A bird on a branch pecking at some berries
Pen and brown ink, 104mm by 115mm
London £55,000($99,000). 28.IV.76
From the Gathorne-Hardy Collection

GIUSEPPE PORTA, called IL SALVIATI
A bearded man with his right arm raised
Coloured chalks, 206mm by 262mm
London £29,000($52,200). 28.IV.76
From the Gathorne-Hardy Collection

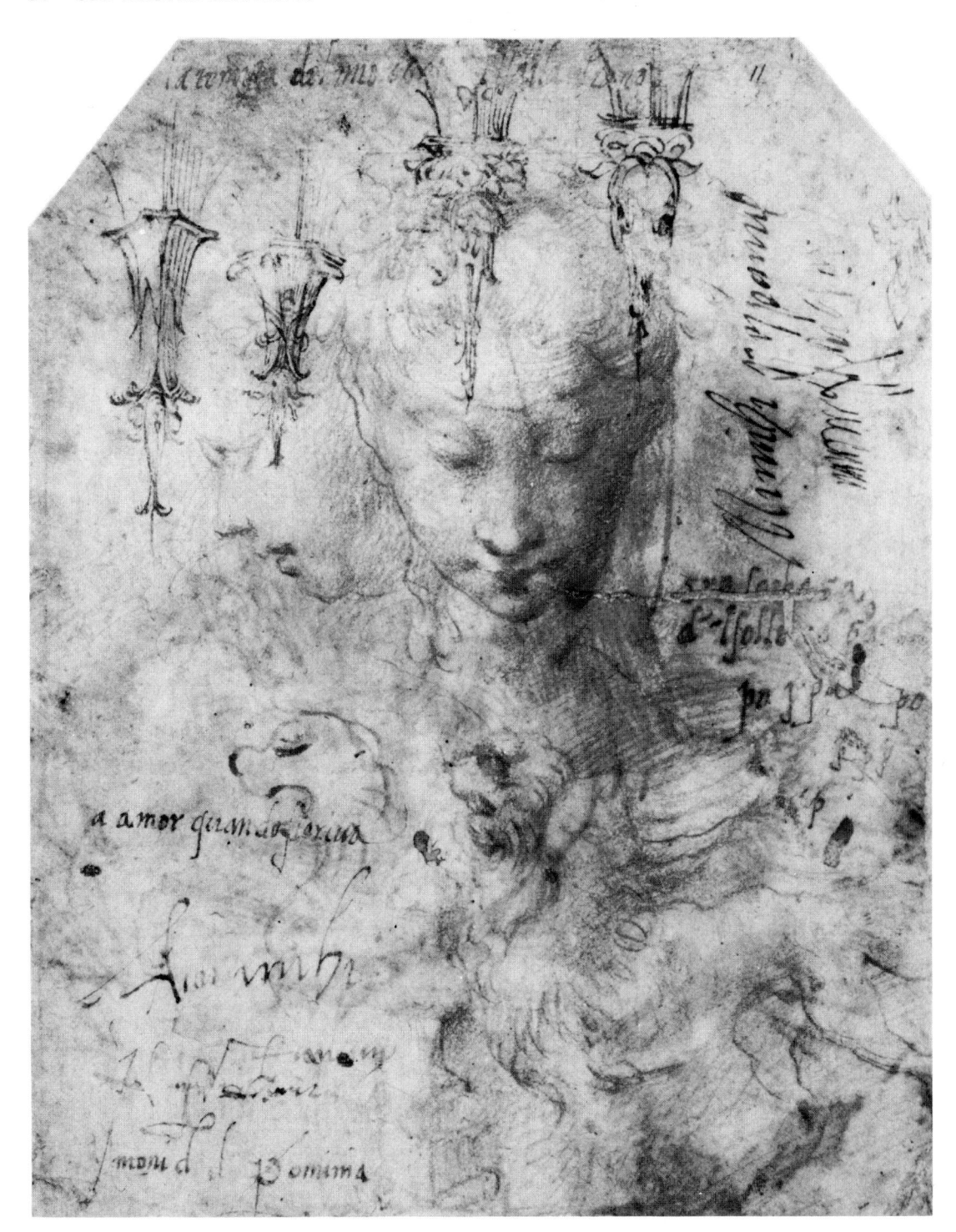

FRANCESCO MARIA MAZZOLA, called IL PARMIGIANINO
Recto: *Studies of female heads, of a winged lion and of finials*
A double-sided drawing, red chalk, pen and brown ink, 188mm by 149mm
London £38,000($68,400). 28.IV.76
From the Gathorne-Hardy Collection

ANDREA MELDOLLA, called LO SCHIAVONE
Doge Francesco Donato attending the mystic marriage of St Catherine
Pen and brown ink and brown and grey wash, heightened with white, 272mm by 317mm
London £25,000($45,000). 28.IV.76

AMICO ASPERTINI
The massacre of the innocents
Red and black chalks and traces of brown ink, heightened with white, 281mm by 426mm
London £15,000($27,000). 28.IV.76

The drawings on this page are from the Gathorne-Hardy Collection

SIR PETER PAUL RUBENS
Christ on the cross
Pen and brown ink and wash over black chalk, heightened with white, 387mm by 202mm
Amsterdam Fl90,000 (£18,334:$33,001). 3.V.76

ABRAHAM BLOEMAERT
Recto: *Studies of an old man's head and hands*
A double-sided drawing, red and black chalk, 190mm by 180mm
Amsterdam Fl29,000(£5,918:$10,653). 3.V.76
From the collection of The Earl Beauchamp

Left
ALLAERT VAN EVERDINGEN
A Norwegian landscape
Pen and brown ink and watercolour, signed, 180mm by 158mm
Amsterdam Fl16,500 (£3,367:$6,060). 3.V.76

Right
ADRIAEN VAN DE VELDE
A seated female nude
Black chalk heightened with white, 305mm by 193mm
Amsterdam Fl16,500 (£3,367:$6,060). 3.V.76

GOVAERT FLINCK
Portrait study of a standing man
Black chalk, heightened with white, 392mm by 240mm
Amsterdam Fl15,000(£2,777:$5,555). 17.XI.75
From the collection of the late Bernard Houthakker

HENDRICK GOLTZIUS
A standing officer, holding a halberd
Pen and brown ink and brown and red wash, 208mm by 158mm
Amsterdam Fl56,000(£11,428:$20,571). 3.V.76

CORNELIS SAFTLEVEN
A camel
Black and reddish-brown chalk and grey wash, signed in monogram *CS* and dated *1646*, 203mm by 310mm
Amsterdam Fl31,000 (£6,326:$11,387). 3.V.76

Right
ALBRECHT DÜRER
The Holy Family beneath a tree
Pen and brown ink, 228mm by 146mm
Amsterdam Fl145,000 (£29,598:$53,276). 3.V.76

Far right
MICHELANGELO BUONARROTI
Recto: *Male nude*
A double-sided drawing, black chalk, 233mm by 100mm
London £42,000($75,600). 28.IV.76

The drawings on this page are from the Gathorne-Hardy Collection

LAMBERT DOOMER
Rebecca and Eliezer at the well
Pen and brown ink and coloured washes, signed and dated *1696*, 263mm by 406mm
Amsterdam Fl25,000(£5,102:$9,183). 3.V.76

HUBERT PIETER SCHOUTEN
The town hall of Amsterdam on the Dam Square
Watercolour, signed and dated 1780, 302mm by 458mm
Amsterdam Fl17,000(£3,148:$6,296). 17.XI.75
From the collection of the late Bernard Houthakker

46 OLD MASTER DRAWINGS

Left
DOMENICO BECCAFUMI
Head of a young man
Tempera and emulsion on paper, 276mm by 210mm
London £21,500($38,700).
5.VII.76

Right
DOMENICO BECCAFUMI
The head of the Madonna
Tempera and emulsion on paper, 246mm by 185mm
London £6,400($11,520).
5.VII.76

JEAN-HONORE FRAGONARD
Le tableau
Pen and brown ink and wash over black chalk, signed, 228mm by 150mm
London £5,500($9,900). 26.III.76

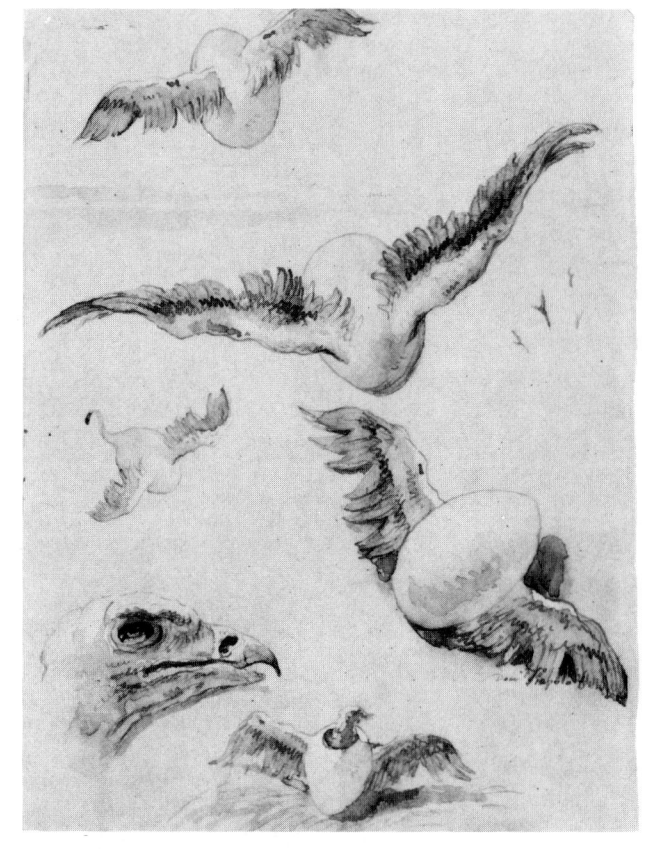

GIOVANNI DOMENICO TIEPOLO
Studies of flying eggs and an eagle emerging from an egg
Pen and brown ink and wash, signed, 245mm by 183mm
London £3,100($6,200). 11.XII.75

OLD MASTER DRAWINGS 47

GIOVANNI DOMENICO TIEPOLO
Venus at the forge of Vulcan
Pen and brown ink and wash over black chalk, 204mm by 380mm
London £5,200($10,400). 11.XII.75
From the collection of Baroness Eugène de Rothschild

GIOVANNI DOMENICO TIEPOLO
A Venetian interior
Pen and brown ink and wash over black chalk, signed, 285mm by 410mm
London £12,000($21,600). 26.III.76

WILLIAM ALEXANDER
Pagoda at Lin-tsin-fou on the banks of the Grand Canal
Watercolour, signed and inscribed and dated *21st Oct 1793* on the mount, 11¼in by 17in
London £3,200($5,760). 1.IV.76

WILLIAM ALEXANDER
The approach of the Emperor of China to receive the British Ambassador on 14 September 1793
Watercolour, signed with initials, 12in by 18in
London £1,700($3,060). 1.IV.76

William Alexander and Lord Macartney's Embassy to China

Dudley Snelgrove

In 1792 it would have been exciting for any young artist to be invited to join a creditable expedition, but twenty-five year old William Alexander must have been highly elated by the honour of his inclusion in Lord Macartney's embassy to China. China at that time was familiar to the Westerner only through the quaintness of costume, custom and landscape depicted on ceramics, furniture and wall decoration, principally distilled through the imagination of artists and decorators from travellers' accounts of the country.

It had become essential, not least for the expansion of commerce in the Orient by the East India Company, to establish a basis of friendly understanding between Great Britain and China which would lead to an interchange of economic and cultural ideas. Previous efforts at trading had been hindered by the harsh restrictions imposed on Europeans and were saved from complete failure only by yielding to the corrupt demands of the powerful Chinese merchants. A diplomatic mission was therefore planned whose aim was to put an end to this harassment and malpractice. The first attempt was made when the Honourable Charles Cathcart was chosen as a potential ambassador and sailed for China in December 1787, but this expedition ended in failure when on reaching Java he became ill with consumption and died there the following June.

Some four years later, Lord Macartney set out with a larger retinue of ninety-five in two ships, the *Lion* and the *Hindostan*, with an escorting frigate. The mission ended in diplomatic failure and general frustration and yet succeeded in broadening the understanding of the China that really existed. The full story has been recorded in diaries and published books, and retold in relevant histories, and needs no lengthy description here.

Macartney's company was composed of carefully chosen diplomats, specialists, soldiers, artisans and musicians. Those concerned with the illustrative requirements were Thomas Hickey, a portrait painter, Lieut Henry Parish to record outlines of coasts and similar data, and William Alexander as draughtsman. Hickey painted two portraits but did little else; Parish, who travelled further into China's mainland than did Alexander, provided some documentary sketches for him to work up for future publication; Sir John Barrow also contributed a few drawings. The mission sailed in September 1792. At Macao they received instructions to proceed to Taku and thence

WILLIAM ALEXANDER
The Hindostan at anchor in the Strait of Mi-a-tau
Watercolour, signed and inscribed and dated *20th July 1793* on the mount, 8¼in by 15in
London £4,200($7,560). 1.IV.76

WILLIAM ALEXANDER
Economy of time and labour exemplified in a Chinese waterman at Han-choo-foo
Watercolour, signed twice with initials and inscribed and dated *12 Nov 1793* on the mount, 7¼in by 9¼in
London £3,200($5,760). 1.IV.76

Right A self-portrait of Alexander wearing an eye-patch. In the collection of the British Museum

Far right Lord Macartney's bookplate from the original folio

to Tientsin, picking up various officials on the way. It was during the final stage from Tientsin that the most difficult obstacle to the success of the venture was presented: Lord Macartney learned that he would be expected to kow-tow before the Emperor Ch'ien-Lung in recognition of him as 'Lord of the World'. As the 'King of Great Britain' sounded to the Earl to be equally, if not more, important, an impasse seemed inevitable. His attitude became even stiffer when a Chinese inscription on a flag flying on his ship was translated as 'Tribute-embassy from Red Barbarians'. Tempers rose when, on arriving at Peking in August 1793, they found that the Emperor was away at his summer palace at Jehol (some six to eight days' journey away) to which they were expected to travel. At Jehol the request for kow-tow was repeated, but this time it was met with a counter demand that a Chinese official of equivalent rank to Macartney should bow to a portrait of George III. Ultimately, the issue was dropped rather than either side should have to concede. When an audience with the Emperor was finally achieved, the party suffered further embarrassment when it became apparent that the gifts they brought on behalf of the King, including clocks, guns and other articles by skilled craftsmen, were greatly inferior when compared with the fine quality of such things already in the palace precincts. However, these difficulties were probably not as much responsible for the failure of the mission as was the general antipathy of the Chinese towards the Europeans.

On the return journey Alexander was disappointed not to be included in the party which travelled overland to Canton; he had to retrace the original route and felt he had been denied the sight of fresh areas of interest. As a result, it was from drawings by Lieut Parish, who had gone with Macartney's party, that he made the very finished versions for Sir George Leonard Staunton's account of the embassy.

The expedition sailed for the long journey home on 9 January 1794 and it may have been during those confined months aboard ship that Alexander made the drawings for the album sold at Sotheby's this year. Its provenance is scanty, but as it contained Macartney's book-plate, it is possible that it was compiled for the Earl's library. The

WILLIAM ALEXANDER
Studies of Imperial infantry soldiers and Chinese watermen
Watercolour, signed with initials and inscribed
(six on two mounts, various sizes)
London £650($1,170). 1.IV.76

volume constituted a splendid survey of every aspect of the expedition and of the works of the industrious draughtsmen on it. Among the drawings of major interest and of the highest quality chosen to be illustrated here, *The Hindostan at anchor in the Straits of Mi-a-tau* would seem the most spontaneous and atmospheric. Alexander travelled in this East Indiaman and probably drew this scene from the shore at Ten-choo-fou. The *Lion*, Macartney's man-o'-war, is visible in the distance among the junks that surround the two ships. A more formal but striking composition is *A Chinese military post on the River Euho*. The turn-out of the Chinese guard, which he must frequently have seen as the ship passed these posts on the riverside, obviously inspired this attractive, if theatrical, scene. Alexander made copious sketches and finished drawings of Chinese soldiery; three assorted warriors appear in a typical sheet of his studies of them. The mechanics of transferring river craft from one water level to another is shown to be both ingenious and simple in *Barges of the Embassy being raised from one canal to another*. The difference in the water level here is six feet and, to paraphrase Staunton's account, the craft is drawn by capstans at either side until sufficiently raised to tip it gently over and down the 'double glacis of sloping masonry, with an inclination of about forty degrees'. It can be presumed from the crowds that Alexander has included on the banks, that there must have been hazards to this exercise.

WILLIAM ALEXANDER
A Chinese military post on the river Euho
Watercolour, signed with initials and dated *19 October 1793* on the mount, 11¾in by 6½in
London £5,200($9,360). 1.IV.76

WILLIAM ALEXANDER
Barges of the embassy being raised from one canal to another
Watercolour, signed with initials and inscribed and dated *16 Nov 1793* on the mount, 10½in by 14½in
London £6,400($11,520). 1.IV.76

The importance of the mission to the annals of British art history is in the part played by Alexander and his chronicling of the things he saw in drawings and words. A self-portrait of him in the British Museum wearing an eye-patch could well have been done on the voyage to China (the inscription leaves off at '179 . . .') and it would be interesting to know whether this was done in fun or to record an incident. Eight hundred and seventy sketches and drawings made on the expedition are in the India Office Library and, penetrating in detail, they capture rare and commonplace scenes in the teeming daily life, the many strange customs, the hilly landscapes crested with forts and the curly quaintness of the architecture.

William Alexander, son of a coach builder, was born on 10 April 1767. From the age of fifteen he studied under Julius Caesar Ibbetson and William Pars before entering the Royal Academy Schools in 1784. At that time the term of studentship there was seven years, so his employment by Lord Macartney would have been his first professional appointment. No drawings by him before this date have been identified by which to judge his ability as a draughtsman, but Ibbetson obviously knew his work was competent and had no hesitation in recommending him for the post.

For several years following his return to England, Alexander worked on the illustrations for Staunton's book and other works which included plates made from his drawings in China, principally Sir John Barrow's *Travels in China* and Alexander's own *Costume of China*. He was also exhibiting regularly at the Royal Academy from 1795 to 1804; including in all sixteen subjects from his Chinese trip.

In 1802 he was appointed to the Royal Military College at Marlow as a drawing master. The post had been offered to Constable who had refused it, considering that the job would stultify his artistic aspirations. During Alexander's time at the College, he spent many of his vacations in the British Museum, making careful copies of ancient terracottas, marbles and Egyptian antiquities, which were afterwards published for the Museum. These are beautifully drawn in monochrome, a method he was particularly inclined to use, especially in his later topographical drawings. It was, therefore, natural that Alexander's name should come readily to the minds of the British Museum authorities when they were looking for a suitable person to become Keeper of the newly-formed Department of Prints and Drawings. The need to create this new section, a break-away from the main library, was due to the exposure of the fraudulent practices of Robert Dighton, a trusted dealer friend of the Librarian who, over a long period, had been stealing fine impressions of Old Master prints and stamping them with his own collector's mark. Alexander was appointed to the keepership in 1808 and maintained the post until he died eight years later.

In character he was a kindly and amiable person, of a serious mind; his tastes were those of the connoisseur and antiquary; his many friends included Sir George Beaumont, Joseph Farington, Constable, Cotman, John Thomas Smith (who succeeded him in the British Museum) and Dr Thomas Monro. His work is well represented in the national museums, the India Office Library, Maidstone Museum, the Paul Mellon Collection and the Huntington Library in the U.S.A. Alexander died on 23 July 1816 at the early age of forty-nine, and it is rightly inscribed on his memorial that 'by the power of his pencil he introduced into Europe a better knowledge of the habits and manners of China'.

THOMAS JONES *Near Tivoli*
Watercolour, signed with initials and dated *12 Novr 1777 (Morn'g)*, 11½in by 16¾in
London £3,100($6,200). 27.XI.75
From the collection of Canon J. H. Adams

SAMUEL PALMER, RWS *Tintern Abbey*
Watercolour, heightened with bodycolour, 10in by 14¼in
London £4,800($9,600). 27.XI.75
From the collection of H. I. Richmond. Formerly in the collection of George Richmond, RA

JOHN FREDERICK LEWIS, RA
A Frank encampment in the desert of Mount Sinai, 1842
Watercolour, heightened with bodycolour, signed and dated 1856, 25¼in by 53in
London £18,500($33,300). 14.IV.76
From the collection of R. T. Laughton, CBE

ENGLISH PAINTINGS 57

JOSEPH MALLORD WILLIAM TURNER, RA
The Dee at Llangollen
Watercolour, circa 1835, 10¼in by 16¼in
London £21,000($37,800). 15.VII.76

58 ENGLISH PAINTINGS

Above left
PETER MONAMY
The evening gun: English men-of-war and barges in a calm sea
Signed, 24¼in by 42in
London £4,200($7,560). 31.III.76
From the collection of G. Loveday

Above right
THOMAS GAINSBOROUGH, RA
A wooded landscape with a farm cart
24in by 29in
London £17,000($30,600). 31.III.76
From the collection of the L. H. Wilson Trust
This picture, together with its pendant now in the Wharton Sinkler Collection, Philadelphia, dates from the late 1750s

Left
ROBERT SALMON
A steamboat and other shipping at the Custom House Quay, Greenock
Signed with initials and dated 1820, 23in by 37in
Gleneagles £8,000($16,000). 29.VIII.75

ENGLISH DRAWINGS 59

GEORGE RICHMOND, RA
A portrait of Samuel Palmer
Sepia ink, signed with initials, inscribed and dated *February 1830*, 7½in by 4¼in
London £1,800($3,240). 15.VII.76
From the collection of Mrs Miriam Hartley

THOMAS GAINSBOROUGH, RA
Study for a portrait of Carl Friedrich Abel (1725-87) playing a Viola da Gamba
Black chalk and stump and white chalk on blue paper, 12¾in by 10in
London £4,800($8,640). 1.IV.76
From the collection of Hubert Gregory

ENGLISH PAINTINGS

JAMES SEYMOUR
The coursing party
34in by 53in
London £21,000($37,800). 28.IV.76
From the collection of Mr and Mrs Jack R. Dick

ENGLISH PAINTINGS 61

GEORGE STUBBS, ARA
The Duke of Grafton's stallion, mares and foals
Signed, 1769, 72in by 108in
London £170,000($306,000). 28.IV.76
From the collection of Mr and Mrs Jack. R. Dick

JOHN FREDERICK HERRING, Snr
Mr Richard Watt's Memnon, a light bay, William Scott up
Signed and dated 1826, 30in by 40in
London £37,000($66,600). 28.IV.76

JOHN FERNELEY, Snr
A game stall at Melton Mowbray
Signed and dated *Melton Mowbray 1841*, 54¾in by 91in
London £14,000($25,200). 28.IV.76

BEN MARSHALL
A portrait of Alexandre le Pelletier de Molimide
Signed and dated 1808, 38¼in by 48in
London £52,000($93,600).
28.IV.76

HENRY ALKEN, Snr
The Meet
One of a set of four fox-hunting scenes, signed, 9½in by 13½in
London £20,000($36,000). 28.IV.76

The pictures on these pages and the two previous ones are from the collection of Mr and Mrs Jack R. Dick. This sale concludes the dispersal of their collection of English sporting and conversational paintings for a total of over £3 million

A portrait of Rosa Bonheur by Edouard Louis Dubufe
In the collection of the Musée National de Versailles

Rosa Bonheur and Sir Edwin Landseer: a study in mutual admiration

Jeremy Maas

The sales of nineteenth-century English and European paintings held at Sotheby Parke Bernet on 5 December 1975 and 14 May 1976 were, by present-day standards at least, of peculiar significance. This collection of pictures had belonged to the late Geraldine Rockefeller Dodge. Although unusually high in quality there was little about the paintings of Ansdell, Bouguereau, Détaille, Harpignies, Meissonier, Herring and Millet to excite more curiosity than they normally command. No, the most remarkable aspect of the sales was the inclusion, for the first time in living memory, of a large number (fifty-one) of works by Rosa Bonheur. Although she was as prolific an artist as any of the above, the appearance of her pictures at auction – even singly – is not a common occurrence. Here, at last, was an opportunity to re-appraise in monetary terms an artist whose reputation, like that of G. F. Watts, has stubbornly resisted any genuine and sustained revival in modern times. No opportunity for such a wholesale re-assessment of an artist of her period had occurred since the Funt sale of Alma-Tadema at Sotheby's Belgravia in 1973. (That had been a revelation in itself: the prices realized then were far in excess of general expectation.) If this was not enough a further aspect of the Dodge sales was to add another, dramatic, new dimension. Also included were sufficient numbers of works of comparable importance by Rosa Bonheur's hero, Sir Edwin Landseer, to afford a rare opportunity of forming a comparative assessment of two separate oeuvres of relatively equal attainment.

In their overlapping careers they were like runners in some Olympic relay-race spanning the greater part of the nineteenth century during one brief moment of which one artist, on the point of exhaustion, passed on his baton to another at the very moment of his first triumph. Marie Rosalie Bonheur (1822-99) was one of four children, three of whom became famous as painters, while the fourth, Isidore, achieved fame as a sculptor. In recent years she has enjoyed a partial, limited revival as one of a group of *animaliers*, but as a sculptor of bronzes her reputation does not stand as high as some of her contemporaries. She was one of the most intriguing figures in nineteenth-century art, a richly-rewarding subject for a modern biographer. In appearance somewhat masculine, though in manner intensely feminine, she was, like George Sand, addicted to dressing like a man (although, usually, only when painting). She was a woman of quite exceptional charm and strength of character and – dare it be said at last? – one of the best animal painters of the last century.

ROSA BONHEUR
Spanish muleteers crossing the Pyrenees
Signed and dated 1857, 45in by 78in
New York $30,000(£16,666). 14.V.76.
From the collection of the late Geraldine Rockefeller Dodge

By far her most celebrated picture (though arguably not her finest) was *The horse fair*. This was first exhibited at the Salon of 1853, failed to find a purchaser, was later bought by her life-long friend, the dealer Ernest Gambart, and exhibited at his gallery in Pall Mall in 1855. This gigantic picture, nearly seventeen feet long, was to become a sensation, ensuring the artist fame throughout her lifetime. Although sent for and admired by Queen Victoria, it was not however until 1857 that the picture was sold. The buyer, William P. Wright of Weehawken, U.S.A., paid less than 30,000 francs for it; he later sold it to Alexander Turney Stewart, the cold, cruel and calculating New York merchant prince, for a price in excess of 50,000 francs. At Stewart's sale in 1887 it passed to Cornelius Vanderbilt for $55,000, who presented it to the Metropolitan Museum of New York, where, ever popular, it is always on view. Gambart was later (1878) to acquire Rosa Bonheur's huge and magnificent *King of the forest*, in title and subject like a tributary gesture to *The Monarch of the glen*.

Although a past master at creating reputations, Gambart at first had little success with his new protégée: her pictures did not sell easily. *Spanish muleteers crossing the Pyrenees*, for instance (which realised $30,000 in the second Dodge sale), failed to find a buyer when it was exhibited at his French exhibition in 1857. It was not in fact sold until May 1861 at Gambart's own first sale at Christie's. Then it fetched £1,995. Its next appearance in a saleroom was again at Christie's, on 2 June 1888, when it sold for £3,780, a notably high price reflecting Rosa Bonheur's ever-advancing reputation, in spite of the still gloomy effects of the 'Great Depression'. (Trade cycles as a factor in assessing artists' reputations in terms of auction prices should always be taken strongly into account; the subject was well treated by Frank Herrmann in the last edition of *Art at Auction*.)

Leslie Towner in *The Elegant Auctioneers* quotes a cynic as remarking of Rosa Bonheur that 'she hugged the taxidermist too closely all her life and loafed too little by the way'. Ruskin was nearer the mark when he observed, while comparing her with Landseer, that 'her feelings for animals were . . . more akin to the menagerie keeper's love', for Rosa Bonheur literally surrounded herself with animals and birds of every description. When painting *The lion at home* she had herself hoisted high up in a cage to observe more closely every detail of behaviour and character of a lion as it prowled up and down. Indeed, one of the reasons for her success was her close affinity with animals and a deep understanding of their ways; she never succumbed to the temptation to endow animals with human characteristics, as Landseer regrettably and with appalling bathos, did on occasion.

Rosa Bonheur had for long been almost a fanatical admirer of Landseer (to her he was 'the greatest painter of animals' and would remain, she believed, 'the greatest of his kind'). While enjoying the fruits of her first success in London in 1855, through the contrivance of Gambart and to her unbounded delight, she was introduced to him. The meeting, at a grand dinner given by the P.R.A., Sir Charles Eastlake, was high-spirited, emotional and crucial. 'Landseer', Lady Eastlake noted, 'was full of impudence, counted up to eight bachelors, and sent a deputation of marriage to her, adding that he would be only too happy to become Sir Edwin Bonheur.' Frith at once offered him congratulations on the prospect of a marriage that was in any case inconceivable. In fact both were to die unmarried.

The horse fair was hung in Gambart's gallery on 17 July. Overnight the artist was proclaimed the 'female Landseer' and on the next day Lady Eastlake drove her to Landseer's studio. Again the occasion was charged with emotion. As Lady Eastlake continued:

'Her whole enthusiasm as a woman has been long given to Landseer. Engravings of his works were the first things she bought with the money she earned; and in his home, surrounded by the most exquisite specimens of his labour and his skill – studies without end of deer, horses, Highlanders, tops of Scotch mountains, &c: and with him pulling out one glorious thing after another, calling her first into one room and then another – his dogs about him, and a horse, as tame as a dog, handed into the painting room – she was in a state of quiet ecstasy. Then he presented her with two engravings of his splendid "Night" and "Morning", writing her name with his upon them, and then pretended to call her attention to the excellence of his brother's work. This was too much for the little great-hearted woman, who is only a man in her unflagging work, and renunciation of all a woman's usual sources of happiness, for one great end; and her face crimsoned and eyes filled. As we drove away, the little head was turned from me, her face streaming with tears.'

Thereafter until the end of her days Rosa Bonheur could scarcely recall the memory of Landseer without some display of emotion.

A few further links between the two artists are worth remembering. *The horse fair* was engraved by Landseer's brother, Thomas; it was during this process that Jacob Bell, the pharmacist and celebrated patron of artists, happened to see the small replica: he promptly wrote to the artist, offering 25,000 francs for it to be included in his collection of Landseers. The offer was accepted. This replica is now in the National Gallery, London. A final expression of Rosa Bonheur's admiration for Landseer may be seen in *A random shot*. The English artist left this large picture unfinished at his death; it was acquired by Gambart and it occurred to Rosa Bonheur to finish it. She duly painted in the landscape. This tribute from one artist to another is now in the Sheffield City Art Gallery.[1]

It is fitting, therefore, that the two Dodge sales, dominated by the works of Rosa Bonheur, should contain at the same time no less than eighteen works by Landseer. Together they seem like one continuous tradition, their overlapping life-spans straddling all but three years of the nineteenth century. Sir Edwin Landseer (1802-73) needs less of an introduction than the French artist. He belongs spiritually to the first half of the century: she to the second. He was more essentially the product of the great age of the print-publishers, followed, perhaps disastrously, by royal and aristocratic patronage. When the two artists met Landseer had already begun his decline into the self-absorbing melancholia that eventually sapped his creative vitality. Although by the standards of Frith, Millais and Holman Hunt, he charged surprisingly moderate prices for his pictures, he nevertheless died a rich man. As his biographer J. A. Manson was at pains to point out, half the fortune of £200,000 he left at his death resulted from the sale of lucrative copyrights.

Landseer's subsequent record as seen in the saleroom differs from that of Rosa Bonheur in one important respect: while her pictures seemed to vanish along with her reputation (Gerald Reitlinger records only ten sales of her pictures in Europe in the fifty years following the Gambart sale of 1903), Landseer's works on the other hand have sold steadily and in sufficient numbers since his death to have made it possible to take his pulse continually ever since. His more important pictures continued to fetch between approximately £1,000 and £7,000 for about thirty years after his death, although it is noticeable that the decline had started some fifteen years previously. After Christie's sale of *The monarch of the glen* for £5,250 in 1916 it is downhill all the way until the Second World War. In the 1960s Landseer prices boomed again. The first of the Dodge sales re-affirmed this revival. *None but the brave deserve the fair*, which sold in 1890 for £4,260 and in 1935 for £152 5s, sold for $13,000; but the most spectacular change in fortunes was reserved for *Alpine mastiffs re-animating a distressed traveller*. From a healthy sale price of £2,257 10s in 1875, its value declined by fits and starts to a mere £37 16s in 1928. In the first Dodge sale this dramatic picture sold for $22,000, *less* than Rosa Bonheur's *Cavaliers in a shower* which made $23,000.

The decline in price of Rosa Bonheur's pictures after her death was faster and sharper than that of Landseer's. For fifty years after the sale of *Sheep in the Pyrenees* for £1,071 in 1906, her pictures, on the rare occasions when they came on to the market in London, barely made £100 to £200 a time. Indeed the rapid decline of her reputation had almost a touch of ignominy about it. After her death in France in 1899 she was widely mourned and confident predictions of the immortality of her art were made on

---

[1] Leon Sarty, *Nice d'Antan* (Nice, 1921), p 191.

SIR EDWIN HENRY LANDSEER, RA
Alpine mastiffs re-animating a distressed traveller
Signed and dated 1820, 74in by 93in
New York $22,000(£11,000). 5.XII.75.
From the collection of the late Geraldine Rockefeller Dodge

every hand. One of the mourners at her funeral was Bouguereau, in whose pocket was secreted a funerary oration which contained grandiloquent assurances of the imperishability of her life's work. When he died six years later taste and fashion were already turning remorselessly against her as they were to turn against him and countless fellow artists. The two Dodge sales (the second underlining the trends set by the first) mark a most convincing return to favour of this great animal painter. The early and continued support from Gambart and wider contemporary patronage on both sides of the Atlantic during her lifetime are now firmly vindicated. All that was needed to set the seal on this revival was a world record. This was achieved by *The duel*, a late, large and dramatic picture of two stallions fighting: in the second sale it

ROSA BONHEUR
Cavaliers in a shower
Signed and dated 1882, 35in by 51in
New York $23,000(£11,500). 5.XII.75.
From the collection of the late Geraldine Rockefeller Dodge

made $62,500, thus overtaking by a wide margin the highest price so far obtained for a Landseer.

It is tempting to suggest many glib reasons for this headlong rush into temporary semi-oblivion, a fate to which animal painters seem peculiarly prone. Changes of fashion in painting cannot fully account for it, nor can it be attributed to the growing influence of the new schools of French painting at the turn of the century as acceptance of these by the general public was then by no means complete or even widespread. Such a dramatic reversal of fortune must have very different, though less easily revealed and defined causes. Paradoxically, these same causes can sometimes be so close to hand as to be suspect for that very reason. When Rosa Bonheur died in 1899 the world was still a horse-drawn society. In spite of the universal proliferation of railways and the invention by Gottlieb Daimler of the internal combustion motor running on petroleum spirit in 1885, the world was still utterly dependent on the horse. It was always in evidence, a part of daily life, as were, to a far greater extent

ROSA BONHEUR
The duel
Signed and dated 1895, 59in by 96in
New York $62,500(£34,722). 14.V.76.
From the collection of the late Geraldine Rockefeller Dodge

than today, other animals – farm-yard, game and domestic. It has been estimated that in the late Victorian era British society required about one horse for every ten people, while in America one horse was needed for every four inhabitants![2] Consequently, when you bought a Rosa Bonheur or a Landseer you bought a picture representing a very familiar world.

In the early years of the twentieth century the increasing rapidity of communications, the further linking of railway systems, the mass production of motor cars, the bicycle, and the advancement of heavy industry at the expense of the rural environment, all helped to change the face of the recognisable world. The popularity of horse and animal painting inevitably declined in the face of scientific and industrial progress. It has often been noted that some fifty years previously portraiture had suffered similarly from the incursions of photography.

[2] F. M. L. Thompson, *Victorian England: the horse-drawn society* (1970).

ROSA BONHEUR
The king of the forest
Signed and dated 1878. 97in by 68½in
New York $21,000(£10,500). 5.XII.75.
From the collection of the late Geraldine Rockefeller Dodge

SIR EDWIN HENRY LANDSEER, RA
None but the brave deserve the fair
Painted in 1838, 28in by 36¼in
New York $13,000(£6,500). 5.XII.75.
From the collection of the late Geraldine Rockefeller Dodge

But, to the discomfiture of historians who crave for symmetry, there is rarely a current without an undertow. While her contemporaries were buying ancestral portraits, Old Masters and Impressionists, Geraldine Rockefeller Dodge, like a few others, was buying in the taste of the nineteenth century. She bought her Landseers and Bonheurs in the twenties, thirties and forties at what must have been bargain prices. To her horses, dogs, cattle and deer clearly represented the most acceptable face of the world. It seems, therefore, perfectly natural, and by no means inappropriate, that the entire proceeds of both sales have been left for the endowment and maintenance of a dog's home in New York.

JAMES JACQUES TISSOT
Going to the city
Signed, 17¼in by 10in
London £8,500($15,300). 9.III.76

FREDERIC, LORD LEIGHTON, PRA, RWS
La Nanna
31½in by 20½in
London £6,500($11,700). 9.III.76

This is the largest of three versions that Leighton painted in Rome of Nanna Risi, mistress and model of Anselm Feuerbach

76   ENGLISH PAINTINGS

Opposite above
DANIEL MACLISE, RA
Robin Hood and his merry men
Signed twice and dated *1839* and inscribed *Retouched 1845*, 72in by 144in
London £6,500($13,000).
11.XI.75
From the collection of
F. V. Cooke

Opposite below
EYRE CROWE
At the pit door
Signed and dated *1873*, 25½in by 43in
London £1,700($3,060).
9.III.76
From the collection of
A. H. Redman

JOHN MORGAN
Ginger beer
Signed, 40in by 27in
London £2,200($3,960). 9.III.76

ENGLISH PAINTINGS

CHARLES FAIRFAX MURRAY and SIR EDWARD COLEY BURNE-JONES, Bt, ARA
Venus Epithalamia
Gouache heightened with gold, inscribed, painted 1871, 14½in by 10½in
London £4,000($7,200). 29.VI.76

The model for Venus was Maria Zambaco. Burne-Jones had made the first version in the same years and probably had a large part in helping Fairfax Murray with the painting

JOHN BYAM LISTON SHAW
Now is the Pilgrim Year fair Autumn's charge
Signed, 33½ in by 47 in
London £3,000($6,000). 11.XI.75

ENGLISH DRAWINGS

LUCIAN FREUD
Unripe tangerine
On board, signed and dated *Oct. '46*,
3⅝in by 3½in
London £1,450($2,900). 12.XI.75

PAUL NASH
In a garden under the moon, 1913
Pencil, blue and black chalk, pen and ink and watercolour with collage, signed with monogram and inscribed, 13¾in by 9¾in
London £2,000($3,600). 17.III.76

SIR WILLIAM ROTHENSTEIN
Portrait of Charles Ricketts and Charles Shannon
Pastel on buff paper, signed and dated '94, 17¼in by 13½in
London £1,400($2,520). 17.III.76
From the collection of N. de Watteville

Below
LUCIAN FREUD
Scotch thistle
Pencil and coloured chalk, signed and dated *July 1944*, 9¼in by 13½in
London £1,500($3,000). 12.XI.75

ENGLISH PAINTINGS AND SCULPTURE 81

Right
FRANCES HODGKINS
Middle Hill, Solva
Signed, 35½in by 35½in
London £3,900($7,020).
16.VI.76

Below
HENRY MOORE, OM, CH
Reclining figure, 1938
Bronze on a wooden base,
length 8½in
London £7,200($14,400).
12.XI.75

HENRY MOORE, OM, CH
Internal and external forms
Bronze, executed in 1952-53 and cast in 1958, height 79in
New York $120,000(£66,667). 26.V.76

BEN NICHOLSON
Corinth
Signed, titled and dated *Jan '63* on the reverse, oil on carved hardboard,
20in by 17in
New York $25,000(£13,889). 26.V.76

PIETRO ANNIGONI
'Eliza', Julie Andrews in 'My Fair Lady'
Signed and dated *(LON.) LIX*, 31½in by 23½in
London £7,000($14,000). 12.XI.75
From the collection of Mrs Charles L. Tucker

DAVID SHEPHERD
Tiger fire
Signed and dated *1973*, 29½in by 48½in
London £15,000($27,000). 17.III.76
From the collection of M. A. Fields

ENGLISH PAINTINGS 85

JOHN SPENCER CHURCHILL
The beach at Dunkirk, 1940
Signed, inscribed and dated, 39½in by 64½in
London £800($1,440). 17.III.76
From the collection of the Officers' Headquarters Mess, Royal Army Educational Corps

LAURENCE STEPHEN LOWRY, RA
Fun fair at Daisy Nook
Signed and dated *1957*,
27¾in by 35½in
London £13,000($23,400).
17.III.76

ISAAK OUWATER
A view in Amsterdam
Signed and dated 1781,
17¾in by 22½in
Amsterdam Fl210,000
(£42,857:$77,142).
26.IV.76

JAN EKELS THE ELDER
A view in Amsterdam
Signed and dated 1776,
18¾in by 22½in
Amsterdam Fl68,000
(£13,877:$24,979).
26.IV.76

The paintings illustrated on this page are from the collection of the late B. de Geus van den Heuvel

CORNELIS SPRINGER
A busy street scene in Gouda
On panel, signed and inscribed on the reverse, 16in by 19¾in
London £18,000($32,400). 19.V.76
From the collection of Prince Thibaut D'Orléans

HENDRIK WILLEM MESDAG
A fishing fleet
Signed, 23½in by 51in
Amsterdam Fl40,000(£8,163:$14,693). 16.III.76

ANDREAS ACHENBACH
A Mediterranean fishing village
On panel, signed and dated 1857, 22in by 30¾in
London £7,400($13,320). 11.II.76

WIJNAND JAN JOSEPH NUYEN
A beach scene
On panel, signed and dated 1836, 12¼in by 16½in
Amsterdam Fl72,000(£14,694:$26,449). 27.IV.76

JOHANNES WEISSENBRUCH
The ferry
On panel, signed and dated '46, 18½in by 25½in
Amsterdam Fl112,000(£22,857:$41,142). 27.IV.76

The paintings illustrated on this page are from the collection of the late B. de Geus van den Heuvel

90 EUROPEAN PAINTINGS

WOUTERUS VERSCHUUR
Watering the horses
Signed, 19¾in by 29½in
New York $21,000($11,666). 14.V.76
From the collection of the late Geraldine Rockefeller Dodge

EUROPEAN PAINTINGS 91

ALFRED VON WIERUS KOWALSKI
Off to market
Signed, 28in by 46½in
London £11,000($19,800). 21.VII.76

92 EUROPEAN PAINTINGS

MARTIN RICO Y ORTEGA
Chiesa dei Gesuati, the Zattere, Venice
Signed, 19in by 26¾in
New York $18,000 (£10,000). 2.IV.76

BAREND CORNELIS KOEKKOEK
A forest scene in summer
On panel, signed and dated 1850, 26in by 33in
Amsterdam Fl235,000(£47,959:$86,326). 27.IV.76
From the collection of the late B. de Geus van den Heuvel

HERMANN KAULBACH
Winding wool
On panel, signed, 19½in by 23¼in
London £24,000($43,200).
21.VII.76

FILIPPO PALIZZI
Rustic playmates
Signed and dated 1866, 25in by 36½in
New York $26,000(£14,444). 14.V.76

94 EUROPEAN PAINTINGS

WILLIAM ADOLPHE BOUGUEREAU
Le ravissement de Psyche
Signed and dated 1895, 82½in by 47in
London £6,200($12,400). 15.X.75
From the collection of the late Sir John Ellerman

Above right
LUCIEN LEVY-DHURMER
L'ésprit d'Automne
Signed and inscribed *Paris* on the reverse,
14in by 23½in
London £11,500($20,700). 19.V.76

ARNOLD BÖCKLIN
Summer
40in by 30in
London £12,500($22,500). 19.V.76
From the collection of J. Hodson

ETIENNE-PIERRE-THEODORE ROUSSEAU
Le four communal
Signed, 24¼in by 38¼in
New York $57,000(£28,500). 5.XII.75
From the collection of the late Geraldine Rockefeller Dodge

Rousseau's visit to the Landes in 1844 inspired a number of paintings. On his return to Paris he executed several full-scale drawings, one of which was *Le four communal*, now in Dijon. In 1852 one of Rousseau's most important patrons, Frédéric Hartmann, saw the drawings in the artist's studio and commissioned paintings to be made from them. Rousseau worked on three of these pictures for the rest of his life: *Le four communal*, *La ferme* and *Le village de Becquigny* (Frick Collection). Although the latter two were exhibited in the Salon, Rousseau never considered any of them completely finished and consequently they were only delivered to Hartmann after the artist's death

PAUL JOSEPH CONSTANTIN GABRIËL
Early morning on Kamper Polder
Signed, 14¼in by 23¼in
Amsterdam Fl44,000(£8,979:$16,163). 27.IV.76

GEORGE HENDRIK BREITNER
A view in Amsterdam from the artist's studio
Signed, 32in by 51in
Amsterdam Fl240,000(£48,979:$88,163). 27.IV.76

JACOBUS HENDRICUS MARIS
A river landscape
Signed, 25¼in by 45¼in
Amsterdam Fl160,000(£32,653:$58,775). 27.IV.76

ISAÄC LAZARUS ISRAËLS
Girls sorting coffee
Signed, 22¼in by 32¼in
Amsterdam Fl155,000(£31,632:$56,937). 27.IV.76

The paintings illustrated on these two pages are from the collection of the late B. de Geus van den Heuvel

GEORGE FRENCH ANGAS
Eagle Hawk gully, Bendigo
Pen and brown ink, and watercolour, signed *G. F. Angas Aug. 1852*, 10in by 13¾in
London £3,300($6,600). 4.XI.75
From the collection of Mrs F. E. Gubbins, great grand-daughter of the artist

CHARLES RAMUS FORREST
Falls on a river near Quebec
Watercolour, one of three
London £2,000($4,000). 4.XI.75
From the collection of Cliff Sinclair, great-great-grandson of the artist

THOMAS BAINES, FRGS
Table Mountain and Bay
Signed and dated *Grahamstown, Nov. 9, 1848*, 17¾in by 26in
Johannesburg R7,500(£4,838:$8,708). 17.III.76
From the collection of D. L. George

CHARLES DECIMUS BARRAUD
Landscape with mountain ranges, South Island, New Zealand
Watercolour, signed and dated 1876, 18in by 30in
London £1,550($3,100). 4.XI.75

WOLF KIBEL
Still life with bird
Mixed media on board, signed, *circa* 1935, 20¾in by 26¼in
Johannesburg R8,800(£5,677:$11,354). 31.X.75
From the collection of Mrs A. H. Halperine

GEORGE FRENCH ANGAS
Young Zulu soldiers of Isangu Regiment and Indabagoombi Regiment
Pen and ink, watercolour and bodycolour, signed in pencil, 17¾in by 12¾in
Johannesburg R7,600(£4,903:$9,806). 31.X.75
From the collection of Mrs F. E. Gubbins, great grand-daughter of the artist

CHINESE SCHOOL
Coastal scenes
One of a pair, nineteenth century, 31in by 49in
Hong Kong £7,000($14,000). 13.XI.71

JOHANN MAURITZ RUGENDAS
Gauchos lassoeing a stee[r]
Signed, 23in by 36in
London £6,500($11,700)
11.V.76
From the collection of Mrs C. L. Clark

TOPOGRAPHICAL PAINTINGS 103

CARL WIMAR
Funeral raft of a dead chieftain
On panel, signed and dated 1856, 11¼in by 15⅞in
London £7,800($14,040).
11.V.76

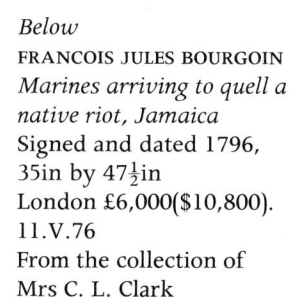

Below
FRANCOIS JULES BOURGOIN
Marines arriving to quell a native riot, Jamaica
Signed and dated 1796, 35in by 47½in
London £6,000($10,800).
11.V.76
From the collection of Mrs C. L. Clark

104 CANADIAN PAINTINGS

ALEXANDER YOUNG
JACKSON, OSA, RCA
Morning, Baffin Island
Signed, titled and dated
1928 on the stretcher,
25in by 32in
Toronto $23,000(£12,777).
20.X.75

TOM THOMSON, OSA
Early spring
On panel, 8½in by 10½
Toronto $35,000(£19,4
17.V.76

JAMES WILSON MORRICE, RCA
On the cliff
Signed, 19in by 23½in
Toronto $26,000(£14,444).
17.V.76

LAWREN STEWART HARRIS,
OSA, RCA
Grocery store in the ward
Signed *'Lawren'* and dated
'20, 32in by 38in
Toronto $44,000(£24,444).
17.V.76

106 THE SALE OF THE GERALDINE ROCKEFELLER DODGE COLLECTION

A front view of 'Giralda', Mrs Dodge's country house at Madison, New Jersey, and some of the 50,000 visitors who came to the pre-sale exhibition

Some of the prospective buyers getting a glimpse of the style in which the 'old wealth' lived. A print of Rosa Bonheur's famous painting, *The duel*, can be seen hanging against the staircase

The Sale of the Geraldine Rockefeller Dodge Collection

Jerry E. Patterson

New Yorkers all know the red-brick house at Fifth Avenue and East Sixty-First Street. Built in subdued Georgian style, it is surrounded by grounds which the owner, the late Mrs Marcellus Hartley Dodge (Geraldine Rockefeller), created by buying and demolishing five brownstone houses on the uptown side along Fifth Avenue and five to the east along Sixty-First Street. For as long as most passers-by can remember, the house overlooking the busy Plaza and Central Park has been silent and shuttered, exuding what one New York City guidebook calls 'a wistful elegance', its overgrown grounds visited only by squirrels from the Park.

In the autumn of 1975 the house was finally opened, as was 'Giralda', Mrs Dodge's country home at Madison, New Jersey, and its secrets revealed, when Sotheby Parke Bernet, New York, began dispersing the Geraldine Rockefeller Dodge collection. There were eight complete sales devoted entirely to the Dodge property, and items from her collection were included in half a dozen more. By the end of the season the sale of 7,950 lots had totalled over $7 million. It was a sale of superlatives: the largest number of objects belonging to one collector ever sold by Sotheby Parke Bernet, the largest house sale ever held by the firm, and the largest amount ever realised by the sale of an estate in the United States.

Although the biggest in recent years, the Dodge sale took its place historically within a long series of auctions of great American houses. Townhouses along Fifth Avenue have been providing landmark sales for Sotheby Parke Bernet and its corporate ancestors for nearly a century, as has the estate country that lies around New York City and along a narrow strip of the Eastern seaboard.

Art price history has been made at auctions like that of the Charles T. Yerkes estate in 1910. Yerkes was a public transportation magnate responsible for a famous financial manipulation known as 'The Chicago traction tangle', who later extended his operations into London's underground. His collection, consisting of more than 2,000 lots removed from his home at Fifth Avenue and East Sixty-Eighth Street, brought $2,207,866. It was especially rich in Persian carpets and contemporary academic paintings by such artists as Joseph Israels, Jan van Beers, and Ludwig Knaus. Mrs Yerkes's collection was sold two years later.

In 1916, the collection of a silk manufacturer oddly named Catholina Lambert was sold from his 'Belle Vista' Castle quite near 'Giralda'. He owned Old Masters and, more importantly for art history, one of the earliest collections of Renoir, Pissarro and Sisley to be sold in the United States. (The Castle, overlooking Paterson, is still standing and is now the home of the Passaic County Historical Society.)

A bronze seated figure of Abraham Lincoln, signed *Daniel C. French* and dated *March, 1916*, height 33in
New York $40,000(£20,000). 31.X.75
This is a working model for the heroic size marble seated figure of Lincoln in the Lincoln Memorial, Washington D.C.

Opposite page
A marble bust of Benjamin Franklin by Jean-Antoine Houdon, inscribed *F. P. Houdon en 1779*, overall height 20$\frac{7}{8}$in
New York $310,000(£155,000). 29.XI.75
The only other known marble version of this bust has been in the Metropolitan Museum since 1872. It is thought that it was brought to America by Houdon in 1785 when he was visiting George Washington

THE SALE OF THE GERALDINE ROCKEFELLER DODGE COLLECTION

The 1928 sale of the collection of Judge Elbert H. Gary, Chairman of the Board of United States Steel, from his Fifth Avenue house, near Mrs Dodge's home, brought records for paintings by Thomas Gainsborough and many other artists, sculpture by Jean-Antoine Houdon (his *Baby Sabina* at $245,000 was the most expensive Houdon ever sold until Mrs Dodge's *Benjamin Franklin* reached $310,000) and palace carpets. The total was $2,293,693.

Older employees at Sotheby Parke Bernet still remember the legendary estate dispersals of Mrs Henry Walters of New York and Newport (1,600 lots, mainly eighteenth-century French furniture, Sèvres, and marble sculpture, between 1940 and 1944); the innumerable Americana (china, glass, quilts, pottery, weathervanes among them) of Mrs Amory Haskell of Red Bank, New Jersey (1944-45); Mrs Hamilton McK. Twombly (Ruth Vanderbilt), last surviving grandchild of Commodore Vanderbilt, at whose palatial 'Florham Park' (almost 'next door' to 'Giralda'), the footmen wore violet liveries to match the Rolls-Royces (1952); Mrs Thelma Chrysler Foy (1959, Impressionists, French furniture and porcelain of the eighteenth century from her townhouse in Manhattan where she reigned as one of the best-dressed women in the world); and Edwin C. Berwind (reputedly the world's largest owner of coal-mining properties, his 'Elms' at Newport, sold by Parke-Bernet in 1962 was remotely inspired by Buckingham Palace).

Within the last ten seasons Sotheby Parke Bernet has sold among other house sales the Newport estate of the late Miss Edith Wetmore, often referred to as 'The Last of the Four Hundred' (1969), and at Glen Cove on the North Shore of Long Island the contents of 'Salutation', home of Mrs Junius Spencer Morgan of the banking family where the amount realised, $1,300,000, was the record total for a house sale until the auction at 'Giralda'.

There is a continuity of objects passed along through these great sales from one collector to another. Mrs Dodge, for example, owned a portrait of the actress Ada Rehan by the Belgian painter Jan van Beers (sold for $1,300) which was in Mrs Yerkes's sale in 1912 and also in Mrs Walters' sale in 1941.

As everyone knows, because few buildings have so caught the public imagination, the American rich in the period between the Civil War and the Second World War created and lived in outsized mansions in every conceivable architectural style and aesthetic taste. The houses are concentrated along the Atlantic between Massachusetts and Pennsylvania. They begin south of Boston, with a spectacular concentration at Newport, where they were modestly called 'cottages' (several are now open to the public after auctions of their contents), and continue down the Connecticut shore, clustering around Greenwich (just this season Sotheby Parke Bernet sold the contents of three estates in eastern Connecticut). The North Shore of Long Island is studded with these homes, and the estate country of northern New Jersey, where Mrs Dodge lived, has produced scores of house sales through the years. Outside this Eastern seaboard strip great houses have been found only in a few other parts of the United States such as Palm Beach or in isolated splendour like 'Biltmore', George Vanderbilt's house in Asheville, North Carolina. Dispersals of the contents of these houses have virtually all been managed by Sotheby Parke Bernet and its predecessor companies.

One of the minor curiosities of American social history has been the almost universal reluctance of the second generation of the rich to live in houses built by their parents. The American pattern has been that a great house is built, often in the old age of the builder and dynasty-founder, and filled with his valuable art collections; when he is dead its contents are sold at auction, and the house itself, often sadly demolished. Some of the great houses have had, therefore, amazingly short life-spans as residences. 'Whitmarsh Hall', the $3,000,000, 130-room Georgian mansion of E. T. Stotesbury near Philadelphia had a typical history: foundations laid 1916, opened 1921, abandoned in 1938, contents sold at Parke-Bernet in 1943. Even more extraordinary was the Senator William A. Clark mansion just around the corner from Sotheby's present location on East Seventy-Seventh Street in New York City, which was eight years under construction and occupied for eleven years (completed 1914, demolished 1925, contents sold 1926). Most second-generation rich say that 'they can't afford to keep up' the parental house, or that they 'can't get staff'. That is not always true even today, and it certainly was not true before the Second World War, in an era of kinder taxation and less restrictive immigration and labour laws. Whatever the reasons, it is a fact that the turnover has been quick in great American houses and collections, and this sets them apart from the 'stately homes' of Britain, lived in for generations and only occasionally sold up.

Several members of Mrs Dodge's family had sales at Parke-Bernet or its predecessors: her father, William Rockefeller, whose house at 689 Fifth Avenue and country home, 'Rockwood Hall' at Tarrytown, New York (a traditional Rockefeller preserve and remaining so even today) were sold in 1923, and her brother Percy A. Rockefeller, whose collection of Barbizon paintings, tapestries, and furniture was sold in 1938. The sale of the collection of Edith Rockefeller McCormick, Mrs Dodge's first cousin, in 1933 was a highlight of that grim depression year. Among other treasures was her *vermeil* dinner service numbering no less than 1,600 pieces which had once belonged to Pauline Bonaparte. Mrs Dodge herself was a lifelong customer of Parke-Bernet: her ledgers show that an astonishing percentage of her art collection had been purchased at the galleries.

Mrs Dodge was a New Yorker, born in 1882. Her father, William Rockefeller, was the younger brother of John D. Rockefeller and was president of the Standard Oil Company. His estate, considered at his death in 1923, to be one of the largest ever probated, came to about $200,000,000, left in trust to his four children. His daughter Geraldine married Marcellus Hartley Dodge, grandson and chief heir of Marcellus Hartley, the arms maker, who at his death in 1902 left a fortune estimated at $50,000,000. When the couple were married in 1907 the press delighted in referring to them as 'the richest young couple in the world'. Mr Dodge was president, later chairman, of the Remington Arms Company. Their only child, Marcellus Hartley Dodge, jnr, died in 1930 at the age of twenty-one. Mrs Dodge's own estate, which is estimated at about $85,000,000, included among other assets $31,000,000 in 400 separate issues of tax-free municipal bonds. Her principal beneficiary is the Geraldine Rockefeller Dodge Foundation, which immediately becomes one of the hundred largest foundations in the United States.

The Dodges built 800 Fifth Avenue in 1922, but never spent much time there (although it was fully furnished and maintained), and paid New York City real estate taxes that in recent years came to $147,000 annually. For decades Mrs Dodge stayed only Thursday nights in the house before a day of business and shopping in town. The half-block occupied by the house and grounds was considered the prime residential plot in the city and through the years offers for it running into millions of dollars were turned down.

EDWARD LAMSON HENRY
Station at Orange, New Jersey (Morris and Essex Railroad)
Signed *E. L. Henry* and dated '73, 10¼in by 18¼in
New York $15,500(£7,750). 31.X.75

Fifty miles from Manhattan, in Madison, New Jersey, Mrs Dodge had her principal home for sixty-two years from 1911, when she bought the 415-acre estate she named 'Giralda', until her death in 1973. It was famous not only for its size and the style in which it was maintained but as the scene from 1927 to 1953 of 'The Morris & Essex', the world's largest one-day dog show. In the last two decades few had seen inside the high fences surrounding 'Giralda', although drivers along the nearby highways were occasionally startled to glimpse deer grazing placidly amidst greenery in a suburban setting.

Mrs Dodge was a generous supporter of the nearby town of Madison, for which she built the municipal building, named after her son. Under her will the local charities receive substantial sums. Her will also contains the unusual suggestion that 'Giralda' be sold to private developers so that it will remain on the tax rolls of the municipality.

Her wealth, the prominence of her name, the mystery attached to the unused Fifth Avenue house, the public record of litigation over her financial affairs after she became incompetent in 1962 and her fame among dog-fanciers, meant there was a lot of public curiosity to be satisfied when Sotheby Parke Bernet began selling the contents of her houses. More than 50,000 visitors came to the pre-sale exhibition at 'Giralda' and thousands more to the sales held there and at the Madison Avenue

THE SALE OF THE GERALDINE ROCKEFELLER DODGE COLLECTION

A group of equestrian bronzes by Antoine-Louis Barye:
Above left Gaston de Foix, height $18\frac{3}{8}$in, $5,000(£2,500)
Above right Charles VII victorious, height $11\frac{5}{8}$in, $4,250(£2,125)
Below left A Tartar warrior, height $14\frac{1}{4}$in, $6,000(£3,000)
Below right An Arab rider killing a lion, height 15in, $3,250(£1,625)

The bronzes illustrated on this page are all inscribed *BARYE* and were sold in New York on 29 October 1975

Part of the living room at 'Giralda', showing some of the bronzes which Mrs Dodge had collected between 1920-61

galleries which included contents removed from 800 Fifth Avenue. More than 15,000 catalogues were sold.

Mrs Dodge began her collecting in the 1920s and was adding pieces until well after the Second World War. Records of her purchases were carefully entered into a series of bookkeeper's ledgers. They show purchases of *animalier* bronzes, for example, as early as 1920 and as late as 1961. Surely few collections of such size have been so personal. There was no trace of the art-historical or curatorial taste that guides so many collectors today, no trace of interior decorator taste, none of 'art for investment' purchases. Mrs Dodge's aversion to modern art, even to the Impressionists, was well-known. She had no ambition whatever to be in the mainstream of twentieth-century collecting. She was buying Landseers and Bonheurs in the 1930s when those artists were utterly unfashionable and Barye bronzes well after enthusiasm for his work had ebbed among American collectors. The individuality, or eccentricity, of the collection intrigued viewers and bidders.

'Giralda' is not a large house as estates go and has only thirty-five rooms. The ratio of objects to rooms, however, must be one of the highest on record. Every flat surface was crowded, and the wallpaper patterns cannot have been detectable for years because so many paintings were hung. Noble stags by Landseer, which seemed almost life-size, gazed across Louis XVI commodes covered with Barye bronzes; vitrines were packed with Chinese porcelains; and the top of every bookcase held a row of silver dog show trophies. The effect was not that of stately halls but rather of a well-to-do family's country place cluttered with cherished if sometimes incongruous objects.

The eye soon sorted out themes in the collecting, however. First was the reflection in art of Mrs Dodge's extraordinary affection, indeed obsession, for animals. This was a lifelong passion beginning as a child when she rescued strays or injured animals. At 'Giralda' she raised dogs, Arabian horses, Welsh ponies, prize bantams and guinea fowls, Canadian geese, and deer, the herd of which eventually numbered over 200 head. She established 'St Hubert's Giralda', a shelter for sick animals named after their patron saint; it is a substantial legatee under her will.

THE SALE OF THE GERALDINE ROCKEFELLER DODGE COLLECTION 115

Two photographs of Mrs Dodge taken at her famous Morris and Essex Dog Shows, which were held in the grounds of 'Giralda'

Dogs came first in Mrs Dodge's affections: for many years she was referred to in the sporting press as 'the first lady of dogdom'. She wrote articles and books on the English Cocker spaniel and the German Shepherd. At the height of her 'Morris & Essex Dog Show' 4,456 dogs competed, and human attendance sometimes ran to 35,000. Lunch was elegantly catered by Longchamps of New York, and silver trophies were lavishly distributed. There were as many as 300 dogs resident in the 'Giralda' kennels for years: the annual meat bill was $50,000. The estate had every variety of housing for the dogs, even a 'whelping house' for the puppies, built on a turntable revolving with the sun so that the puppies could get maximum sunshine. There were, of course, dog cemeteries. Access to the main house was provided for the dogs through a runway which they could use without assistance. Each night fourteen were allowed to sleep in Mrs Dodge's rooms; they were chosen on a rotating basis in order to avoid jealousies. In New York the sixth floor of 800 Fifth Avenue was reserved for the dogs with a special bathtub for their ablutions. The grounds had been created primarily to exercise them and were referred to by the neighbours as 'the most expensive dog run in the world'. There were still 169 dogs at 'Giralda' when Mrs Dodge became ill in 1962. No new dogs were added but the gradually diminishing pack was kept in style by court order. The last of the dogs, which survived his mistress, was 'Bert', an ancient pointer estimated to be more than twenty years old.

Mr Dodge, who died in 1963, was a horse breeder who lived on an adjoining and even larger estate called 'Hartley Farms'. From its dining room the dining room of his wife's 'Giralda' was visible down a long vista of carefully planted trees.

In Mrs Dodge's art collection there must have been nearly every nineteenth-century bronze made of a dog or group of dogs: greyhounds, bloodhounds, pointers, setters, Great Danes, retrievers, terriers, and many other breeds. Among the paintings was a group of watercolours that Mrs Dodge commissioned from Reuben Ward Binks, a British-born artist who was assigned the job of portraying every dog in the 'Giralda' kennels. He was artist-in-residence, off and on, from 1929 to 1939. There were almost one hundred of his paintings in the house sale, bringing a total of $17,340.

116 THE SALE OF THE GERALDINE ROCKEFELLER DODGE COLLECTION

A bronze entitled *The end of the trail* by James Earl Fraser, signed and dated *1913*, height 44in
New York $42,500(£21,250). 31.X.75

This is one of the most famous sculptures of the American West and dramatises the absolute despair of the American Indian at the loss of his native land

A bronze figure of *The Indian warrior*, signed *A. Phimister Proctor* and dated *1898*, height 39in
New York $51,000(£25,500). 31.X.75

The Indian warrior was completed in Paris while Proctor was there on the Rinehart Scholarship which he had won in 1896. The bronze was exhibited at the Paris Exposition of 1900 and won a gold medal

Among the *animalier* bronzes were other domesticated animals – horses, donkeys, and cows (but no cats) and fiercer specimens such as tigers, jaguars and wild boars, many of them shown devouring lesser species in grisly fashion. And the paintings, headed by Rosa Bonheur's and Sir Edwin Landseer's work (see pp. 64-73 for further discussion), largely portrayed dogs, horses, sheep and stags.

Also among the bronzes, and obviously a second theme in the collection, were models of hands, the majority being of the left hand. There were the clasped hands of Robert and Elizabeth Barrett Browning, and the right hand of Arthur Kaley, 'the Manx Giant', who was 7 ft 8 in tall and whose hand measured $12\frac{1}{4}$ in. There were Paderewski's hands and those of many lesser celebrities.

Abraham Lincoln was much admired by Mrs Dodge. She had bronzes of his hands, his portrait in oil, and life-masks, busts, and standing figures. Her Lincoln collection was headed by the bronze of Daniel Chester French's great seated figure in the Lincoln Memorial, Washington, D.C. ($40,000).

A major theme of the Dodge collection was the American Indian portrayed by many major American artists. The bronzes included James Earl Fraser's *The end of the trail* ($42,500) and A. Phimister Proctor's *The Indian warrior* ($51,000). There were even bronze andirons in the form of Indians (Louis Potter, *Kneeling Indian braves*, $3,750; these had been in the collection of Mrs Dodge's brother Percy Rockefeller).

The most important Indian subject was *The passing of the buffalo* by the Utah artist, Cyrus Dallin, which Mrs Dodge had commissioned for $12,000 in 1931. Dallin himself came to 'Giralda' to see it installed on the grounds on an enormous boulder brought from Massachusetts. For the sale the 9-ft figure of an Indian brave was moved into Sotheby Parke Bernet's lobby where it was an object of wonder to Madison Avenue shoppers and sold for a world record for an American bronze. The Margaret Ball Petty Foundation of Muncie, Indiana, bought it and has placed it in Walnut Plaza in Muncie – on the original thirty-eight-ton boulder which was hauled a thousand miles from 'Giralda' to Muncie by a heavy equipment moving firm.

Dallin was one of Mrs Dodge's favourite artists: she owned eighteen of his works. Among artists whom she knew personally she much admired the American sculptress Malvina Hoffman: there were forty-two lots of her work in the sale. Among sculptors of the past she had many works by Jean-Antoine Houdon, in addition to the record *Benjamin Franklin* and, rather surprisingly, considering her expressed disdain for 'modern art', she avidly collected Rodin. Her twenty-one marbles and bronzes by Rodin brought a total of $360,000. Among painters she favoured Rosa Bonheur (fifty-two works sold for a total of $325,450) and Sir Edwin Landseer (seventeen works sold for a total of $96,150).

Other themes in her collecting were Buddhas and buddhistic figures, many of them executed in bronze and scattered about both house and grounds at 'Giralda'. There were also many Madonna figures in various media, and an astonishing number of bells headed by Paul Revere's church bells ($4,200 and $4,500). Bells were hung over many doors at 'Giralda'. Although Mrs Dodge was a country gentlewoman who rarely wore jewellery, hers sold for $2,431,025 and established a world record for a single-owner collection. Her 'pigeon blood' rubies, brought a total of $690,000.

The art collection and the jewellery excited dealers and collectors and broke records, but many of the 50,000 visitors to 'Giralda' were drawn to lesser items, the innummerable necessities of a way of life which, if not entirely vanished, is at least

Cyrus Dallin's 9-ft bronze, *The passing of the buffalo*, as it stood in the grounds at 'Giralda'. It was sold in New York on 31 October 1975 for $150,000(£75,000)

fading, and is seldom seen spread out before one as on this occasion. Mrs Dodge was a great hoarder, and it did not appear that much had been thrown out during her sixty-year tenancy of the house. There was ample staff for maintenance: 'Giralda' had employed more than 125 people at one time and even during Mrs Dodge's final illness there was a full-time staff of forty-seven. It has always been the custom at house sales to sell everything down to the last bootscraper. At 'Giralda' these objects ran into the thousands, and exhausted cataloguers made up lots with titles like 'Group of Miscellaneous Equine Related Items' in their effort to organise them. Dozens of vehicles including such rariora as pony sulkies, phaetons, jogging carts, and 'runabouts' were sold. The former stables were set up for 'a tag sale' with fixed prices (5,000 lots

REMBRANDT PEALE
Self portrait
Signed *R. Peale* and dated *1846*, 27in by 22in
New York $45,000(£22,500). 31.X.75

ALBERT BIERSTADT
View on the Hudson River looking across the Tappan Zee towards Hook Mountain
Signed *A. Bierstadt* and dated *1866*, 36¼in by 72¼in
New York $115,000(£57,500). 31.X.75

The largest-known landscape painting of the Hudson River by Bierstadt, who lived at Irvington-on-Hudson during the years 1866-82

totalling $22,192) and became an emporium of carriage rugs, Vuitton luggage, shawls, picnic hampers, china, kitchenware, driving-whips and hay-forks. Tweedy ladies who looked as though they had kennels of their own, rubbed shoulders with dealers from the city as both hunted through the accoutrements. Professional buyer or amateur, all were fascinated, and awed, by the glimpse they were getting into the style in which 'old wealth' lived.

After eight months 'the sale of the century', as the American press called it, eventually drew to a close and Number 800 Fifth Avenue has also been sold (developers have elaborate plans for luxury apartments on the site). The 415 acres of 'Giralda' will be put on the market and will eventually, no doubt, house entire new communities. The Geraldine Rockefeller Dodge Foundation 'for the prevention of cruelty to animals and for the encouragement of art' and St Hubert's Giralda, remain as richly-endowed memorials to Mrs Dodge's interests; and hundreds of homes and collections now have one or more of the Dodge possessions. Each will be proudly shown by the successful bidder, one may be certain, along with anecdotes of the glimpse he caught of the extraordinary way of life at 'Giralda'.

WILLIAM ROBINSON LEIGH
Fleeing bandit
Signed *W. R. Leigh*, 28in by 22in
Los Angeles $30,000(£15,000). 20.X.75

FREDERIC REMINGTON
Watching the dust of the hostiles from the bluffs
Wash, heightened with white, signed, 20in by 26in
Los Angeles $30,000 (£16,666). 8.III.76
From the collection of Walter B. Ford III

FREDERIC REMINGTON
Return of a Blackfoot war party
Signed *Frederic Remington '87*, 28in by 50in
Los Angeles $155,000 (£77,500). 20.X.75

WILLIAM SIDNEY MOUNT
The disagreeable surprise
Signed *Wm S. Mount* and dated *1843*, 8in by 10in
New York $65,000($32,500) 12.XII.75

THOMAS HART BENTON
Swing your partner
Watercolour on paper, signed *Benton* and dated '45, 23¼in by 32½in
New York $22,000(£12,232). 29.IV.76
From the collection of Dr and Mrs Kane Zelle

A bronze entitled *On the war trail*, signed *A. Phimister Proctor* and dated *1921*, height 48in
New York $43,000(£21,500). 31.X.75
From the collection of the late Geraldine Rockefeller Dodge

This is a reduction of the heroic size bronze commissioned for the plaza at the Civic Center in Denver, Colorado, which was dedicated in 1920

A polychromed bronze bust of an Indian chief by Carl Kauba, signed *C. Kauba,* height 21½in
New York $21,000(£10,500). 31.X.75
From the collection of the late Geraldine Rockefeller Dodge

128 IMPRESSIONIST AND MODERN PAINTINGS

JEAN-FRANÇOIS MILLET
Petite bergère assise
Left: Drawing in black chalk, signed, 11in by 8in
Amsterdam Fl45,000(£8,333:$16,666). 17.XI.75
From the collection of the late Bernard Houthakker

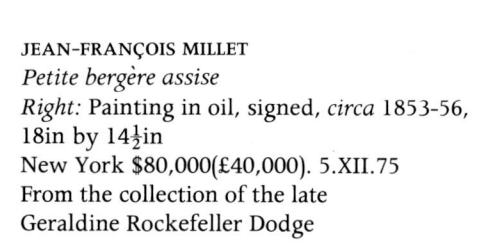

JEAN-FRANÇOIS MILLET
Petite bergère assise
Right: Painting in oil, signed, *circa* 1853-56,
18in by 14½in
New York $80,000(£40,000). 5.XII.75
From the collection of the late
Geraldine Rockefeller Dodge

The drawing above is a preliminary study for the painting here reproduced and for another very similar in the Minneapolis Institute of Art

ETIENNE-PIERRE-THEODORE ROUSSEAU
Village de Barbizon
On panel, signed, 8¾in by 13in
London £9,500($19,000). 3.XII.75

NARCISSE-VIRGILE DIAZ DE LA PENA
Landscape near Fontainebleau
Signed and dated '75, 21½in by 29in
New York $22,000(£11,000). 5.XII.75
From the collection of the late Geraldine Rockefeller Dodge

EDOUARD MANET
Pêches
Signed, painted in July 1882, 13in by 15¾in
London £75,000($135,000). 28.VI.76

PIERRE-AUGUSTE RENOIR
Portrait de Cézanne
Pastel, signed and dated '80, 21⅛in by 17½in
New York $230,000(£127,777). 17.III.76
From the collection of Mr and Mrs Josef Rosensaft

132 IMPRESSIONIST AND MODERN PAINTINGS

CLAUDE MONET
L'église de Vernon
Signed and dated '83, 23¼in by 29in
New York $310,000(£172,222). 17.III.76
From the collection of Mr and Mrs Josef Rosensaft

IMPRESSIONIST AND MODERN PAINTINGS 133

ALFRED SISLEY
La Seine à Bougival au printemps
Signed and dated '76, 18¼in by 24¼in
London £120,000($216,000). 7.IV.76

PIERRE-AUGUSTE RENOIR
Jeune fille au bouquet de tulipes
Signed, painted *circa* 1878, 22in by 18¼in
London £202,000($404,000). 3.XII.75
From the collection of Gérard Leclery

IMPRESSIONIST AND MODERN PAINTINGS 135

PAUL GAUGUIN
Nature morte à l'estampe japonaise
Signed and dated '89, 28½in by 36⅞in
New York $1,400,000(£777,777). 17.III.76
From the collection of Mr and Mrs Josef Rosensaft

136 IMPRESSIONIST AND MODERN PAINTINGS

EDGAR DEGAS
Danseuse rajustant son chausson
Pastel and charcoal, signed, executed *circa* 1890-95, 19¼in by 24½in
London £60,000($120,000). 3.XII.75

IMPRESSIONIST AND MODERN PAINTINGS 137

HENRI DE TOULOUSE-LAUTREC
Fille à l'accroche-coeur
On board, signed with the monogram, painted in 1889, 26¾in by 21¼in
London £230,000($460,000). 3.XII.75

This girl was one of the dancers at the Moulin de la Galette

PAUL GAUGUIN
Les premières fleurs
Signed and dated '88, 28¾in by 36½in
London £220,000($396,000). 28.VI.76

IMPRESSIONIST AND MODERN PAINTINGS 139

VINCENT VAN GOGH
L'heure de midi
Signed *Vincent*, painted in Arles in August 1888, 25in by 20¾in
London £480,000($864,000). 28.VI.76

PAUL GAUGUIN
Recto: *Standing nude*
A double-sided charcoal drawing, executed *circa* 1892, 18¾in by 12⅜in
New York $40,000(£22,222). 18.III.76
From the collection of the late Lester Avnet

PAUL CEZANNE
L'église de village
Pencil and watercolour, executed *circa* 1888, 13¼in by 20¼in
London £39,000($70,200). 7.IV.76
From the Bernheim-Jeune family collection, Paris

PAUL SIGNAC
Le brick à Marseille
Signed, painted in 1911, 32$\frac{1}{8}$in by 25$\frac{3}{4}$in
New York $145,000(£80,555). 17.III.76
From the collection of Mr and Mrs Josef Rosensaft

GIOVANNI BOLDINI
Portrait de Mademoiselle Béatrice de Comando
Pastel, signed and dated *1900*, 43in by 32¼in
London £10,000($18,000). 7.IV.76

Béatrice de Comando was the daughter of the Comte de Comando (whose house in Paris is now a museum), and Mademoiselle Irène Cahen d'Anvers

KEES VAN DONGEN
Trinidad Fernandez
Signed, painted *circa* 1907, 39¾in by 32in
New York $160,000(£88,888). 17.III.76
From the collection of Mr and Mrs Josef Rosensaft

MARC CHAGALL
Composition imaginaire
Signed, painted in 1920, 36¾in by 29in
New York $205,000(£113,888). 17.III.76
From the collection of Mr and Mrs Josef Rosensaft

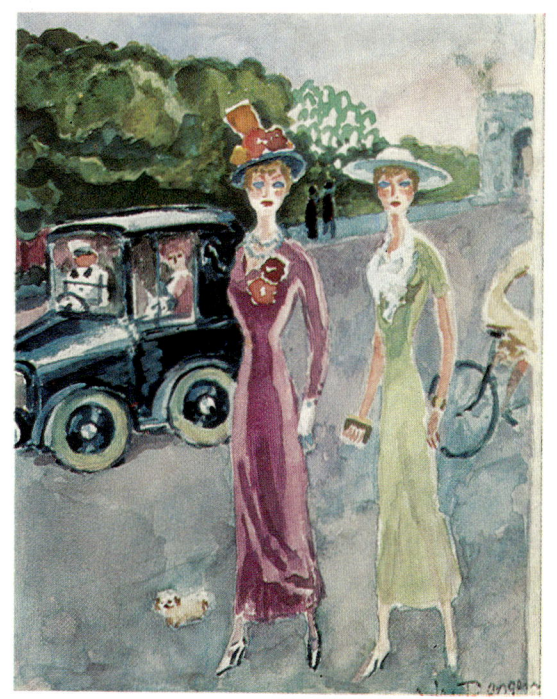

KEES VAN DONGEN
A la recherche du temps perdu
A selection from 70 illustrations in gouache, commissioned by the publishers Gallimard in 1946-47 to illustrate Marcel Proust's book, each measures 9½in by 8¾in
London £100,030($180,054). 30.VI.76
Formerly in the collection of the Proust family

LEON BAKST – *Cléopâtre*
Costume design for the Jewish dancer
Pencil, watercolour and gold paint, signed and dated *1910*, 31.5cm by 23cm
Monte Carlo Fr68,000(£8,095:$14,571). 26.VI.76

Diaghilev in Monte Carlo[1]

Julian Barran

In the ballet world the names Diaghilev and Monte Carlo are linked as closely as M.G.M. and Hollywood. As the story of their association is a success story with all the ingredients except a happy ending, I have permitted myself to touch only on the highlights and the triumphs. For the serious scholar or student of ballet the dark days of despair are recorded faithfully and objectively elsewhere. Diaghilev was on the side of the angels and as such created such moments of beauty, combinations of music, dancing and painting that their survival is assured by the intensity of the artistic achievement. It is those moments that I would like to commemorate, but like Jean Cocteau: 'Je devine que, je ne suis pas le seul à ressentir sa présence et que de Londres à Monte Carlo, de Paris à New York le fantôme de Diaghilev circule et observe nos entreprises.'

Was it Diaghilev's Roman patrician attitude or the influence of his Russian landowning ancestors which made him feel the need for winter quarters? Geographically, Monte Carlo was a central point in western Europe; it was ideally situated as a place where his company could withdraw, rehearse and perform new works. Diaghilev announced to his 'committee' his intention of visiting it in the winter of 1911. At that time there was a full season created by visitors from Europe, Russia and America which ensured an international and socially-brilliant audience. What Diaghilev started in 1911 and which ended in 1929, with a break for the war, left the Principality the capital of dance.

When Diaghilev descended on Monte Carlo for that first season he took with him as artistic director Alexandre Benois (later to be succeeded by Léon Bakst), Mikhail Fokine as choreographic director of ballets, Tcherepnine as conductor (to be replaced by Pierre Monteux from 1912-14). Nijinsky, Karsavina and Bolm headed the list of dancers. The company, not unnaturally, was known simply as *Les Ballets Russes*. Following the opening night on 6 April 1911 the triumph of the season was the first performance on 19 April of *Le spectre de la rose*. Of all ballets this delightful choreographic poem to music by Weber lives in the memory. If Nijinsky's reputation needed enhancing this ballet achieved it. His final leap through the window as the rose carried from the room on a gust of wind, staggered the audience. The second première of Diaghilev's Monte Carlo début was *Narcisse*, Tcherepnine's mythological poem with Léon Bakst's setting of classical Greece. A ballet that combined such music and painting with the dancing of Nijinsky and Karsavina was certain to appeal and was another success.

---

[1] My thanks are due to Richard Buckle for his advice in the preparation of this article.

Serge Grigoriev in *The Diaghilev Ballet 1909-29* is full of praise for the appointments of the Monte Carlo theatre (designed by Garner, architect of the Paris Opera). The luxury of the auditorium and the front of the house was extended backstage, a very unusual feature in his experience. The theatre was small which limited the size of some productions: the great backcloths for *Schéhèrazade* and *Cléopâtre* had probably to be folded in on all sides to permit their effective use. The company for the 1911 season was small and manageable so that the stage would not have been overcrowded.

The *Ballets Russes* season in Monte Carlo in 1912 took place during March and April. Although no new ballets were presented the rehearsals for *L'après-midi d'un faune* were well under way. The première of this ballet, which was to shock its audiences, took place in Paris on 29 May 1912. Richard Buckle in his book, *Nijinsky*, gives an impressive list of people staying in Monte Carlo in the 1912 season:

'Puccini had arrived to rehearse *The Girl of the Golden West*, the Aga Khan was at the Hôtel de Paris, and there were a number of distinguished English visitors. Lord Curzon was at the Grand Duke Michael's villa Kazbeck, Lord and Lady Dunsany at the Jersey's villa Cap di Monte, the Joseph Chamberlain family were at the villa Victoria and Lady Ripon and Lady Juliet Duff . . . joined their devoted friends at the Rivièra Palace.'

In 1912 the rift between Fokine and Diaghilev widened. Diaghilev's wish to promote Nijinsky as a choreographer undermined Fokine's position and he left the company in June. In August the following year Nijinsky was also to leave Diaghilev. Physically, he sailed with a reduced company to South America, but emotionally he moved beyond Diaghilev's influence when he married Romola de Pulsky. When the ballet returned to Monte Carlo in 1914, Fokine was back as choreographic director and Massine had joined the company ostensibly to dance as Joseph in the Strauss ballet (a part which had been intended for Nijinsky), but in reality as Diaghilev's new star. The first performance of *Papillons* was given during the 1914 season. War broke out that summer and the company dispersed, Diaghilev retaining his faithful band of intimates. Tours were arranged outside the war zone in Spain, the United States and again in South America. The company did not return to Monte Carlo until 1920.

Much had altered in society during the war and a great deal had happened to the Diaghilev ballet. Most striking was the change in Diaghilev's attitude towards the ballet world and the type of ballet he wished to produce. Musically, Debussy and Ravel were out, the 'six' were in. Picasso, Derain and Matisse, with Max Ernst and Miró joining their ranks a little later, had replaced Bakst and Benois. Massine had 'arrived' as a choreographer, but Bronislava Nijinska and Balanchine were soon to follow. Black tie had not quite replaced white tie and tails, but the change was of that order. Of all the 'isms' 'Modernism' was the cry. By 1920 when Matisse created the décors and costumes for *Le chant du rossignol*, the public knew that the Diaghilev ballet no longer meant visions of the exotic East, the wastelands of the Steppes or half-cosy Butter-week fairs in St Petersburg. It meant 'Le dernier cri'. It has been observed that the more fashionable a dress the less often it can be worn. So it was with Diaghilev's ballet. Of the twenty-seven productions created after 1920, in broad terms only *The sleeping princess, Noces, Le fils prodigue* and possibly *Les biches* have entered the world ballet repertoire as had *Petruschka, Schéhèrazade, Spectre de la rose*,

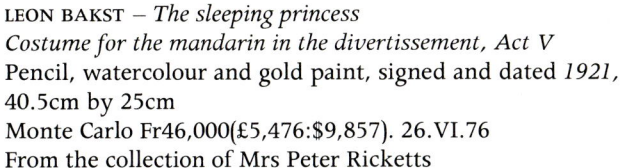

LEON BAKST – *The sleeping princess*
Costume for the mandarin in the divertissement, Act V
Pencil, watercolour and gold paint, signed and dated *1921*,
40.5cm by 25cm
Monte Carlo Fr46,000(£5,476:$9,857). 26.VI.76
From the collection of Mrs Peter Ricketts

HENRI MATISSE – *Le chant du rossignol*
Costume design for a warrior
Indian ink, executed in 1920, 18cm by 8cm
Monte Carlo Fr15,000(£1,785:$3,214). 26.VI.76
From the collection of Monsieur Malville

L'après-midi d'un faune and *Oiseau de feu* before them. Of those three post-1920 ballets one was a nineteenth-century 'classic'.

Monte Carlo from 1920 to 1929 became even more the Diaghilev ballet base. Of the new productions from that period, eight were first performed there. Most years the Monte Carlo season extended well into May and even into June or July. As sea-bathing became more popular the south coast was replacing the northern French coast resorts.

JEAN COCTEAU
Caricature of Diaghilev and Bakst in 'Le spectre de la rose'
Indian ink, inscribed on the back Léon Bakst Serge de Diaghilev (Spectre de la Rose), executed *circa* 1912, 20cm by 25.5cm
Monte Carlo Fr6,000(£714:$1,285). 26.VI.76

The ballet was probably at its height in 1924. Of six new productions that year, four were first given in the Théâtre de Monte Carlo, *Tentations de la bergère* (décor by Juan Gris), *Les biches* (décor by Marie Laurencin), *Les fâcheux* (décor by Braque) and *Le nuit sur le Mont Chauve* (décor by Gontcharova). *Le train bleu*, the ballet conceived on the beach at Monte Carlo which satirised the vacuous life lead by society there, was in fact first shown in Paris. Perhaps Diaghilev feared it was too near the mark for his glittering, twittering Monte Carlo audience.

Artists, composers, dancers and promoters flocked to see *Les Ballets Russes de Monte Carlo* and Diaghilev's dream of making the Principality a cultural centre was realised. The final triumphant year of his life was marked by its Monte Carlo season. In May 1929 *Le bal* was first performed there: De Chirico and Kochno collaborating in this metaphysical masque. In the same year Diaghilev died in another watering place, Venice, having lived and worked so happily in Monte Carlo. I promised no happy ending; I can only make this a tribute to Sergei Pavlovitch Diaghilev.

DIAGHILEV IN MONTE CARLO 151

LEON BAKST
Costume for 'Roxane'
Pencil, gouache and silver paint, signed, inscribed *Roxane Mme Gilda Darte* and dated *1911*, 37.5cm by 26.5cm
Monte Carlo Fr74,000(£8,809:$15,857). 26.VI.76

GEORGES ROUAULT
Trio (Cirque)
Signed, painted *circa* 1938, 29⅞in by 41⅞in
New York $280,000(£155,555). 17.III.76
From the collection of Mr and Mrs Josef Rosensaft

IMPRESSIONIST AND MODERN PAINTINGS 153

MAURICE UTRILLO
La rue Chappe et le Sacré Coeur
Signed, painted *circa* 1910, 20¾in by 28¼in
London £34,000($61,200). 30.VI.76

OSKAR SCHLEMMER
Reihung
Watercolour and pencil, executed in 1929, 21$\frac{5}{8}$in by 13$\frac{3}{4}$in
New York $29,000(£16,111). 18.III.76
From the collection of the late Lester Avnet

FERNAND LEGER
Homme dans la rue
Watercolour, signed and dated '19, 16in by 11¾in
London £22,000($39,600). 30.VI.76

JACQUES VILLON
Portrait de Marcel Duchamp
Signed and dated *'13* on the reverse, oval: 23¾in by 19in
Los Angeles $42,500(£23,611). 10.III.76
From the collection of the late Florence Howald Shawan

ALBERT GLEIZES
Dans le port
Signed and dated *New York 1917*, $60\frac{3}{8}$in by $47\frac{1}{2}$in
New York $42,000(£21,000). 22.X.75
From the collection of the Solomon R. Guggenheim Foundation

158 IMPRESSIONIST AND MODERN PAINTINGS

PIET MONDRIAN
Composition in a square
Signed and dated '22, 21in by 21¼in
New York $220,000(£110,000). 22.X.75

FERNAND LEGER
Composition à 1 profil
Signed and dated '34-35, $38\frac{1}{4}$in by $57\frac{1}{2}$in
New York $92,500(£51,388). 26.V.76
From the collection of the late Sara Murphy

Gerald and Sara Murphy invited Leger in 1931 for his first trip to the United States. They arranged for him to meet all the right people and, to thank them, Leger presented them with this work three years later

160 IMPRESSIONIST AND MODERN PAINTINGS

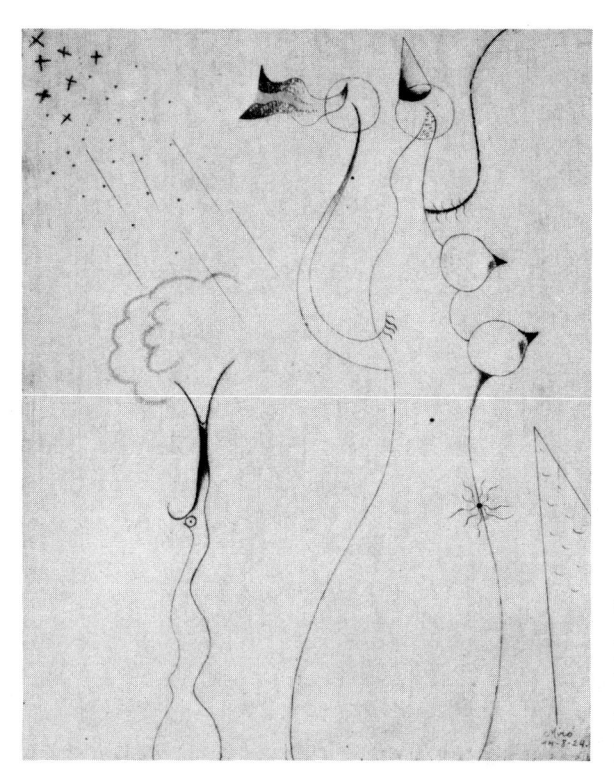

JOAN MIRO
Portrait de femme
Pencil, black crayon, watercolour and gouache on panel, signed and dated *14-8-24*, 10½in by 8½in
London £13,000($23,400). 30.VI.76

PABLO PICASSO
Nu allongé
India ink and wash, signed and dated *10.9.38*, 17½in by 26¾in
New York $39,000(£21,666). 18.III.76
From the collection of the late Lester Avnet

SALVADOR DALI
Cygnes reflétant des éléphants
Signed and dated *1937*, 20in by 30¼in
London £79,000($142,200). 30.VI.76
From the collection of Edward F. W. James

In a letter dated 2 May 1976, Edward James writes that Dali referred to the man standing on the rocks on the left as 'quelque petit bourgeois' and that he was intended to resemble a chemist in a neighbouring village called Ampurdam, north of Barcelona. He continues: 'I believe from what Dali once told me, that such figures are recollections of uncles and cousins from his early childhood – or simply sometimes just of business associates of his fathers; in fact, the sort of people who dominated a dry, materialistic and prosaic world from which he was already as a small boy fighting to escape. He is thus defeating them, getting the best of those ''petits bureaucrats'' by putting them in landscapes and in situations where they would find themselves totally lost.'

From the end of 1937 to the end of 1938, Edward James had a contract with Dali whereby Dali received a monthly pension in return for two or three paintings and ten drawings a month. Only two were delivered to Edward James before the war, and of the remainder most disappeared in France during the war. This picture and another were recovered in 1944 from the last train of loot that was stopped on its way from Paris out of France the day after the Liberation of Paris.

JEAN DUBUFFET
Train arrière autobus Gare Montparnasse-Porte des Lilas
Pen and ink, gouache and pencil, signed with initials and dated *25/2/61*, 19$\frac{3}{8}$in by 26$\frac{1}{8}$in
New York $27,000(£15,000). 18.III.76
From the collection of the late Lester Avnet

PABLO PICASSO
Scène orientale
Mixed media on paper, signed and dated *5.1.68.I, 8.1.68*, and *9.1.68*, 18¾in by 23⅛in
New York $50,000(£27,777). 17.III.76
From the collection of Mr and Mrs Josef Rosensaft

164 MODERN SCULPTURE

AUGUSTE RODIN
Le penseur
Bronze, signed and stamped *Alexis Rudier Fondeur Paris*, executed in 1880, height 28in
New York $67,500(£33,750). 22.X.75
From the collection of the late Geraldine Rockefeller Dodge

MODERN SCULPTURE 165

JACQUES LIPCHITZ
Draped woman
Bronze, signed and numbered *6/7* and stamped
MODERN ART FDRY, N.Y., executed in 1919,
height 37in
New York $38,000(£21,111). 26.V.76

ALBERTO GIACOMETTI
Tête d'homme sur tige
Bronze on plaster base, executed in 1947 (one of a
cast of six), height $21\frac{3}{4}$in
New York $35,000(£19,444). 26.V.76
From the collection of William N. Eisendrath Jnr

MARK ROTHKO
Sienna, orange and black on dark brown
Signed, titled and dated *1962* on the reverse, 76in by 69in
New York $190,000(£105,555). 27.V.76

CONTEMPORARY ART 167

FRANCIS BACON
Reclining man with sculpture
Painted in 1960-61, $65\frac{1}{2}$in by 56in
New York $160,000(£88,888). 27.V.76

ROY LICHTENSTEIN
Artist's studio
Signed and dated '73 on the reverse, 60in by 74in
New York $90,000(£50,000). 27.V.76

DAVID HOCKNEY
The sprinkler
Acrylic on canvas, signed, titled and dated *Los Angeles 1967* on the reverse, 48in by 48in
London £18,000($36,000). 4.XII.75

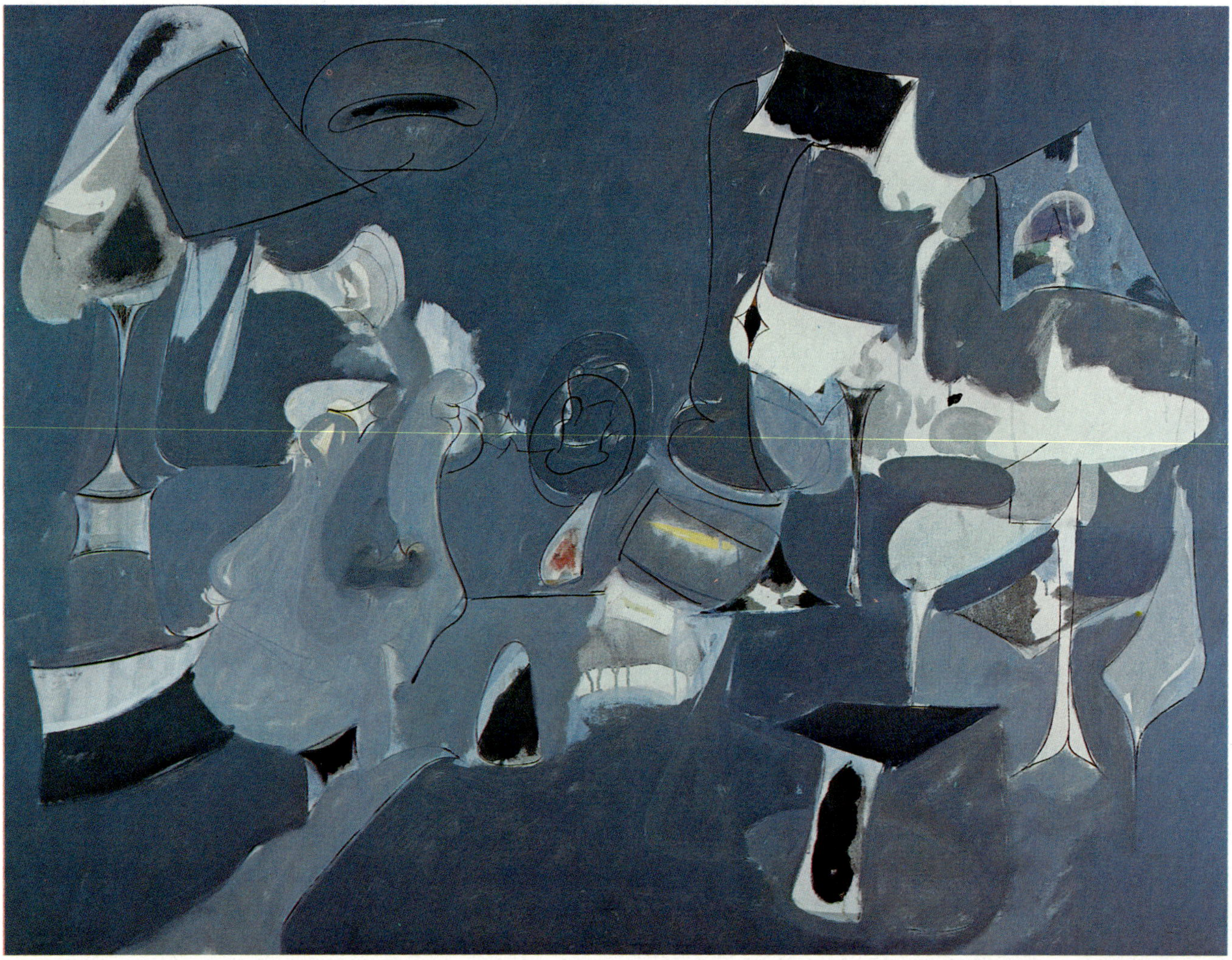

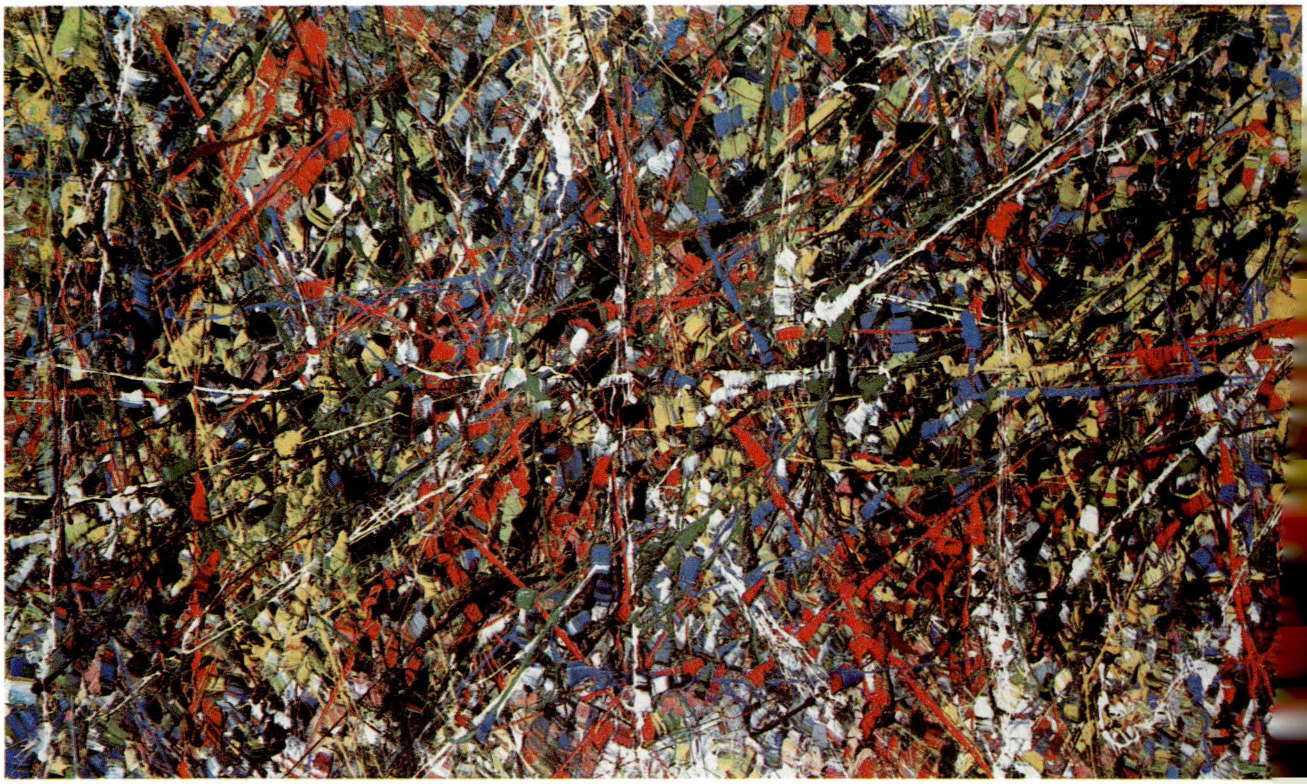

LARRY RIVERS
Africa III
Painted in 1963, 112in by 133in
New York $37,000(£20,555). 27.V.76

Opposite above
ARSHILE GORKY
Soft night
Signed and dated '47, 38in by 50in
New York $140,000(£77,777). 27.V.76

Opposite below
JEAN-PAUL RIOPELLE
Composition
Painted in 1952, 44¾in by 76½in
New York $32,500(£18,055). 27.V.76

ANDY WARHOL
Single Marilyn
Silk screen on canvas, executed in 1962, 20¼in by 16in
London £11,000($19,800). 1.VII.76

Below
SAM FRANCIS
Mascotte
Gouache, signed on the reverse, executed in 1958, 30in by 21¾in
London £6,400($12,800). 4.XII.75

Left
KENNETH NOLAND
Mesh
Acrylic on canvas, titled and dated *1959* on the reverse, 65¾in by 63¼in London £15,500($31,000). 4.XII.75

Right
MORRIS LOUIS
Narrow gauge
Acrylic on canvas, painted in 1962, 89in by 14in
London £15,000($27,000). 1.VII.76

MARK TOBEY
Changing of the square
Tempera on board, signed and dated '65, titled and dated '65 on the reverse, 39¼in by 27½in
London £15,000($30,000). 4.XII.75

Prints

EDVARD MUNCH
Frauen am Meeresufer
Woodcut printed in colours on thin japan, signed in pencil, 1898, 456mm by 512mm
London £29,000($52,200). 27.IV.76

176 PRINTS

FRANCISCO JOSE DE GOYA Y LUCIENTES
The bulls of Bordeaux
A set of four lithographs, 1825, 418mm by 538mm
New York $160,000(£88,888). 6.V.76

These magnificent large-scale compositions, executed only a quarter of a century after the invention of lithography, are Goya's only published works in this medium

FRANCISCO JOSE DE GOYA Y LUCIENTES
La Tauromaquia
Plate 2, etching with aquatint, a proof impression of a previously unknown state (before burnishing between the tree trunks and in the foreground), included as part of a set of thirty-three plates in the first edition of 1816
London £36,000($64,800). 25.III.76
From the collection of the Edward James Foundation

FRANCISCO JOSE DE GOYA Y LUCIENTES
La Tauromaquia
Etching with aquatint, one of the set of thirty-three plates in the first edition of 1816, 248mm by 355mm
London £33,000($59,400). 20.V.76
From the collection of Brinsley Ford

MARCO RICCI
The set of landscapes
Etchings, in all twenty numbered plates, second state with sequence numbers, 290mm by 430mm
London £5,100($9,180).
25.III.76

After ANTOINE WATTEAU
L'assemblée galante
Etching, first state of four, before the engraved work, 408mm by 528mm
London £650($1,170).
20.V.76

REMBRANDT HARMENSZ. VAN RIJN
Saint Jerome reading in an Italian landscape
Etching and drypoint, second state of two on 'oatmeal' paper, 258mm by 209mm
New York $65,000(£36,111). 7.V.76

180 PRINTS

GIORGIO MORANDI
Natura morta con il panneggio a sinistra
Etching, 1927, first state of two, signed in pencil, dated, and numbered 24/40, 243mm by 353mm
New York $9,000(£5,000). 6.V.76

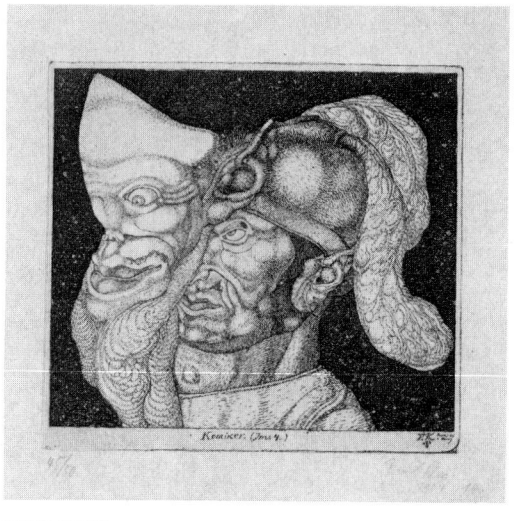

PAUL KLEE
Komiker
Etching, second state, signed in pencil, numbered 45/50, dated 1904 with work number 14, 153mm by 168mm
London £7,200($12,960). 27.IV.76

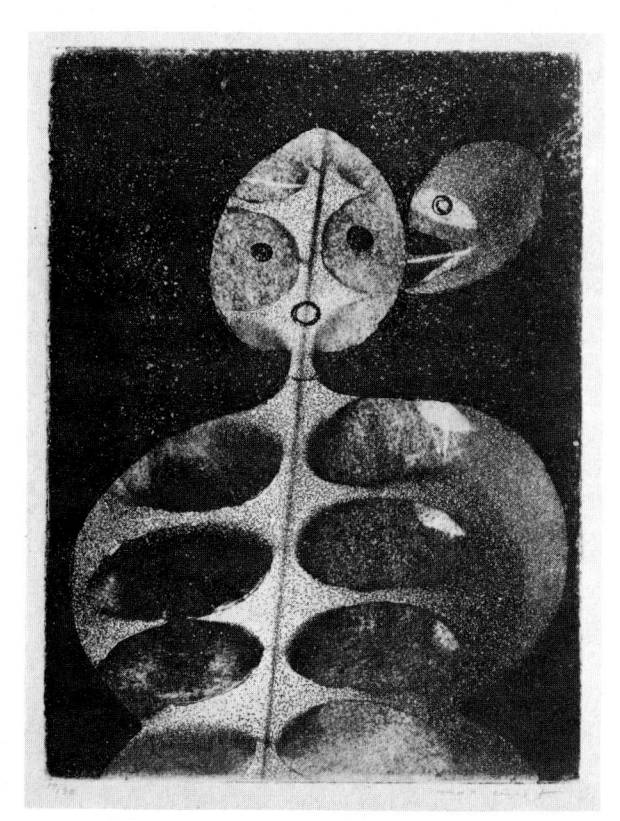

HENRI DE TOULOUSE-LAUTREC
Femme au tub
Lithograph printed in colours, plate four of *Elles*, 1896, 400mm by 520mm
Los Angeles $26,000(£14,444). 10.III.76

The complete set of Toulouse-Lautrec's *Elles*, comprising the cover, frontispiece and series of ten lithographs printed in colours and published by Gustave Pellet in an edition of 100 in 1896, realised $119,950(£66,668)

Opposite page left
MAX ERNST
Figure (Le secret)
Aquatint, signed in pencil, number 19/30, 1950, 236mm by 178mm
New York $3,400(£1,700). 13.XI.75

Opposite page right
CHARLES MERYON
Le stryge
Etching, fourth state of eight, 1853, 170mm by 130mm
New York $3,900(£2,166). 6.V.76

MAX BECKMANN
Gruppenbildnis Edenbar
Woodcut, 1923, hand-printed proof impression of the second state of two, signed in pencil, dated, and annotated *Eden-Hotel (Handprobedruck)*, 490mm by 495mm
New York $6,500(£3,250). 13.XI.75

PABLO PICASSO
Buste de jeune femme
Woodcut, 1906, signed in pencil and number 2/15, 555mm by 385mm
New York $37,500(£20,833). 6.V.76

This is the artist's major work in this medium. The edition of only fifteen impressions was printed in 1933 (only two earlier impressions, one incomplete, are known)

PAUL KLEE
Jungfrau in baum
Etching, signed in pencil, numbered 24/30, dated 1903, inscribed by the artist with title and the work number 2, 236mm by 298mm
London £11,700($21,060).
27.IV.76

PAUL GAUGUIN
Manao Tupapau
Lithograph, 1894, signed in ink and numbered 74, from the edition of 100 included in *L'Estampe Originale*, April-June 1894, 183mm by 272mm
New York $12,000(£6,000).
13.XI.75

EDVARD MUNCH
Weibliche aktfigur – Die Sünde
Lithograph, printed in colours on Japan paper, signed in pencil, 1901, 695mm by 400mm
New York $42,500(£21,250). 14.XI.75

After GEORGE STUBBS, ARA
Dungannon by George Townley Stubbs
Stipple engraving printed in colours, 1791, 403mm by 502mm
London £460($920). 18.XI.75
From the collection of W. J. Gray

After JOHN JAMES CHALON, RA
The Turnpike gate by Charles Turner
Mezzotint printed in colours, one of a pair, 485mm by 560mm
London £1,200($2,160). 13.IV.76

After AMBROSE LOUIS
GARNERAY
Whale-fishery: Harpooning the whale by Frederick Martens
Coloured aquatints, one of a pair
London £1,100($1,980).
13.IV.76

GABRIEL LUDWIG LORY
Switzerland: Voyage pittoresque de l'oberland bernois
Coloured aquatints, thirty plates, 1822
London £5,200($9,360).
13.IV.76

188 PRINTS

WELBY SHERMANN
The shepherd
Engraving on chine appliqué, 124mm by 80mm
London £620($1,116). 3.II.76
From the collection of H. I. Richmond, formerly in the collection of George Richmond, RA

This print was made after a design by Samuel Palmer

GEORGE RICHMOND, RA
The good shepherd
Engraving, second and final state, inscribed *Geo. Richmond, R.A. designed and engraved 1829*, 176mm by 116mm
London £1,100($1,980). 25.V.76

Manuscripts and Printed Books

190 ORIENTAL MANUSCRIPTS AND MINIATURES
194 WESTERN MANUSCRIPTS
214 AUTOGRAPH MANUSCRIPTS AND LETTERS
220 PRINTED BOOKS AND DRAWINGS

S. MANETTI
Storia naturale degli Uccelli
5 volumes with 600 hand-coloured plates, Florence, 1767-76
London £9,500($19,000). 10.XI.75

FIRDAUSI
Shahnama
Persian manuscript with 53 miniatures [Shiraz, mid sixteenth century]
London £90,000 ($180,000).
9.XII.75

ORIENTAL MANUSCRIPTS AND MINIATURES 191

The Defeat of Hemu
A leaf from the Victoria and
Albert Museum *Akbarnama*,
[Mughal, *circa* 1595-1600]
London £22,000($39,600).
12.IV.76
From the collection of the
Hagop Kevorkian Fund

The Bible
An Armenian manuscript on vellum illuminated by Malnazar and Aghaphir,
[New Julfa], 1637-38
London £19,000($34,200). 12.IV.76
From the collection of the Hagop Kevorkian Fund

MUHAMMAD AZIMA
Shahid u Mashud
A Persian manuscript composed, written and illustrated by the author, [Delhi or Murshidabad], 1750
London £7,500($13,500). 14.IV.76

Scenes from the lives of Gideon and Moses
Hours of the Virgin, use of Rome
With 84 large miniatures by Gerard Horenbout and other artists, [Ghent or Bruges, *circa* 1510]
London £370,000($666,000). 5.VII.76

An unrecorded Flemish Book of Hours

Christopher de Hamel

Books of Hours are probably the most common of all surviving medieval manuscripts. They are essentially lay prayerbooks and each family of importance would be likely to possess at least one such book. Their name derives from the central cycle of prayers and psalms intended for each of the canonical hours of the day and most were written and illuminated in secular workshops between the late fourteenth and the early sixteenth centuries. Many of the manuscripts are standard in size and decoration and were apparently written for sale on bookstalls in the cathedral and commercial towns. The more expensive and grandly-illuminated Books of Hours (the Duc de Berry's *Très Riches Heures* is a well-known example) were produced on commission for specific wealthy lay patrons and were often decorated by artists of the first rank.

One extraordinary Book of Hours, which was apparently completely unknown before being brought into Sotheby's Munich office late last year, was illuminated in Ghent or Bruges about 1510 by a group of remarkable Flemish artists. The manuscript is in every way a grand production. Every one of its 312 leaves is decorated with a border completely surrounding the script and decorated with birds, flowers, animals and other devices. In addition to the usual daily cycle of hours, the text also contains offices for every day of the week. It begins with a calendar for the liturgical year with miniatures not only of the peasants' occupations for each month – with some extraordinary landscapes and farmyard scenes – but also little pictures of saints and the games associated with each month. These include a snow fight, piggy-back, a game of golf (one of the earliest depictions), skittles, hoops, a water tournament and other similar subjects. The majority of the large paintings throughout the manuscript are arranged in pairs with a New Testament subject, representing the theme for each office, with its Old Testament parallel on the facing page. At the end of the various Hours themselves are the Penitential Psalms, the Office of the Dead, and a long series of prayers to particular saints with large miniatures of each one.

The principal artist of the manuscript is Gerard Horenbout and at least twenty-three of the miniatures are in his hand. In addition to his work as an illuminator he is also known as a panel painter. He was a member of the artists' guild in Ghent in 1487 and a decade later was working on the Breviary of Isabella the Catholic; his work can be seen in the Grimani and Mayer van den Bergh Breviaries and in 1521 he is documented as completing the Sforza Hours as court painter to Margaret of Austria. About 1528 he received an annuity from the English court and he died in Ghent in 1541. The present manuscript shows him at the peak of his career.

The Crucifixion and *Moses and the brazen serpent* (the Old Testament prefiguration of the Crucifixion) A pair of miniatures by Gerard Horenbout

One of the other major hands in the Book of Hours is the Bruges artist, known as the Dresden Master, who painted the Nativity scene with the shepherds dancing with each other and with their dog. Five other miniatures are either by him or his assistants. The calendar and many of the saints' portraits in the manuscript were painted by the Master of the Emperor Maximilian I; others of this group are undoubtedly in the hand of Simon Bening (died 1560) – the miniatures of Saints Julian, Francis, Anthony and Dominic are certainly his – and others are hard to separate between Bening and the Maximilian Master. Several of this series were later copied into the celebrated Grimani Breviary now in Venice and this new Book of Hours helps our understanding of the models for that manuscript. A tantalising and intriguing problem is presented by the artist of five of the miniatures: scenes from the lives of Saint John, Christ, Solomon, David and of the Death of the Virgin. The short, bustling and intensely human little figures are characteristic of the great and elusive Master of Mary of Burgundy, perhaps the best Flemish illuminator of the fifteenth century, whose late work has never been satisfactorily identified; if it exists, it will almost certainly look like the five miniatures in this manuscript.

The attribution of the book to a certain locality is not easy. Books are very portable things. There are various stylistic links with altarpieces in Ghent. The group of artists, however, frequently moved between Ghent and Bruges as work became available and a lavish commission could take them to work in a patron's own residence elsewhere.

The original owner of the manuscript is not yet known. A coat-of-arms (*azure*, a cross *ancrée* between four bezants *or*) appears in one miniature but, if it is a clue, it has proved elusive. The same group of artists produced books for James IV of Scotland, Maximilian I, Charles V, the Infanta of Portugal and the Grimani and Sforza families of Italy, and yet possibly none is finer in quality than the present manuscript. It is difficult to suggest who, in 1510, could have afforded to pay more than the crowned heads of Europe for this Book of Hours.

The Bible in Latin
Illuminated by William de Brailes, the earliest English artist of whom the name is known, [Oxford, *circa* 1230-35]
London £23,000($41,400). 5.VII.76
Formerly in the collection of Robin Howard, CBE
Now in the Bodleian Library

Bestiary
A German manuscript on vellum with 86 coloured drawings, [Erfurt(?), second half of the fourteenth century], £60,000($120,000)

Opposite page
The Freudenberg Breviary
Latin manuscript on vellum, [Bavaria, Diocese of Eichstätt], 1487, £36,000($72,000)
Both these manuscripts are from the collection of the late Sir Thomas Phillipps Bt (1792-1872) sold in London on 26 November 1975

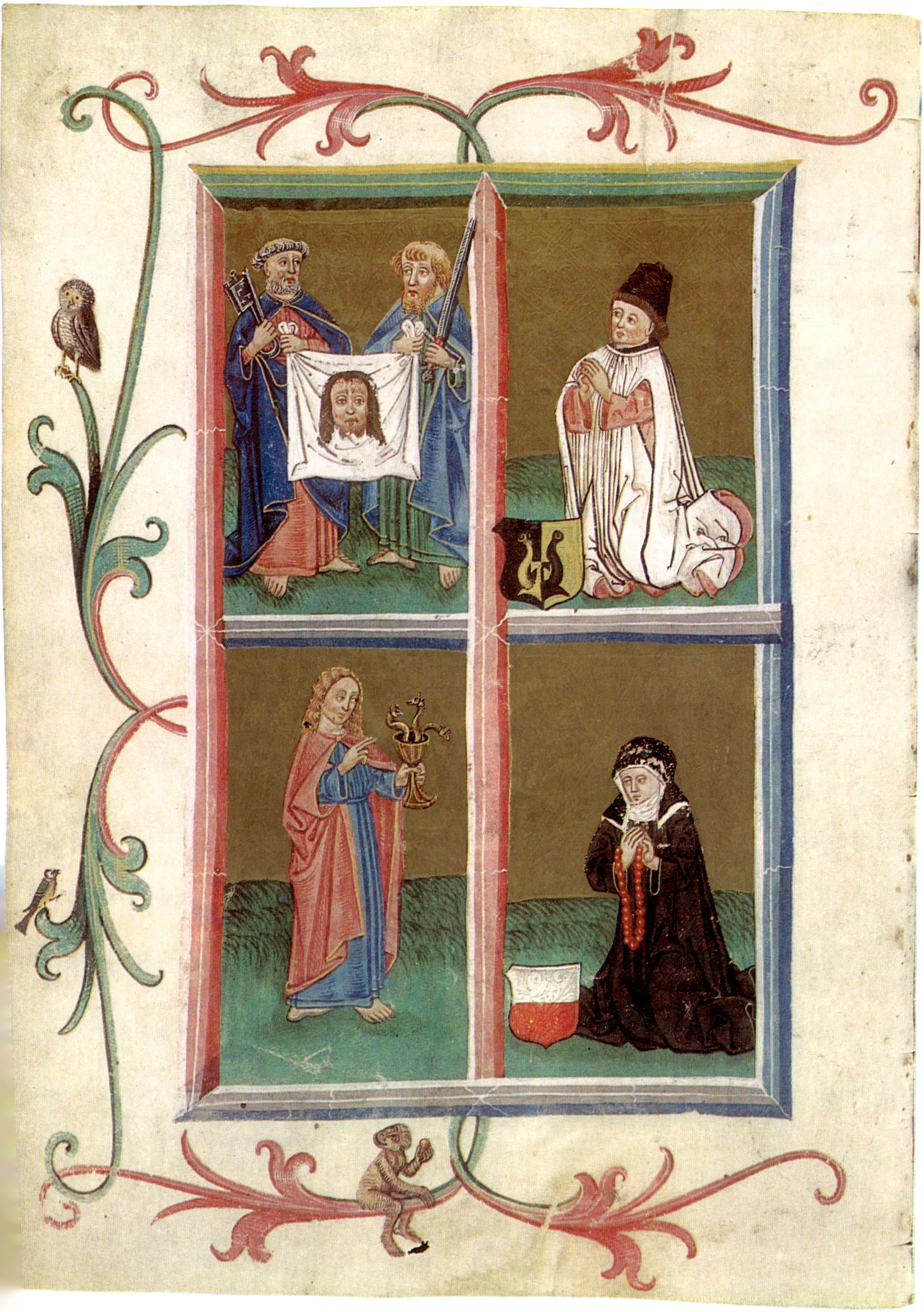

E. SWEERT *Florilegium Amplissimum et Selectissimum*
Text on large paper with 110 engraved plates (Amsterdam, 1647-54)
London £2,800($5,040). 15.III.76

The Botanical Library formed by the late Dr Arpad Plesch

Wilfrid Blunt

Dr Arpad Plesch was a born book-collector. Though a Doctor of Law and the author of a number of treatises on international law and kindred subjects his tastes were catholic, and the fine library that he formed between the Wars in the villa La Léonina, at Beaulieu-sur-Mer on the French Riviera, covered a wide field. Then came the Germans, and when Dr Plesch returned from exile he found his shelves bare.

Men like Dr Plesch rise above adversity. Thanks to shrewd dealings in Japanese stocks and shares he was soon in a position to replace many of his books of reference, and to form fresh collections of eighteenth-century French classics, finely-bound limited editions of works illustrated by artists such as Derain and Picasso, and a choice little nest of erotica. In particular, he began the acquisition of a superb library of botanical books, then absurdly cheap by today's standards, and to found a *Stiftung für Botanik* and a large garden at Beaulieu devoted mainly to the scientific acclimatisation of exotic plants. He also published a *de luxe* catalogue of his botanical books, copiously illustrated and prefaced by a reproduction of his portrait by Graham Sutherland. On his death in 1974 at the age of eighty-four, estate duties necessitated the disposal of his botanical library, which was auctioned at Sotheby's in three two-day sales on 16-17 June and 17-18 November 1975, and 15-16 March 1976. The total hammer price for the three sales was £568,379, by far the highest for the sale of any natural history library.

It is immediately evident that Arpad Plesch was more interested in the sumptuously-illustrated botanical productions of the seventeenth and, more especially, eighteenth and nineteenth centuries than in the early herbals with their modest woodcuts. However, two *incunabula* in his library deserve mention: a *Herbarius Patavie* (Passau, 1485) formerly in the collection of that distinguished historian of botany Dr F. W. T. Hunger, and a German *Hortus Sanitatus* (Strasbourg, *circa* 1485), the latter neither a first edition nor a perfect copy yet a rarity deservedly fetching £3,200. In both these the woodcuts have been coloured by an early hand, and were, indeed, possibly issued in this state by the publishers.

The great herbals of the first half of the sixteenth century are those of Brunfels and Fuchs. Of the three parts of Brunfels' *Herbarum Vivae Eicones* (Strasbourg, 1530-36), a landmark in the history of botanical illustration as the earliest of the printed herbals to be illustrated throughout with naturalistic figures, Dr Plesch possessed only the

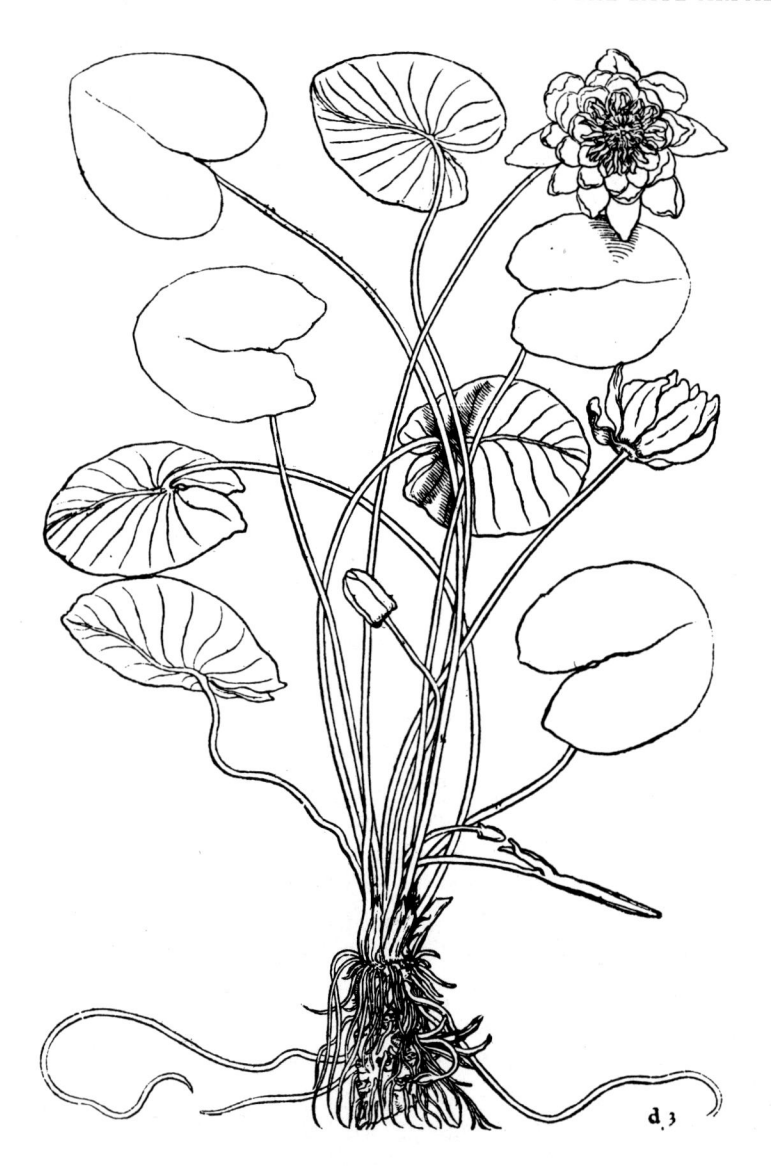

O. BRUNFELS
Herbarum Vivae Eicones ad Naturae Imitationem
The first part only of three with 86 text woodcuts (Strasbourg, 1530)
London £900($1,800). 16.VI.75

first; but it is unusual to find so clean and crisp a copy of it. The artist was Hans Weiditz, who was closely associated with Dürer. Far more impressive and far better known as the *De Historia Stirpium* of Leonhart Fuchs, published in Basel by the Isingrin Press in 1542. Perhaps Ruskin and William Morris, who so admired this great folio, may not have been acquainted with the Brunfels; if they were, then they must surely have found the latter aesthetically the more satisfying. The woodcuts in Dr Plesch's Fuchs have also been coloured by a contemporary hand, and a further example of his preference in this respect is a copy of Hieronymus Bock's *De Historia Stirpium* (Strasbourg, 1552) the first Latin edition of a work published in German at Strasbourg in 1539.

The second half of the century is dominated by the works of Pierandrea Mattioli, Rembert Dodoens, Carolus Clusius and Mathias Lobel. Many by the last three of these were issued by the famous Plantin Press. Christophe Plantin, a Frenchman by birth, set up his printing works in Antwerp about 1550 and accumulated there a large collection of botanical drawings, blocks made from which constituted a kind of pool at the disposal of authors needing such illustrations. The Plesch collection includes an unusual, though not unique, item – one of the original woodblocks used by Mattioli in the later and more nobly-illustrated edition of his *Commentarii* (from 1558 onwards) – and a fine hand-coloured copy of Dodoens' *Cruydeboeck* (Antwerp, [1552]-54), the first and the rarest of his herbals. There were also several other works by Mattioli, Lobel and Clusius in the sale. A book of much importance to Englishmen is Turner's *Herbal* (Köln, 1568). William Turner, known as 'the father of British botany', after publishing the first part of his herbal in London in 1551, fled the country because of his religious opinions, but returned there on Elizabeth's accession. The woodcuts that illustrate his magnum opus are largely derived, as so often in herbals of that time, from those in Fuchs's *De Historia Stirpium*.

As the sixteenth century drew to its close, the woodblock began to give place to the metal plate, and the herbal, with its emphasis on *useful* plants, to the florilegium with illustrations of flowers that only had their beauty to commend them. Among the earliest of botanical books in which metal plates were employed are Fabio Colonna's *Phytobasanos* (Naples, 1592) and *Ekphrasis* (Rome, 1606 and 1616), but their subject matter places these closer to the herbals. Dr Plesch possessed what is probably the dedication copy, in a handsome binding, of the first part of the *Ekphrasis* (1606), and other editions of both works.

A number of delightful florilegia were published in the opening years of the seventeenth century. Of these Dr Plesch's fine copy of Basil Besler's *Hortus Eystettensis* (Eichstätt and Nuremberg, 1613) realised the considerable sum of £16,000, and Emanuel Sweert was represented by a magnificently hand-coloured *de luxe* copy of a later edition (Amsterdam, 1647-54) of his *Florilegium*, originally published in Frankfurt in 1612. Besler's gigantic work, often to be found in two volumes, was described by Sir Thomas Browne as the massiest of herbals; massive it certainly is, and Sir Arthur Church was justified in saying that it was best transported in a wheelbarrow, but it is a florilegium rather than a herbal. Sweert was a Dutch florist at one time employed by the Emperor Rudolf II as Praefectus of his gardens. In spite of Sweert's assurance on the title-page that his plants were 'drawn from life', many of the plates are derived, or even in some cases directly copied, from the works of de Bry and other far better artists.

At the same time that metal engraving was becoming the accepted method of illustration on the Continent, the woodcut was still employed in England in such works as Gerard's *Herbal* (1597; 1633 and 1636) and John Parkinson's ever-popular *Paradisus* (1629) and *Theatrum Botanicum* (1640) – the latter sometimes described as 'the last British herbal'. These books, as the sale showed, still realise relatively modest prices.

Dr Plesch's most precious prize of the later part of the seventeenth century was a copy of Dionys Dodart's *Mémoires pour servir à l'Histoire des Plantes* (Paris, Imprimerie Royale, 1676), with thirty-nine superb plates engraved, after drawings by Nicolas Robert, by Robert himself and Abraham Bosse. After many delays the main work was published with 319 plates but no text, and yet later in the form originally intended. Nicolas Robert is best remembered for his famous *chef d'œuvre de la galanterie*, the *Guirlande de Julie* – an album of paintings of flowers supported by verses by Corneille and other poets of the Rambouillet circle inscribed by Jarry, the greatest calligrapher of the day. This enchanting book, which was shown in London in 1950 at the exhibition of 'Flower Books and their Illustrators' held that year at the National Book League, was the birthday gift of the baron de Sainte-Maure (the future duc de Montausier) to his fiancée, Julie d'Angennes, before he left to join the army.

Reaching the eighteenth century, we find the majority of the more important items in the Plesch library to be British. Here the highest price realised (£10,000) was for a work begun in this century but continuing publication to this day; a complete run of Curtis's immortal *Botanical Magazine* from its start in 1787 down to 1968. Earlier in the century we have John Martyn's *Historia Plantarum Rariorum* (London, 1728[-37]), the first botanical book to be illustrated with plates printed in colour (mezzotint, finished by hand); this is therefore the humble predecessor of such masterpieces as Redouté's *Les Liliacées* (1802-16).

Catesby's *The Natural History of Carolina*, the most famous of colourplate works dealing with the flora and fauna of America, first appeared in 1730-48; it was represented in this sale by the second edition, published in London in 1754. There was also a fine copy of Sir Hans Sloane's *A Voyage to the Islands Madera . . .* (London 1707-25), the first volume bound by Robert Steel, royal binder to William III, and the second similarly by an unidentified craftsman. The twenty-six folio volumes of *The Vegetable System* (London, 1759-75) of that extraordinary man Sir John Hill, half genius and half charlatan, realised £7,200. The collation of this copy, which was acquired by Plesch at the Leyel sale in 1958, has presented considerable problems to the compiler of the Plesch sale catalogue; in some volumes the plates are coloured, in others not, and presumably we are dealing here with a composite set. Among other works by Hill in the sale was his *Exotic Botany* (London, 1759), with plates as decorative as they are fanciful.

Possibly the greatest of all botanical artists was an Austrian, Franz (Francis) Bauer, whose superb plates of heaths for his *Delineations of Exotick Plants* (London, 1796-97) fully justify the £1,900 that the book fetched. His only rival as a botanical draughtsman was his younger brother, Ferdinand. Franz came to England in 1790 at the invitation of Sir Joseph Banks, then virtually Director of Kew Gardens, and until his death fifty years later worked at Kew making paintings of the flowers brought back to this country by men of more adventurous spirit than himself. Among these botanist-explorers was Ferdinand, who accompanied Sibthorp to the Levant in 1786 and Matthew Flinders to Australia in 1801; Ferdinand's famous *Flora Graeca* will be discussed in due course.

France was represented by the only known complete copy of P. P. Alyon's *Cours de Botanique* (Paris, 1787-88), its great rarity being largely responsible for the high price (£9,200) realised. Far more beautiful, and scarcely less rare is the Plesch copy of the *Cornus* (Paris, 1788 [1789]) of L'Heritier de Brutelle — one of six printed on vellum with six plates hand-coloured by Redouté and his younger brother Henri-Joseph. Another uncommon French work — a fine and complete copy of J. P. Bergeret's *Phytonomatotechnie Universelle* bound in contemporary morocco — was included in the library, as was a remarkable collection of engraved suites of designs, mostly of flowers, by L. Tessier and others. There were also two copies of François Regnault's *La Botanique* (Paris, 1774) — an impressive folio whose author engagingly describes the potato as 'possibly the only good thing that ever came out of America'.

C. L. L'HERITIER DE BRUTELLE *Cornus*
One of six copies printed on vellum (Paris, 1788)
London £8,000($16,000). 17.XI.75

Among the greatest German publications of the eighteenth century are Weinmann's immense florilegium, *Phytanthoza Iconographia* (Regensburg, 1737-45) and Christopher Trew's *Plantae Selectae* (Nuremberg, 1750-52) with one hundred plates by Georg Dionysius Ehret. Weinmann was the director of a long-established pharmacy in Regensburg, and the importance of his book, which has more than a thousand plates printed in colour and finished by hand, is that it affords us a wonderful survey of the plants grown in German gardens at that time. It contains some amusing plates of cacti in brightly-coloured pots. Ehret – who might perhaps be described as the Handel of flower-painting in that he left his native Germany to settle in England, where he was endlessly industrious and much admired – was in his early days employed for a time, at starvation wages, by Weinmann in the production of the *Phytanthoza Iconographia*. He did well to break away and find fame in the country of his adoption.

Austria was represented by J. J. von Plenck's *Icones Plantarum Medicinalium* (Vienna, 1788-1803) and by several important works by Nikolaus von Jacquin including his *Hortus Botanicus Vindobonensis* (Vienna, 1770-76) of which only 162 copies were printed. Turning to Holland, we find Linnaeus there with his *Hortus Cliffortianus* (Amsterdam, 1737), his only work with handsome plates; but the most spectacular product of the Dutch presses in the sale was Seba's zoological-botanical *Thesaurus* (Amsterdam, 1734-65), this sumptuous set of four folio volumes with contemporary colouring deservedly fetching £8,000. Seba, an internationally famous apothecary of German birth, formed a remarkable cabinet of curios which he sold in its entirety to Peter the Great of Russia; but like Dr Plesch himself he was an incurable collector, and starting all over again built up another which surpassed the first. Seba died in 1736, and it was only by the auction of his new collection that the publication of the final part of the great *Thesaurus*, completed by his collaborators, could ultimately be published.

By the time we come to the nineteenth century, the volume of fine flower books has become so great that we inevitably find many important works not included in the Plesch library. For example, of Van Spaëndonck, Redouté's master, we have only the very indifferent posthumous *Souvenirs* (Paris, *circa* 1826), not his lovely *Fleurs dessinées d'après Nature* (Paris, *circa* 1800). W. H. Fitch, most prolific of British nineteenth-century botanical draughtsmen, is represented by his lithographs for three books by Sir Joseph Hooker, but not by those of orchids that he made for the works of J. Bateman and Robert Warner or those of lilies used in H. J. Elwes's *Monograph on the Genus Lilium*. However, let us rather consider those treasures that Dr Plesch did possess.

It is only fitting that in the age of Redouté, we should take France first. An unforgettable word-portrait of Redouté, as given by J. F. Grille in his *La Fleur des Pois* (1853), may be compared with the more flattering lithograph of him here reproduced:

'A stocky figure with elephantine limbs; a head like a large, flat Dutch cheese; thick lips; a hollow voice; crooked fingers; a repellent appearance; and – beneath the surface – an extremely delicate sense of touch; exquisite taste; a deep feeling for art; great sensibility; nobility of character; and the application essential to the full development of genius: such was Redouté, painter of flowers, who counted all the prettiest women in Paris among his pupils.'

Portrait of Redouté lithographed by Ferogio
after Mlle Godefroy, from *Le Bouquet Royal*
Four hand-coloured plates (Paris, 1843)
London £600($1,080). 15.III.76

Though he was born in that part of Belgium then belonging to the Duchy of Luxembourg, France was the country of Redouté's adoption, and in the Empress Joséphine, and later in the duchesse de Berry, he found the enthusiastic and generous patronesses that made possible the production and publication of his wonderful folios. He was probably less gifted than Turpin or Van Spaëndonck; but he was far luckier. On 19 June 1840, while examining a white lily brought him by one of his pupils, he received a stroke from the result of which he died the following day. On his coffin was laid a wreath of roses and lilies bearing the inscription:

> 'O peintre aimé de Flore et du riant empire,
> Tu nous quittes le jour ou le printemps expire.'

Redouté himself is, of course, represented in strength with fine copies of his *Les Liliacées* (Paris, 1802-16: £19,000), *Choix des plus belles Fleurs* (Paris, 1827: £10,000) and *Les Roses* (Paris, 1817-24: £9,500). He is also there as the principal illustrator of the seven magnificent volumes of H. L. Duhamel du Monceau's *Traité des Arbres et Arbustes*; and as the sole illustrator of A. de Candolle's *Plantarum Succulentarum*

TAB. III.

P. J. REDOUTÉ *Choix des plus belles Fleurs*
144 plates after Redouté (Paris, 1827)
London £10,000($18,000). 15.III.76

Opposite page
A. SEBA *Locupletissimi Rerum Naturalium Thesauri*
Text in French and Latin with 449 plates of natural curiosities (Amsterdam, 1734-65)
London £8,000($14,400). 16.III.76

G. BROOKSHAW
Pomona Britannica
90 coloured stipple engravings finished by hand (1805-12)
London £2,800($5,600). 16.VI.75

Historia (Paris, 1799[-1805]), Ventenat's *Jardin de la Malmaison* (Paris, 1803-4) and Rousseau's *La Botanique* (Paris, 1805).

Other splendid French works of the period include an almost complete set of the immense *Voyage aux Régions équinoctiales du Noveau Continent* by Baron Friedrich von Humboldt and others (Paris, *circa* 1805-29), a fine copy of J. H. Jaume Saint-Hilaire's *La Flore et la Pomone Françaises* (Paris, 1828-33), and one of the limited edition, with plate captions printed in gold, of J. L. M. Poiret and P. Turpin's lovely *Leçons de Flore* (Paris, 1819-20); Turpin's original drawings for the last-named, once the property of 'un souverain de l'Allemagne', are in the Lindley Library of the Royal Horticultural Society.

Among English books, pride of place must be accorded to the ten volumes of Sibthorp's famous *Flora Graeca* (London, *circa* 1845: £22,000), with nearly a thousand hand-coloured plates after paintings by Ferdinand Bauer. This set was one of forty of a second printing, the first and even smaller edition having appeared between 1806 and 1840; but except for the watermarks there is little to distinguish them. The illustrations for this magnificent work were the fruits of the expedition made by

Sibthorp and Ferdinand Bauer to the Levant in 1786-87. In addition to the purely botanical plates, Bauer produced a number of landscapes which were used in the title-pages of the ten volumes; and there is also in Oxford a large collection of unpublished Greek zoological drawings which ought certainly one day to be given to the world by an enterprising publisher. Another uncommon work of the turn of the century is the *Plants of the Coast of Coromandel* (London, 1795-1819) by William Roxburgh, an energetic Scot in charge of the Calcutta Botanic Garden who employed native artists to provide drawings for plates executed by British engravers. George Brookshaw was represented by no less than six works, his magnum opus, *Pomona Britannica* – the most splendid fruit book ever produced – fetching £2,800. Mrs Bury's *A Selection of Hexandrian Plants* (London, 1831-34) owes most of its beauty to the skill of the engraver, Robert Havell, junior, who much improved upon the mediocre watercolours he had to work from.

German and Austrian publications, in general much less known and appreciated in this country than those of England and France although hardly inferior to them, were strongly represented. There is space only to mention one or two of the more important. From Vienna in the golden age of the two Jacquins we have the elder Jacquin again represented, now by his *Fragmenta Botanica* (1809), and his son by a number of works including his *Eclogae Plantarum Rariorum* (1813-44). Other rare Viennese publications which fetched good prices were those of N. J. Host, F. Schmidt, J. E. Pohl, L. Trattinick and Graf von Waldstein.

The German presses provided a copy of the extremely uncommon *Flora Monacenis* of F. von Paula von Schrank (Munich, 1811-18), with 400 hand-coloured lithographs by J. N. Mayrhoffer, the first botanical artist to use a medium which was soon to become so popular. From Munich we also have C. F. P. von Martius' rare and important *Flora of Brazil*; from Hanover, J. C. Wendland's *Ericarum Icones et Descriptiones* (1798-1813), and from Berlin the 14 volumes (bound in seven) of F. G. Hayne's *Getreue Darstellung* (1845-46), a very uncommon work on medicinal plants – and K. L. Willdenow's *Hortus Berolinensis* (1816).

Outside France, England, Austria and Germany there were only two nineteenth-century books in the sales that call for special mention. P. F. von Siebold, a German doctor who spent many years in Japan, was principally responsible for the two volumes of *Flora Japonica*, published in Leyden between 1835 and 1870, which realised £3,000. And lastly, from Belgium we have the only known complete copy of J. de Liron d'Airoles *Album de la Civélière* (Brussels, 1855-58).

It must seem probable that never again will so important and representative a collection of finely-illustrated botanical books be seen in the saleroom, for the only comparable library in this field to be formed in recent years, that assembled by Mr and Mrs Roy Arthur Hunt, is now, through their generosity, in the possession of the Carnegie-Mellon University of Pittsburgh. The Hunt library is, of course, considerably larger, is far more fully representative where early botanical books are concerned and far richer in works that are unillustrated or in which the text is of more importance than the plates. But Dr Plesch was not a botanist, he was a bibliophile. His aim was to assemble a collection of beautifully-produced and beautifully-illustrated flower books, and this he triumphantly achieved.

J. SIBTHORP, J. E. SMITH and J. LINDLEY   *Flora Graeca*
In ten volumes, 1806-45
London £22,000($39,600). 15.III.76

N. J. VON JACQUIN *Fragmenta Botanica*
138 engraved plates, all but two being coloured by hand (Vienna, 1809)
London £6,000($12,000). 17.XI.75

214　AUTOGRAPH MANUSCRIPTS AND LETTERS

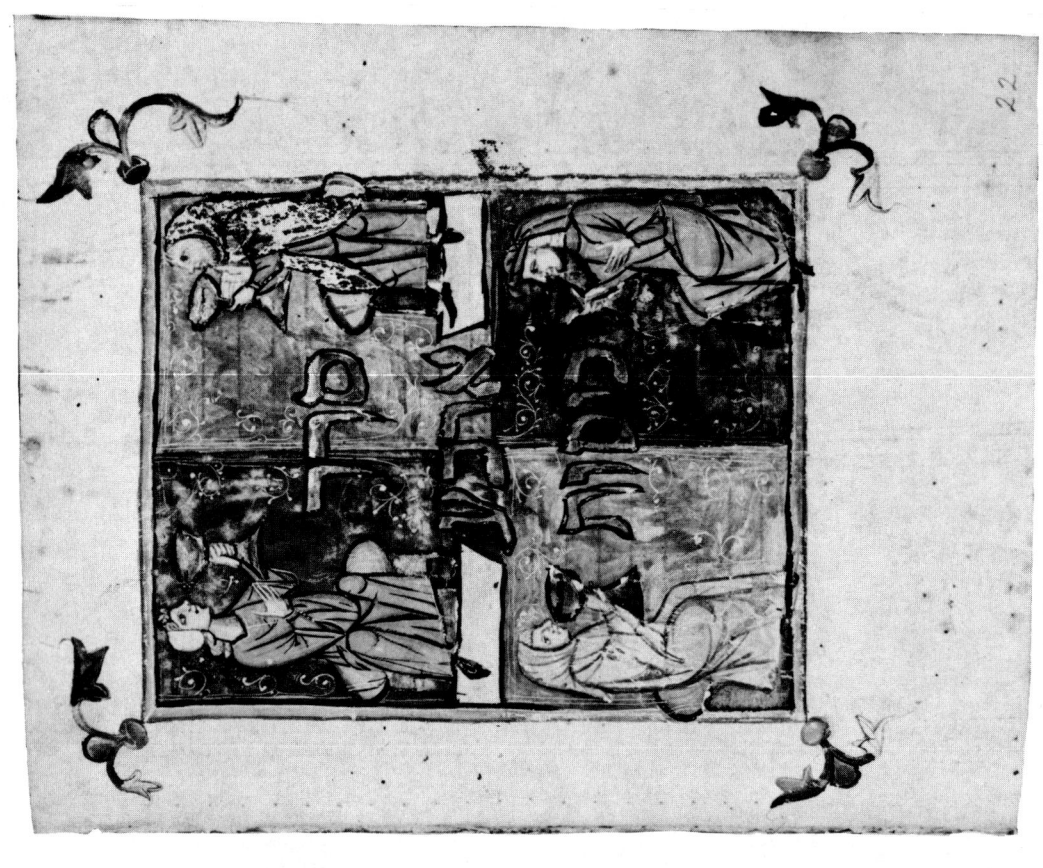

Haggadah according to the Spanish Provencal Rite
Manuscript on vellum [Spain(Barcelona?), circa 1300]
Zürich SF580,000(£105,454:$210,908). 5.XI.75
From the collection of the late David Solomon Sassoon

MOSES MAIMONIDES
Commentary on the second and third orders of the Mishnah
Judaeo-Arabic manuscript [Cairo, circa 1160-68]
Zürich SF1,200,000(£218,182:$436,364). 5.XI.75
From the collection of the late David Solomon Sassoon

AUTOGRAPH MANUSCRIPTS AND LETTERS 215

JOSEPHUS
De bello Judaico
Greek manuscript on vellum, [Byzantine Empire, first(?) half of the eleventh century]
London £27,000($54,000). 26.XI.75
From the collection of the late Sir Thomas Phillipps Bt (1792-1872)

Machzor according to the old Roman Rite
Manuscript on vellum written and illuminated by Abraham Ben Matatiah, Pesaro, 1480
Zürich SF260,000(£47,273:$94,544). 5.XI.75
From the collection of the late David Solomon Sassoon

ELIZABETH I, QUEEN OF ENGLAND
Letter written by her secretary, Roger Ascham, and signed by the Queen, Hampton Court, 1568
London £3,200($5,760). 22.VI.76
Formerly in the collection of Robin Howard, CBE

PETER I, EMPEROR OF RUSSIA
Autograph document, a draft for a *ukaz*, [Russia, *circa* 1700-1720]
Zürich SF5,500(£1,000:$2,000). 5.XI.75

THOMAS TELFORD
An extensive archive of his papers, including 70 autograph reports, 900 letters and two drafts of his autobiography
London £5,000($9,000). 22.VI.76

LORD BYRON
Autograph manuscript of his poem *Beppo*, Venice, 1817-18
London £50,000($90,000). 22.VI.76

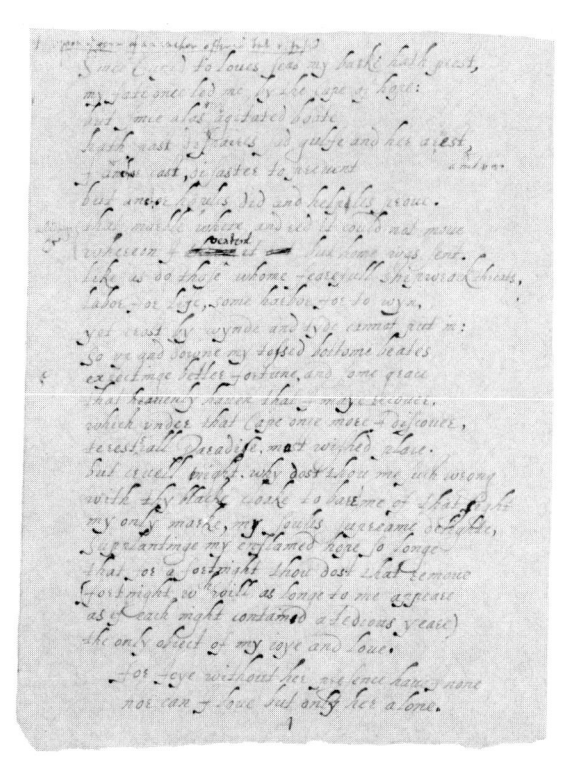

DUDLEY NORTH
Two poetical manuscript notebooks, [early seventeenth century]
London £9,500($19,000). 29.X.75

GEORGE WASHINGTON
118 autograph letters concerning his estate at Mount Vernon, 1793-98
New York $250,000(£138,888). 24.II.76
From the collection of the Long Island Historical Society

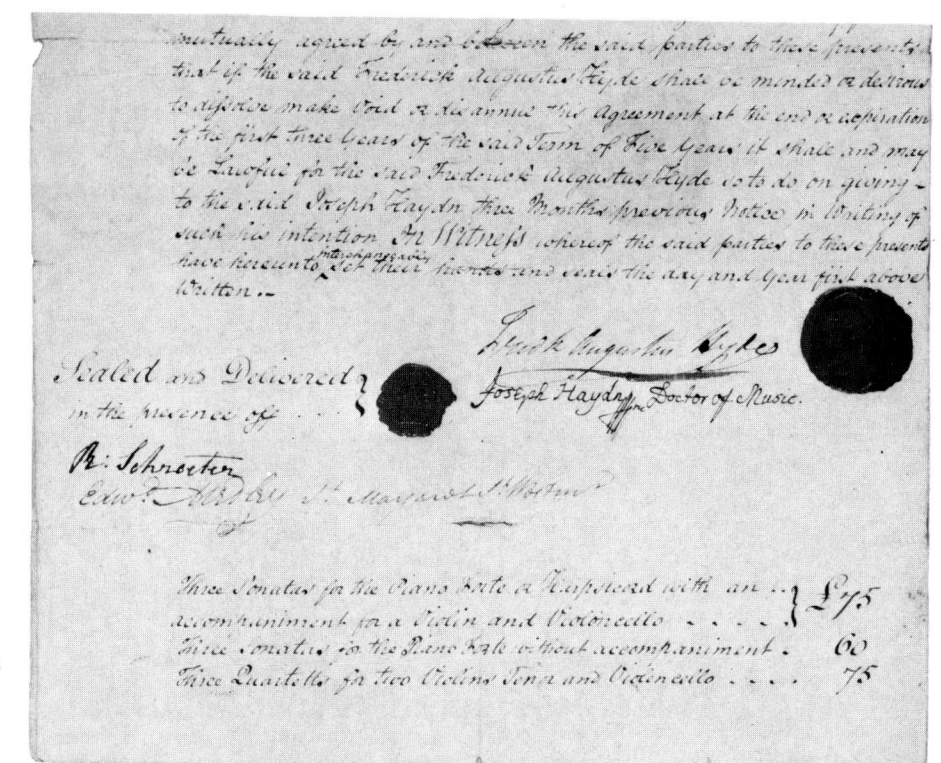

JOSEPH HAYDN
A signed manuscript contract with F. A. Hyde, a music publisher, agreeing to write 55 compositions in five years, London and Vienna, 1796
London £2,600($4,680). 9.II.76

VIRGINIA WOOLF
The Voyage Out
First edition, extensively revised by the author in manuscript and typescript, 1915
London £1,150($2,070). 14.V.76

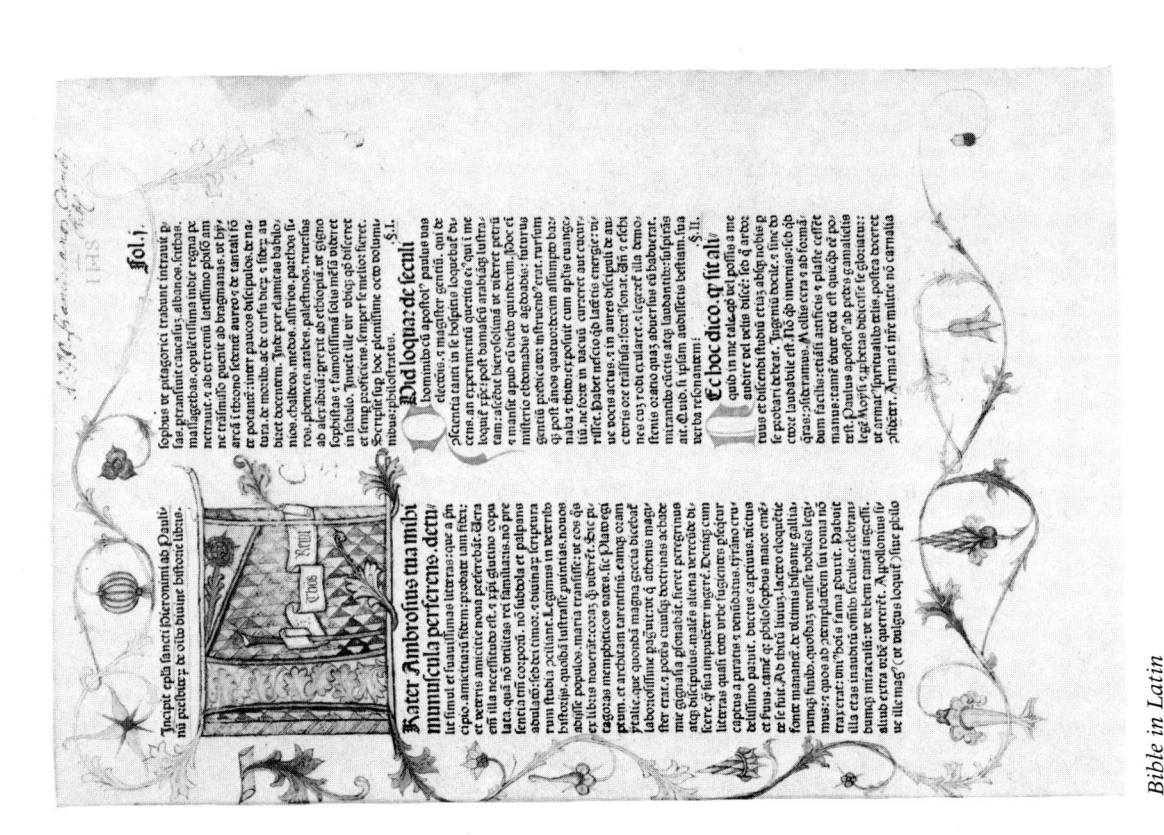

The Gutenberg Bible
Twelve leaves comprising the Book of Daniel, Mainz, [1455]
New York $45,000(£25,000). 7.IV.76
From the collection of Allan Bluestein

Bible in Latin
With considerable contemporary illumination, Nuremberg, Antonium Coburger, 1480
London £1,600($3,200). 3.XI.75
From the collection of Sven Ericsson

PRINTED BOOKS 221

Apostol (The Acts and Epistles of the Apostles).
Moscow, 1564
Monte Carlo, Fr62,000(£6,888:$13,777). 28.XI.75
From the collection of Serge Lifar
This is the first book printed in Moscow by Ivan Fedorov, the father of Russian printing

ST JEROME
Opera
The binding is of contemporary Bolognese brown morocco, Basel, 1526
London £300($540). 23.II.76

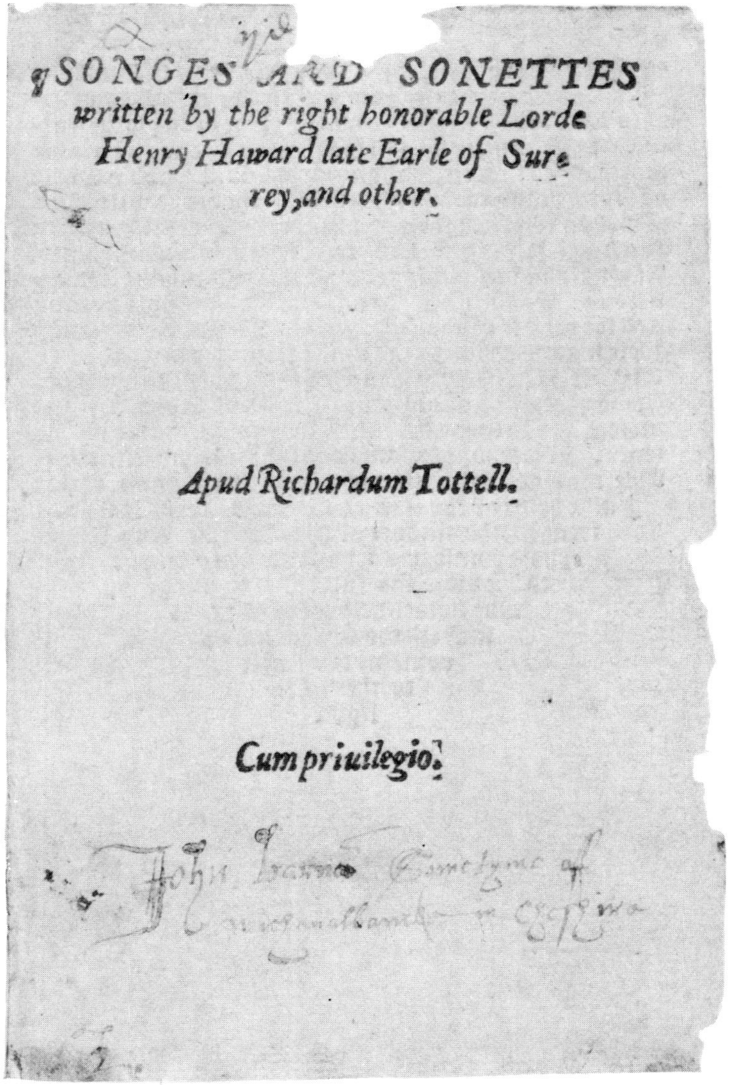

WILLIAM SHAKESPEARE
Comedies, Histories and Tragedies
The first folio, London, 1623
New York $35,000(£19,474). 7.IV.76
From the collection of Allan Bluestein

Songes and Sonettes, 'Tottell's Miscellany'
Fifth edition, 1559
London £16,000($28,800). 1.III.76
Formerly in the collection of Robin Howard, CBE

NICHOLAS BEYARD(BAYARD) and CHARLES LODOWICK
A Journal of the late Actions of the French at Canada
London, 1693
New York $17,000(£8,500). 25.XI.75

ELIZABETH BARRETT BROWNING
Sonnets [from the Portuguese]
'Reading, 1847', but a Wise-Forman forgery of *circa* 1890
London £1,800($3,240). 24.III.76
From the collection of the late John Carter, CBE

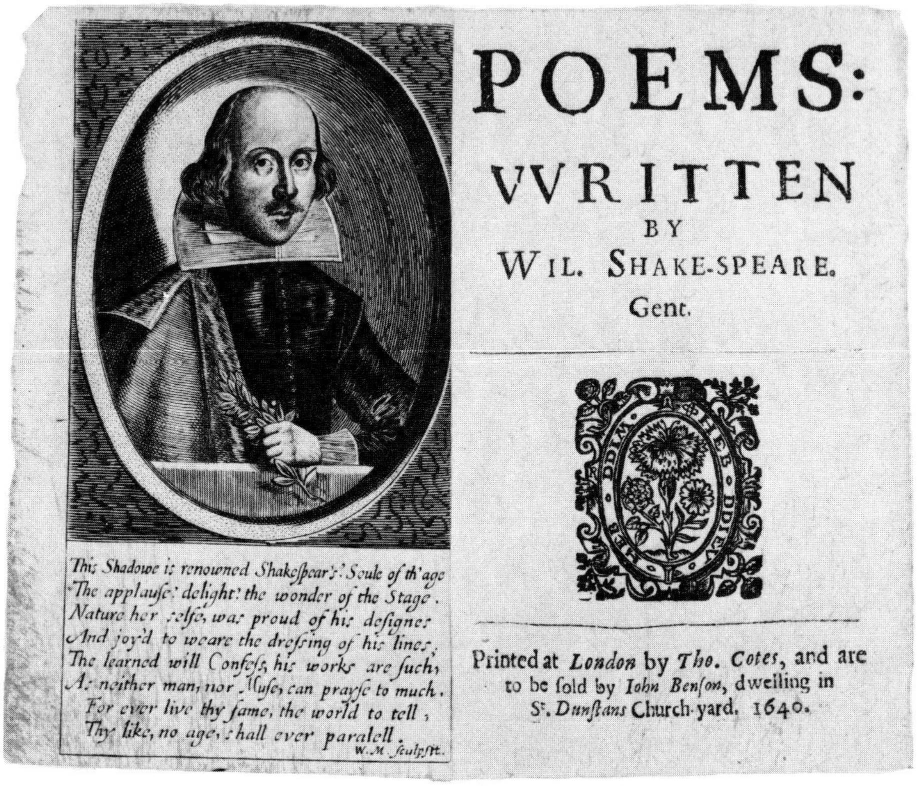

WILLIAM SHAKESPEARE
Poems
First edition, 1640
London £16,500($29,700).
1.III.76
Formerly in the collection of Robin Howard, CBE

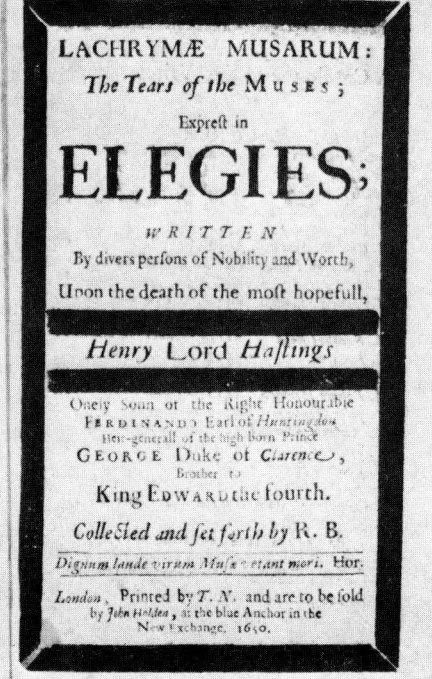

RICHARD BROME
Lachrymae Musarum: the Tears of the Muses, 1650
London £520($1,040).
24.XI.75
From the collection of the late Sir Thomas Phillipps Bt (1792-1872)

The History of Little Goody Two-shoes
Second edition, John Newbery, 1766
London £1,250($2,500). 16.X.75

The Lady-Bird's Lottery
London, 1813
London £52($94). 25.II.76

The Poetic Garland
Four volumes, J. Harris, 1806-9
London £520($936). 25.II.76

226 PRINTED BOOKS

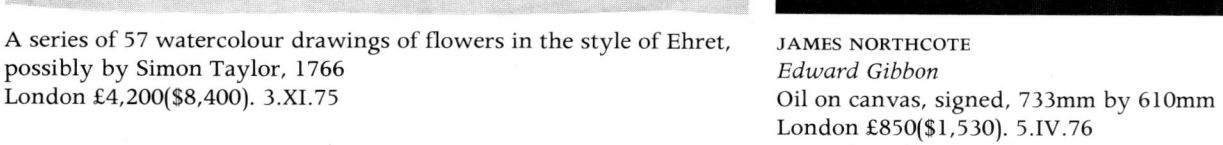

JAMES NORTHCOTE
Edward Gibbon
Oil on canvas, signed, 733mm by 610mm
London £850($1,530). 5.IV.76
From the collection of the late A. N. L. Munby, TD, DLitt

A series of 57 watercolour drawings of flowers in the style of Ehret, possibly by Simon Taylor, 1766
London £4,200($8,400). 3.XI.75

PRINTED BOOKS 227

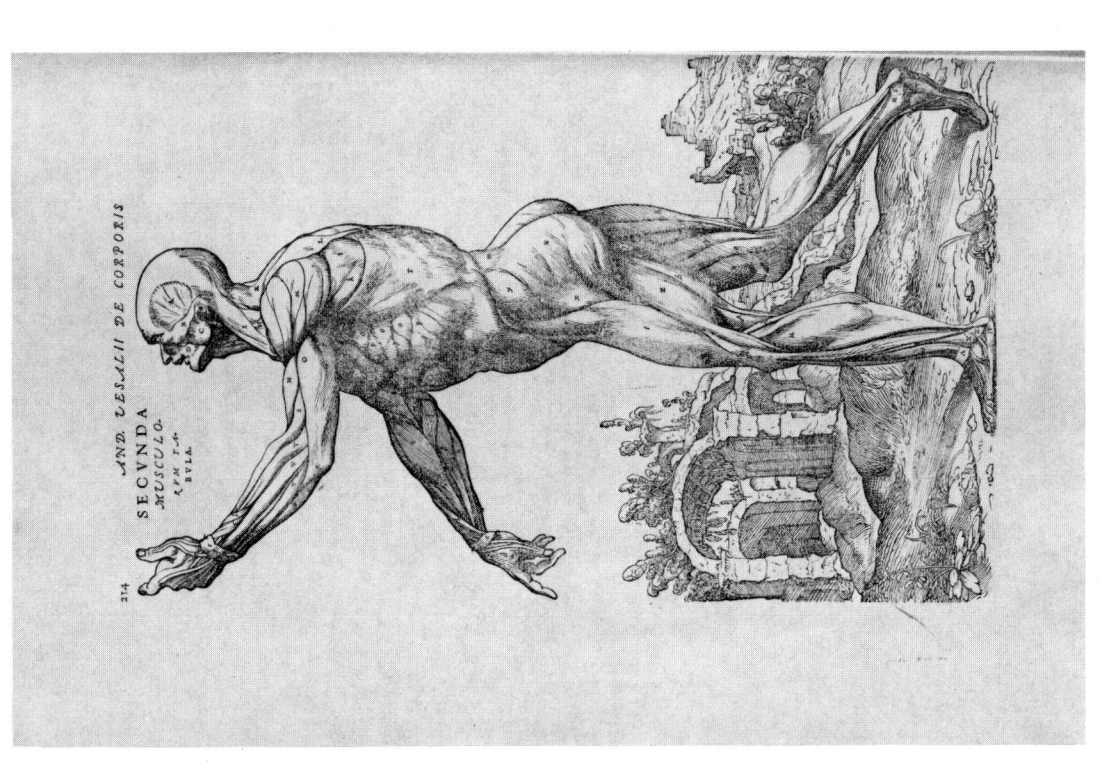

[JOHAN KOBEL]
Wapen. Des heyligen Romischen Reichs Teutscher Nation
Frankfurt, 1545
London £1,200($2,160). 23.II.76

ANDREAS VESALIUS
De humani corporis fabrica
Second edition, Basel, 1555
New York $7,750(£4,305). 18.V.76

228　PRINTED BOOKS

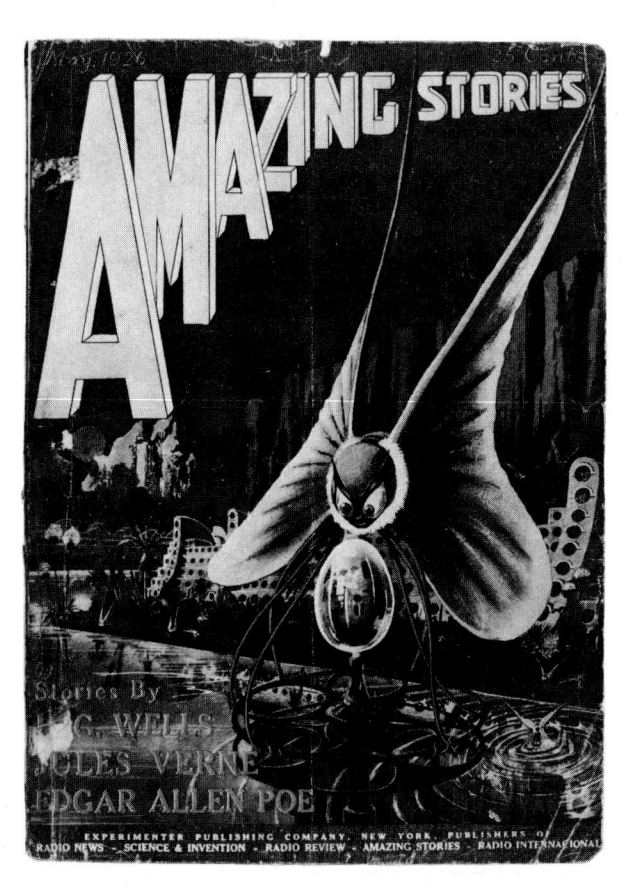

Amazing stories
An incomplete run of 263 issues, 1926-66
London £300($540). 14.V.76

Below
Horrible details . . . Trial of John William Holloway for the Murder of his Wife
Pictorial broadside, Smeeton, 1831
London £22($44). 28.XI.75
From the collection of the late Sir Thomas Phillipps Bt (1792-1872)

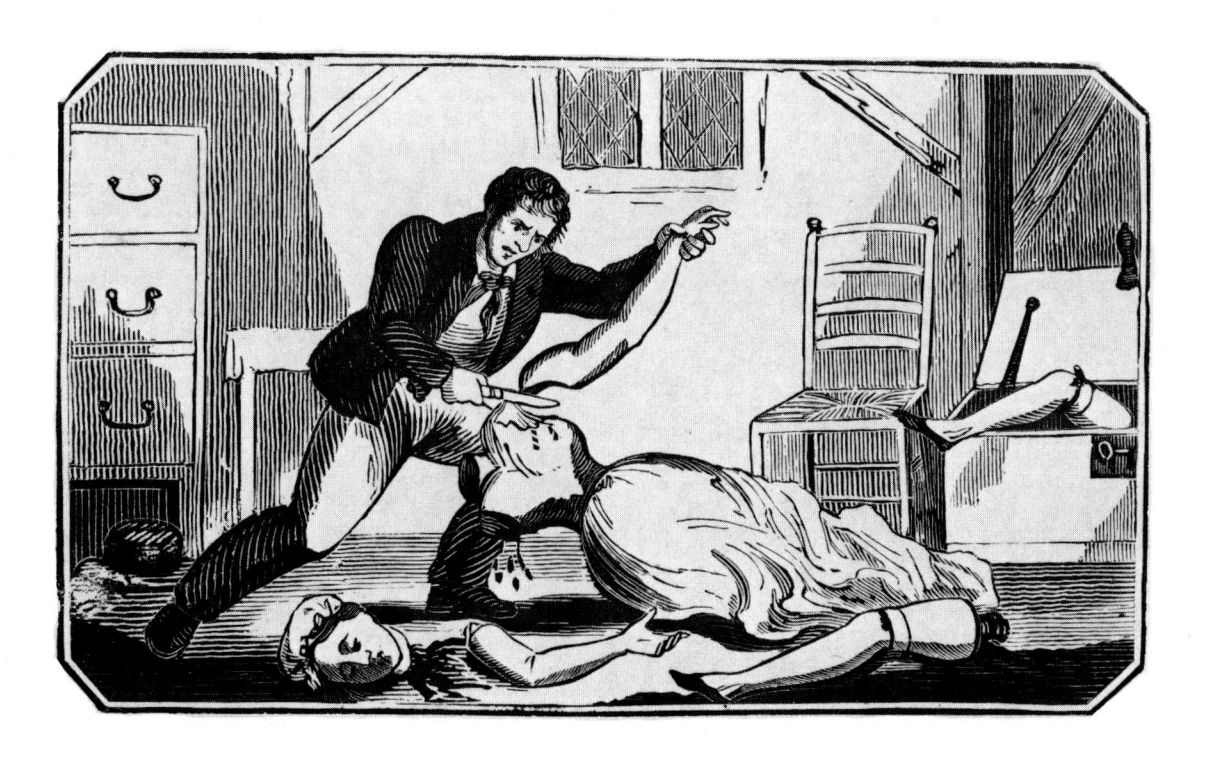

MAX ERNST
Une Semaine de Bonté
5 parts, 182 wood engravings, Paris, 1934
London £520($1,040). 13.XI.75

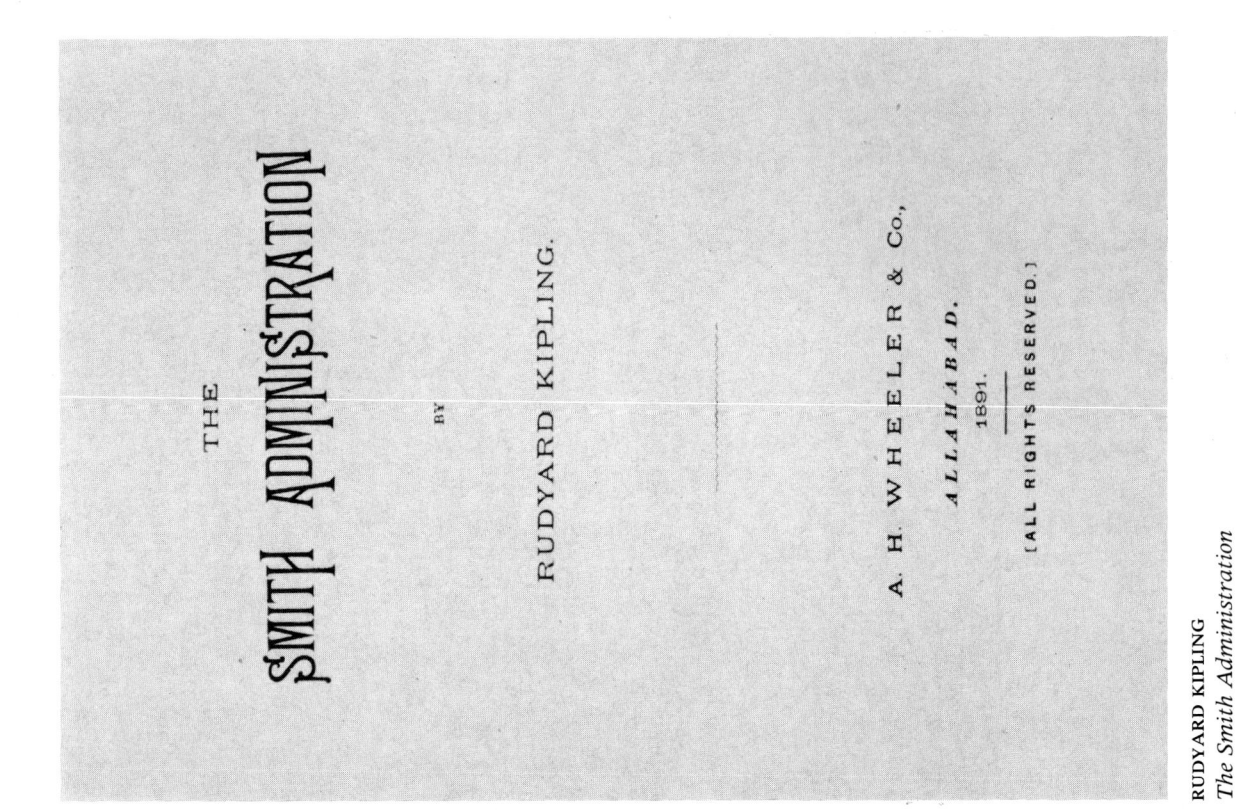

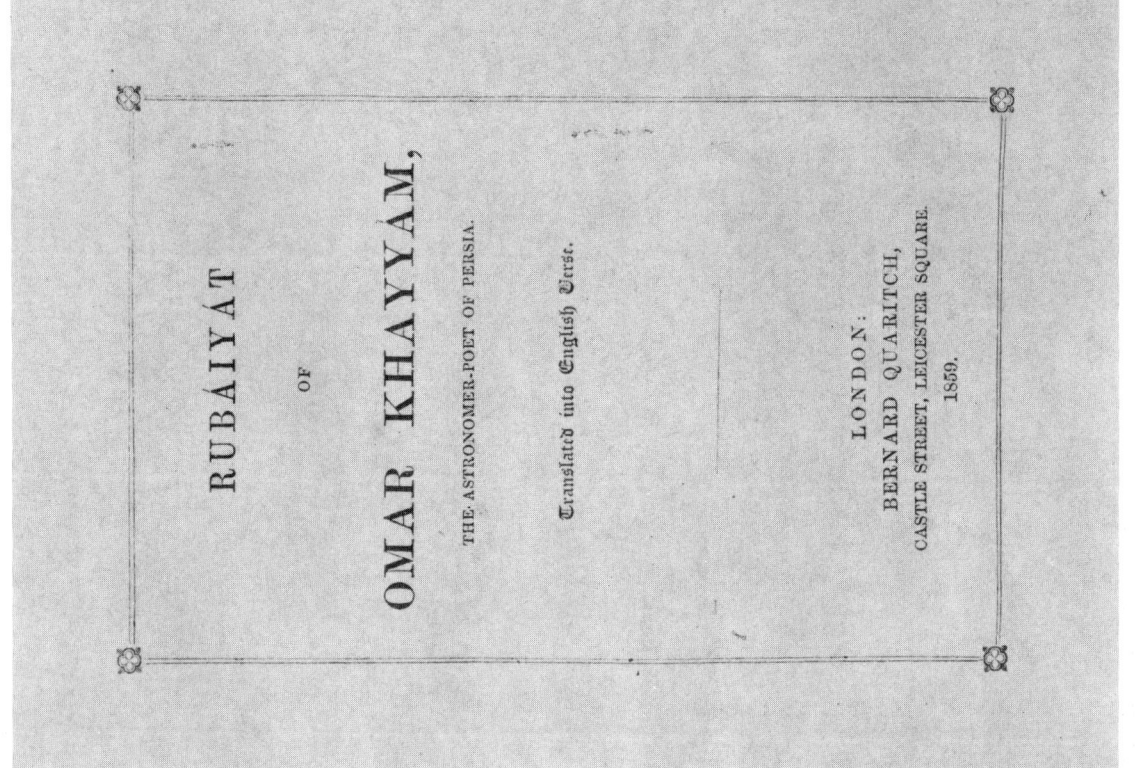

RUDYARD KIPLING
The Smith Administration
Allahabad, 1891
New York $10,000(£5,000). 26.XI.75

EDWARD FITZGERALD
Rubaiyat of Omar Khayyam, 1859
New York $10,500(£5,833). 7.IV.76
From the collection of Allan Bluestein

PRINTED BOOKS 231

foi de laboureur, que Chloé jamais ne seroit à autre que lui. DAPHNIS aussitôt, sans vouloir ni boire ni manger, s'en recourut vers elle, et l'ayant trouvée qui tiroit ses brebis et faisoit des fromages, il lui annonça la bonne nouvelle de leur futur mariage, et de là en avant ne feignoit de la baiser devant tout le monde, comme sa fiancée, et l'aider en toutes ses besognes, tiroit les brebis dans les seilles, faisoit prendre le

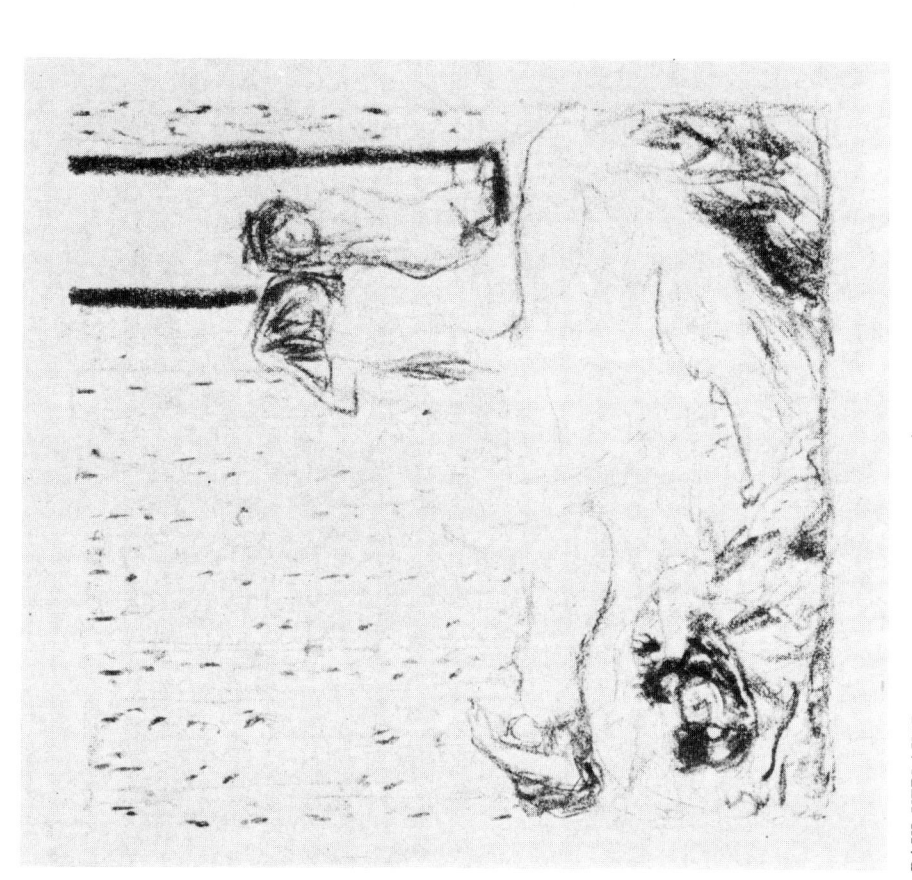

163

PAUL VERLAINE
Parallèlement
With numerous illustrations by Pierre Bonnard, morocco binding by G. Cretté, Paris, 1900
London £2,600($4,680). 10.VI.76

Right
LONGUS
Daphnis and Chloé
One of 20 copies on vellum, numerous illustrations by Aristide Maillot, Paris, 1937
London £1,150($2,070). 11.VI.76

LOUIS DUPRE
Voyage à Athènes et à Constantinople
12 black and white lithographic vignettes and 40 full-page coloured lithographs after Dupré, Paris, 1825
London £6,500($13,000). 10.XI.75

PRINTED BOOKS 233

A selection of the books from the library of William Beckford (1759-1844) which realised a total of over £180,000 ($360,000).

From the collection of the Rt Hon the Earl of Rosebery sold in London on 27 and 28 October 1975

ARTHUR RACKHAM
Two girls gathering berries
Watercolour on card, signed and dated 1914, 325mm by 482mm
London £1,120($2,016). 9.IV.76

JOHANN GEILER VON KAISERBERG
Navicula, Strasbourg, 1511
London £900($1,800). 27.X.75
From the collections of William Beckford and the Rt Hon the Earl of Rosebery

Works of Art

235 GOTHIC, RENAISSANCE AND BAROQUE WORKS OF ART
248 NINETEENTH-CENTURY WORKS OF ART
252 ICONS AND RUSSIAN WORKS OF ART
260 OBJECTS OF VERTU
276 PORTRAIT MINIATURES

A pair of Gothic ivory triptych wings (the top two panels illustrated), probably North Italian, *circa* 1300, 1ft 1in by 3in
London £7,200($12,960). 18.III.76

An Upper Rhine relief of the Annunciation, *circa* 1520-30,
4ft 3¾in by 2ft 11½in
London £5,500($9,900). 8.VII.76

This Annunciation relief, the 'Schöne' Madonna on the opposite page and the Bavarian figure of St Benedict (p. 241) formed part of an interesting group of about fifty Gothic and Baroque wood carvings from a Continental private collection sold on the 8 July. The sale of the collection totalled about £105,000($189,000) and contained interesting examples of Swabian, Franconian, Bavarian, Austrian and North Italian sculpture. A fifteenth-century Austrian figure of St Cosmos made £4,000($7,200), an attractive Austrian figure of St Catherine from about 1480, with much original colour, £5,000($9,000) and an Italian wood figure of St Peter seated, *circa* 1300, £8,000($14,700). Similar figures are to be found near the west doors of many churches in Tuscany and Lombardy

An Austrian wood group of the Virgin enthroned, *circa* 1425, height 3ft 10½in
London £16,000($28,800). 8.VII.76

This carving of the Madonna and Child belongs to the so-called group of 'Schöne' Madonnas, or 'Fair' Madonnas, that were so popular in Austria at the end of the fourteenth and the beginning of the fifteenth century. The best known of the group is the Virgin of Seeon in the Bayerisches Nationalmuseum. The practice of using sweeping clusters of drapery and gentle features was admired to such an extent that it spread to Bohemia and even as far as Poland, and is now known as the 'International Style'. The Seeon Madonna and a number of other examples from private collections and museums are included in an exhibition this year at the Salzburg Carolino Augusteum Museum, entitled *Spätgotik in Salzburg (1400–1530)*, and the present example has been purchased by this Museum not only for their own collection but also for inclusion in the exhibition. The piece will help to show very clearly the development of this famous style and to fill an essential gap in the Museum's collection

Left
A South German polychrome sandstone group of the Virgin and Child, *circa* 1350, height 5ft 6½in
Monte Carlo Fr170,000(£20,238:$36,428). 23.VI.76
This monumental group, while suggesting a French influence, can be compared with contemporary South German Madonnas such as the one in the cathedral at Augsburg

Opposite page
Below
A North Italian Romanesque marble lion, probably Venetian, twelfth century, length 3ft 8in
London £5,400($10,800). 13.XI.75
From the collection of the late Baron Descamps
This lion probably supported the base of a column and would have been one of a pair flanking the portal of a church or cathedral

Two from a group of six Gothic altar pieces which came originally from a church in Boussu, Belgium, sixteenth century, height 1ft 1in
Amsterdam Fl72,000(£14,694:$26,449). 26.III.76

A South German limewood figure of St Barbara, *circa* 1520, height 3ft 3½in
London £14,000($25,200). 18.III.76

An Old-Bavarian figure of St Benedict, School of Leinberger, *circa* 1520, height 3ft 9¼in
London £5,000($9,000). 8.VII.76

An Italian marble statue of a Vestal Virgin by Antonio Corradini, signed, mid eighteenth century, height 4ft 6in
Monte Carlo Fr140,000 (£16,666:$30,000). 23.VI.76
Now in the permanent collection of the Musée du Louvre

Corradini was famous for his veiled sculptures and his talent for conveying mystery through the use of diaphanous draperies was well in advance of his time. He worked for the courts of Vienna, Prague and Dresden while being mainly based in Venice

An Italian red wax equestrian figure of Carlo III, King of Naples and the Two Sicilies, *circa* 1760, height 2ft 10in
London £9,200($16,560). 8.VII.76

Carlo III later became Carlos VII, King of Spain (1759–1788). This statue is apparently a working model for the equestrian monument to Carlo III, intended to be set up in the exedra designed by Vanvitelli for the Palace of Caserta outside Naples.

A bronze turkey, from the workshop of Giovanni da Bologna, Florence, late sixteenth century, height 1ft 4½in
Monte Carlo Fr150,000(£17,857:$32,142). 23.VI.76

The present model is derived from a series of birds and animals made by Giovanni da Bologna for Cosimo I de' Medici, to decorate a grotto at the Villa Reale, outside Florence

A putto, from the model by Battista Lorenzi, early seventeenth century, height 2ft 7¼in Monte Carlo Fr100,000(£11,905:$21,428). 23.VI.76

This putto derives from one of the figures decorating the *Lamp of Galileo* in Pisa Cathedral

A gilt-bronze and silver figure of Christ, South German, seventeenth century, height 1ft 2⅜in
New York $4,750(£2,375). 29.XI.75
From the collection of the late Geraldine Rockefeller Dodge

An Italian gilt-bronze bust of a man, mid-seventeenth century, height 1ft
Monte Carlo Fr42,000(£5,000:$9,000). 23.VI.76

Left
A Limoges enamel pyx, thirteenth century, height 4¾in
London £1,750($3,150). 18.III.76

Right
A prayer nut, the interior carved with seven scenes from the story of David and Goliath, Antwerp, *circa* 1500, diameter 2in
Monte Carlo Fr78,000 (£9,286:$16,714). 23.VI.76

A Neapolitan tortoiseshell and piqué ewer and basin, *circa* 1720, length of basin 1ft 2½in, height of ewer 8¾in
London £9,500($17,100). 18.III.76
From the collection of Anthony Whitaker

248 WORKS OF ART

A French gilt-bronze and enamelled figure of *Corynthe* set with semi-precious stones, inscribed *L. GEROME/SIOT-FONDEUR, PARIS/FRANCE NON LICET OMNIBUS ADIRE CORINTHUM*, height 2ft 5$\frac{3}{8}$in
New York $8,500(£4,722). 20.II.76
From the collection of the late Geraldine Rockefeller Dodge

WORKS OF ART 249

A French bronze figure of a girl playing a violin, inscribed *F. Barbedienne Fondeur, Paris*, mid-nineteenth century, height 3ft 3½in
London £780($1,560). 26.XI.75

A French marble figure of 'Susanna Surprised', by Jean Baptiste Carpeaux, signed *J. Bte Carpeaux; 1873*, height 2ft 5in
London £1,150($2,070). 21.IV.76

250　WORKS OF ART

Left
A Russian bronze equestrian group, by Eugène Lanceray, signed and dated 1878, length 2ft 8⅝in
New York $7,000(£3,888). 20.V.76
From the collection of the Kimbell Art Foundation

Below left
A Russian wax maquette of a cossack by Eugène Lanceray, *circa* 1870, height 10½in
London £480($864). 21.IV.76

Below right
A Russian bronze portrait group by Prince Peter Paul Troubetskoy, signed and dated 1910, height 1ft 6in
London £2,700($4,860). 21.IV.76

Above
A French silver figure of an eagle, inscribed *BARYE*, height 10in
New York $2,300(£1,150). 29.X.75

Above right
A French bronze allegorical group of Peace, inscribed *BARYE* and *F. Barbedienne, Fondeur*, height 3ft 3⅜in
New York $13,000(£6,500). 29.X.75

Right
A French bronze group of three jockeys taking the jump, inscribed *I. BONHEUR*, length 5ft 1¼in
New York $17,500(£8,750). 4.XII.75

The works on this page are from the collection of the late Geraldine Rockefeller Dodge

252 ICONS

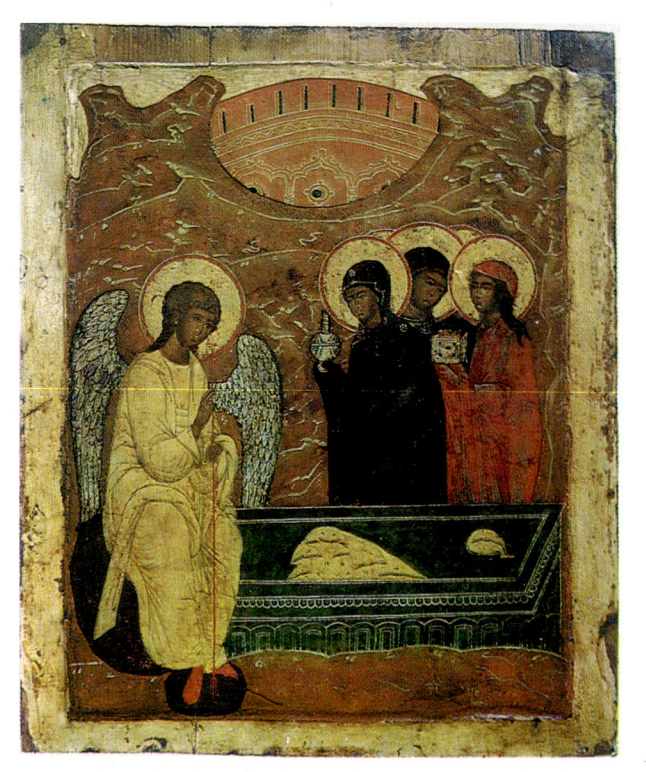

An icon of the Three Holy Women at the sepulchre, North Russian probably Vologda school, early seventeenth century, 28in by 24in
London £3,000($5,400). 29.III.76

An icon of St Anastasia, Moscow-Novgorod school, sixteenth century, 12¼in by 10¼in
London £2,600($5,200). 22.IX.75

An icon of the Resurrection and Descent into Hell, Central Russian, probably Yaroslav, seventeenth century, 35in by 27in
London £3,800($6,840). 29.III.76

Opposite page below left
An icon of the Mother of God of Jerusalem, Moscow school, sixteenth century, 7¼in by 6in
London £2,300($4,600). 1.XII.75

Opposite page below right
An icon of the Entry into Jerusalem, North Russian, *circa* 1600, 25in by 22¼in
London £2,500($4,500). 9.II.76

254 ICONS

An icon of the Birth of the Virgin, North Russian, probably Vologda school, *circa* 1600, 28in by 22in
London £2,900($5,220). 9.II.76

An icon of the Mother of God of Kazan, with a repoussé and chased silver-gilt and shaded enamel riza, enamelled by Ivan Alexiev, Moscow, *circa* 1900, 12¼in by 10½in
New York $12,000(£6,000). 11.XII.75

256 RUSSIAN WORKS OF ART

A Russian silver-gilt and enamel tea set, Moscow *circa* 1910, height of teapot 24.7cm
New York $13,000(£7,222). 20.V.76

Opposite above
A Fabergé silver-gilt and enamel 'jewelled' *kovsh*, Moscow *circa* 1900, length 51.5cm
New York $30,000(£15,000). 12.XII.75
Opposite below
A silver-gilt and enamel jewel casket by Ivan Chlebnikov, Moscow *circa* 1910, 9.9cm by 17.8cm
New York $16,000(£8,888). 20.V.76

A Fabergé cameo pendant set in gold and enamel and decorated with diamonds, workmaster August Holmström, St Petersburg *circa* 1890, diameter 3.2cm
Monte Carlo Fr24,000(£2,857:$5,142). 25.VI.76

The agate cameo is a portrait of Grand Duke Vladimir (1848-1908), second son of Tsar Alexander II. He had a large collection of pictures and was a patron of the young Diaghilev. The pendant has remained in the family of the Grand Duke's descendants until the present day

A Fabergé gold and enamel presentation box mounted with the Russian imperial eagle in diamonds, workmaster Johann Victor Aarne, *circa* 1900, length 14cm
New York $41,000(£22,777). 20.V.76

RUSSIAN WORKS OF ART 259

A Fabergé silver presentation model of a Volga paddle-steamer, workmaster Henrik Wigström,
St Petersburg *circa* 1913, length 71cm
New York $31,000(£17,222). 20.V.76
Formerly in the collection of Franklin D. Roosevelt

Centre above A gold and enamel cigarette case, workmaster Henrik Wigström, St Petersburg *circa* 1910, length 8.9cm $2,300(£1,277)
Left A striated agate kovsh mounted in gold and enamel, workmaster Michael Perchin, St Petersburg *circa* 1890, length 10.8cm $5,250(£2,916)
Right A gold and translucent enamel cigarette case, workmaster August Hollming, St Petersburg *circa* 1900, length 9.5cm $4,000(£2,222)
Centre below A silver and enamel bell push, workmaster Henrik Wigström, St Petersburg *circa* 1900, diameter 5cm $950(£527)

These Fabergé objects were sold in New York on 20 May 1976

260 OBJECTS OF VERTU

Far left A Swiss gold and enamel musical automaton spyglass with watch movement, struck with French *garantie* mark, 1809-19 and Dutch import mark, *circa* 1800, length 82mm
Fr200,000 (£22,000:$44,000)

Left An English gold and enamel *nécessaire* by George Michael Moser, signed *Moser F.*, London *circa* 1760, length 120mm
Fr10,000 (£1,111:$2,222)

A Swiss four-colour gold 'magician' snuff-box, *circa* 1820, width 95mm
Fr90,000 (£10,000:$20,000)

The objects illustrated on this page were from the collection of the late Mrs Charles E. Dunlap and were sold in Monte Carlo on 29 November 1975

Above A German gold and enamel snuff-box, probably by Daniel Baudesson, *circa* 1765, width 82mm
Fr170,000(£18,889:$37,777)

Below A German gold and bloodstone box, *circa* 1750, diameter 92mm
Fr122,000(£13,555:$27,111)

The boxes illustrated on this page were from the collection of the late Mrs Charles E. Dunlap sold in Monte Carlo on 29 November 1975

262 OBJECTS OF VERTU

A gold and enamel snuff-box by Jean-François Breton, Paris 1753, width 85mm
Monte Carlo Fr400,000(£44,444:$88,888). 29.XI.75
From the collection of the late Mrs Charles E. Dunlap

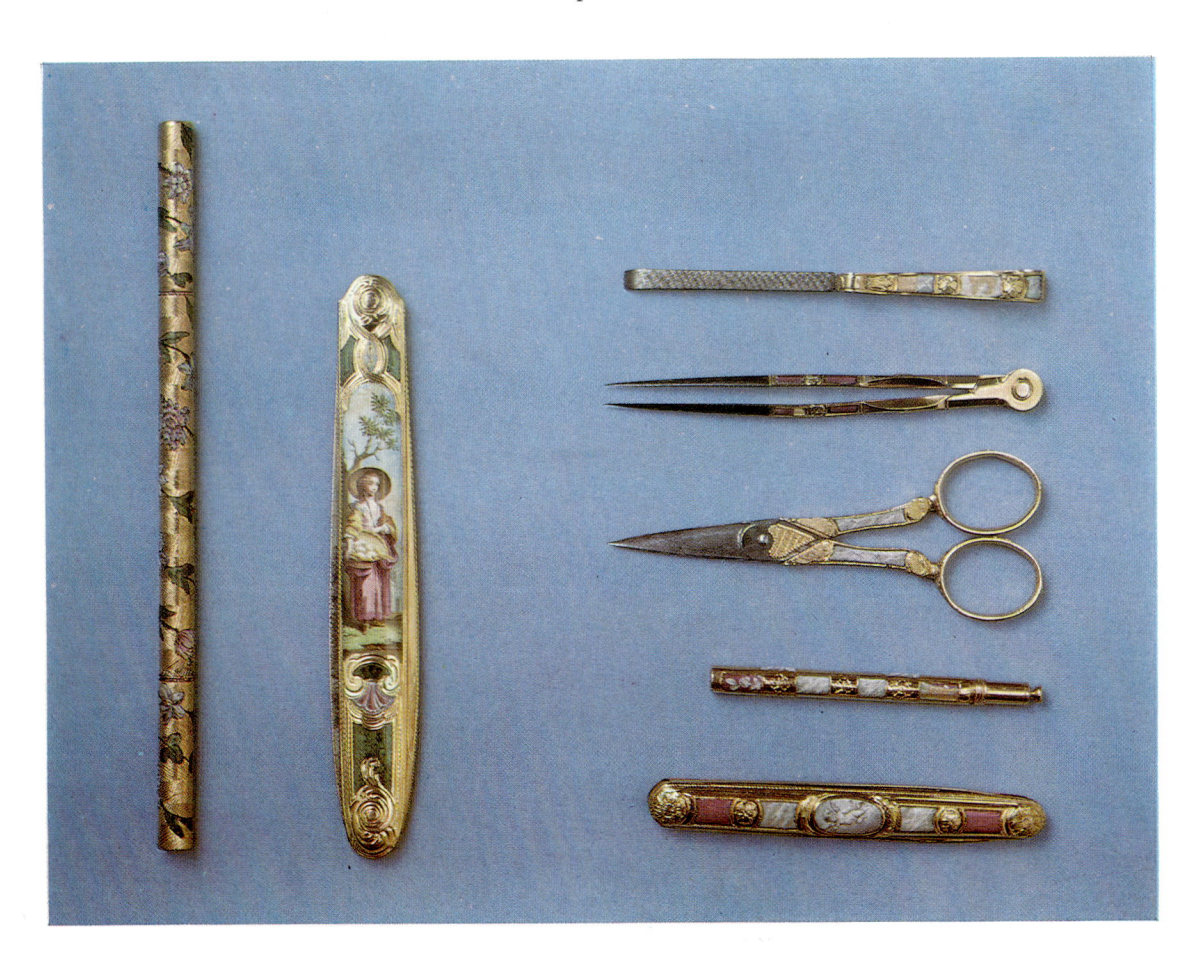

A gold snuff-box by Jean Ducrollay, inset with miniatures attributed to Jacques Charlier, Paris 1750-51, length 82mm
Monte Carlo Fr180,000(£21,415:$38,692). 25.VI.76

A gold and enamel snuff-box by Pierre-Etienne Buron, Paris 1750, length 81mm
Monte Carlo Fr180,000(£21,415:$38,692). 25.VI.76

Opposite below
A gold and enamel pen and pencil holder, Paris 1750-56 Fr12,000(£1,333:$2,666); a travelling knife, Paris 1756 Fr38,000(£4,222:$8,444); and a *nécessaire de voyage* by Pierre-Nicolas Pleyard, Paris 1768 Fr19,000(£2,111:$4,222)
These objects were sold in Monte Carlo on 29 November 1975

264 OBJECTS OF VERTU

A Swiss gold and enamel musical singing-bird box with watch, *circa* 1800, width 96mm
Monte Carlo Fr110,000(£12,222:$24,444). 29.XI.75
From the collection of the late Mrs Charles E. Dunlap

A Swiss gold and enamel musical singing-bird box by Jean-George Remond et Cie, movement with mark of Frères Rochat, Geneva, *circa* 1800, length 96mm
Monte Carlo Fr96,000(£11,429:$20,571). 25.VI.76

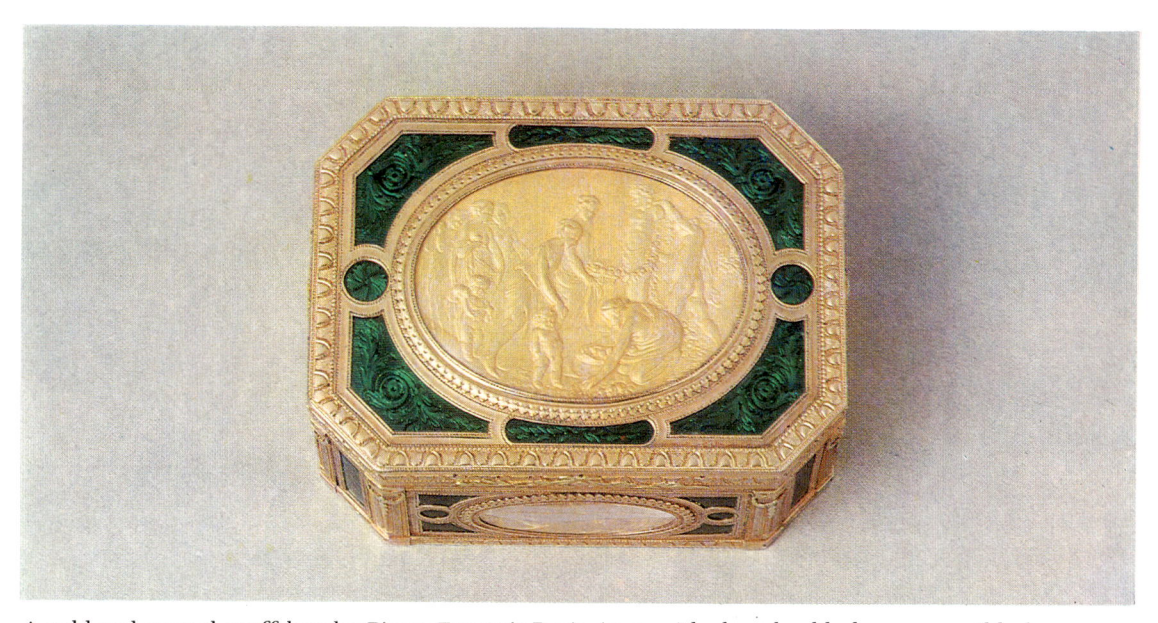

A gold and enamel snuff-box by Pierre-François Drais, inset with chased gold plaques, possibly by Gérard Debèche, Paris, 1771-72, width 80mm
Zürich SF68,000(£12,363:$24,726). 7.XI.75

A gold and hardstone snuff-box by Johann Christian Neuber, inset with a miniature by Petitot, and inlaid with 107 specimens of individually-numbered stones, Dresden, *circa* 1780, width 82mm
Monte Carlo Fr160,000(£17,777:$35,555). 29.XI.75
From the collection of the late Mrs Charles E. Dunlap

266 OBJECTS OF VERTU

A London enamel counter box containing forty-eight enamel miniature playing cards and eight tokens, *circa* 1755-60, width of box 65mm £1,700($3,060)

A London enamel snuff-box with gilt-metal mounts and corded thumbpiece, *circa* 1760, width 75mm £820($1,476)

Left A Bilston enamel mustard pot, *circa* 1770, height 115mm £360($648)
Right A London enamel tobacco box, *circa* 1760, height 150mm £1,800($3,240)

The objects on this page were formerly in the collection of the late Hon Mrs Nellie Ionides sold in London on 24 May 1976

An enamel scent flask with silver-gilt mounts attributed to Lucien Besche, maker's mark of Henry William and Louis Dee, London, 1872
London £2,500($5,000). 6.XI.75

Fig 1
MAXIMILIAN VON GEER
The Schloss at Schleissheim, view from the garden
Gouache on vellum, 170mm by 125mm

One of a set of thirteen miniature paintings of the Wittelsbach castles around Munich executed *circa* 1730, which were sold in Monte Carlo on 25 June 1976 for a total of Fr260,700(£31,035:$55,864)

Baths, Baroque and Bavaria

T. H. Clarke

It is half a century since Sacheverell Sitwell wrote *German Baroque Art*, an appreciation which made the English aware of a style which they, and others, had for so long despised. But, as the author pointed out, whereas the music of the period, that of Bach, Handel, Mozart and Haydn, was readily accepted, few people realised that 'those geniuses had been supported by an equivalent architecture and beauty of life'. It is this latter that we are enabled to explore for a while by a closer examination of the series of thirteen miniatures painted in gouache on vellum by the court miniaturist and steward, Maximilian von Geer (1690-1768), about whose career virtually nothing is known. This enchanting set of bird's-eye views of the houses and gardens of the Wittelsbach family in the countryside around Munich formerly helped to adorn the walls of the Blarenberghe Room at Mentmore; they were sent for sale by Eva, Countess of Rosebery at Monte Carlo, where they realised a total of Fr260,700.

A similar series of von Geer's gouaches can be seen – from behind a rope – in the miniature cabinet in the Residenz in Munich, in a place of honour either side of the fireplace: this is the last of the *Reiche Zimmer* (literally, Rich Rooms) designed by that brilliant Walloon, François Cuvilliés, in 1731 and executed shortly after. The exaggerated rococo framework is a pleasing foil to the more sedate baroque of the miniatures. These are not the only series; two more, or parts of them, are believed to exist. But until the present sale, when the miniatures could be viewed and handled in London and Munich as well as in Monaco, it has been impossible to enjoy them in privacy, to examine with a glass the details of architecture, of fashion and of garden design. We can now abandon the convention of the bird's eye view and descend from the heights to join the mortals on the ground. Fortunately we can call on the help of two German travellers, contemporary witnesses, to bring the scenes to life.

The two were in Munich in 1729 and 1730, within a year or so of the presumed date of these gouache drawings; they might even have met. And both had their works translated into English, so that by letting them accompany us the verbal as well as the visual atmosphere of the time is preserved. The more reliable observer was Johann Georg Keysler (1683-1743), tutor and bearleader to the young Bernstorfs; his *Neueste Reisen* was first published in Hanover in 1740 and in London in 1756. Our second source is Charles Louis, Baron de Pöllnitz (1692-1775), adventurer and eventual protégé of Frederick the Great, whose *Mémoires* were published in the polite language of French in 1734 and translated into four English volumes in 1738; he also wrote guides to the watering-places of Spa and Aachen and a rather scandalous account of the amours of Augustus the Strong.

Before losing ourselves in the gardens or on the lakes, brief biographies of the two Electors of Bavaria who built the main country palaces of Schleissheim and Nymphenburg are called for. The first was Max Emmanuel (1662-1726), who reigned for forty-seven years, but many of them in exile. Distinguishing himself as a general in the service of the Hapsburgs after the raising of the siege of Vienna in 1683, he then did a ten-year stint as Stadtholder of the Netherlands, where he began seriously to collect paintings. Deserting his Emperor in the War of the Spanish Succession, he was unlucky enough to be defeated by Marlborough at Höchstadt (Blenheim), but had some consolation in that he was exiled to Paris, whence he returned in 1715 to Munich, where he built and ran into debt. His son Karl Albrecht (1697-1745), then, had only ruled for six years or so when von Geer painted his views. He was to enjoy brief fame as Holy Roman Emperor from 1742-45.

Pöllnitz had visited the Bavarian court under Max Emmanuel, and so was in a position to compare the son to the father. 'The Elector Charles-Albert', he writes,

'delights in Pleasures and bodily Exercise, and acquits himself therein with a Grace. He is a comely Personage, and has a grave, noble, and majestic Air. . . . He sticks to Business, and above all seems to be very earnest in redressing his Finances which he found in great Disorder when he succeeded to the Electorate.' And of his wife Amalia, daughter of the Emperor Joseph I, he comments: 'The Electoress, who is a little Woman . . . prefers Hunting to all other Pleasures, and there are few Days but she partakes of that Diversion with the Elector, who, as well as the Princes his Brothers, is fond of it.'

'Of all the Sovereigns in *Europe*, next to the King of France, the Elector of *Bavaria* has the finest Pleasure-Houses, for which he may thank the Elector his Father who had a wonderful good Fancy and Judgment'; so Pöllnitz again, who no more than our other source, Keysler, was interested enough to mention by name any of the architects of these 'Pleasure-Houses'. That Max Emmanuel's Italian architects, Viscardi and Zucalli, were replaced by the French-trained Joseph Effner and the Walloon, François Cuvilliés, that French gardeners took over from Italians likewise, was of less moment to these chroniclers than the fact that the Electress had in her bedroom at Schleissheim a tent and a cushion of silver damask 'for a favourite dog', while her husband whose bed-chamber was directly below had 'a sort of kennel for a dog' next to his bed, 'and the like for twelve others, in a fine closet adjoining': here we quote from Keysler. So when looking at the first of our illustrations, the Palace or Neues Schloss of Schleissheim seen from the garden side (colour plate, Fig 1) we must eschew art-historical questions and be content with having Keysler as a matter-of-fact guide walking at our side. Under the date 21 June 1729, he writes:

'in the garden behind the palace of Sleisheim [sic], in the canals each side the middle walk, are little fountains up to the large bason. . . . From thence begins a mall planted on both sides with large and beautiful lime trees, and, though it be nine hundred and fifty paces long, the late elector [Max Emmanuel] used to drive a ball to the end of it in three strokes.'

If you look with a magnifying glass at the foreground of von Geer's gouache you will note a bewigged nobleman with club in hand and a teed-up ball; is this perhaps the Elector in person, the earliest Bavarian golfer?

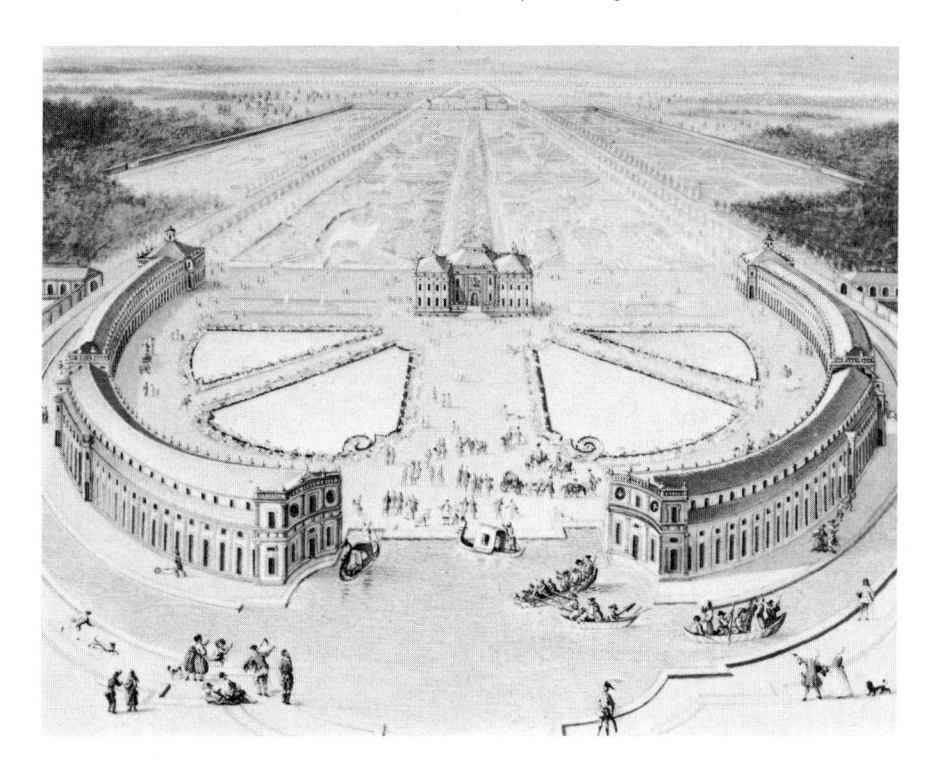

Fig 2
MAXIMILLIAN VON GEER
Schloss Lustheim, from the east (detail from a miniature painting)

The Schleissheim complex, eleven miles north of Munich, depends for much of its effect on the lavish use of water for its fountains, basins and canals, as indeed does the better-known Nymphenburg. The water came from the rivers Isar and Würm, the latter bringing the clear water of the Starnberger See, via a series of canals, one of them completed as early as 1692; materials for building were thus more easily transported, and Schloss was linked to Schloss by water. Some of the heavy work digging the canals, so Keysler tells us, was carried out 'by the Turkish prisoners taken at Buda', in particular the canal that led from Schleissheim to Lustheim, Max Emmanuel's fairway, as it were. Lustheim, which is shown in our next illustration (Fig 2) was built by Zuccali in 1684-89. Now restored to its former splendour, it houses the Ernst Schneider collection of Meissen porcelain, perhaps the greatest outside Dresden. Seen from the east, the amphitheatre once contained the 'lodgings for the officers of the household', as well as 'a stable for sixteen of the elector's horses'. Keysler adds that when he wrote in 1729

> 'partly for economical reasons, and partly from Nymphenburg's being the favourite both of the elector and the electress, the buildings do not go forward either here or at Sleisheim; otherwise Sleisheim for architecture might be justly set in competition with the so much boasted palace of Versailles.'

And so to Nymphenburg, just west of Munich, perhaps travelling along the straight canals in one of the gondolas to be seen in the foreground of the view of Lustheim. For there are gondolas in the garden of Nymphenburg too, as we look at the palace from the west (Fig 3), a view familiar from the painting by Bellotto. The palace grew slowly, Italians and Germans were for ever improving and altering it, while the

Fig 3
MAXIMILIAN VON GEER
The Schloss at Nymphenburg, from the west (detail from a miniature painting)

Frenchman Girard laid out the garden when Max Emmanuel got back from exile at St Cloud. Let Pöllnitz be our cicerone:

> 'When the court is at Nymphenburg the Electress has a Drawing-Room three times a week where there is Gaming, and when that is over the Ladies sup with their Electoral Highnesses, who sometimes admit Gentlemen of their Court to their Table, but commonly all Foreigners. They who prefer taking the Air to Gaming, find open Calashes every Evening drawn by two Horses, at the Bottom of the Steps on the side of the Garden. A Gentleman drives the Calash, two Ladies ride in it, and a Gentleman stands behind. And such as prefer the Water find very neat Gondolas finely gilt upon the Canal at their Service.'

A closer look at the parterre in our next illustration (Fig 4) reveals 'a great Bason ornamented with a Group of Figures of mill'd lead gilt with Water-Gold representing *Flora* receiving Flowers from *Nymphs* and *Cupids*'. The fountain is no more, the figures were melted down during the Napoleonic wars. A later English visitor, William Beckford, was less appreciative.

> 'We were driven in the evening to Nymphenburg, the Elector's country palace, the bosquets, jets-d'eaux, and parterres of which are the pride of the Bavarians.... The queen of Golconda's gardens in a French opera are scarcely more gaudy and artificial.... We paraded by a variety of fountains in full squirt, and though they certainly did their best (for many were set going on purpose) I cannot say I greatly admired them.' (*The Travel Diaries*, 1780)

This set of gouaches lacks one of the Pagodenburg, a chinoiserie delight, but happily it contains a view of the Badenburg (1716-19), a creation of Effner's for Max Emmanuel, and earliest survivor of such a building (Fig 5). 'A delightful structure,'

Fig 6
MAXIMILIAN VON GEER
View of the Starnberger See, with the replica of the Bucintoro

notes Keysler, 'consisting of elegant grottos, and a large bath, into which both cold and warm water may be conveyed.' There is no record that it was ever used as a bath, but on the other hand it is said to have served as a model for a swimming bath on an Atlantic liner.

We end with water, (and with the most expensive miniature in the series, Fr40,000) on the broad acres of the Würm or Starnberger See, where there are Wittelsbach

Fig 4
MAXIMILIAN VON GEER
Fountain in the west gardens of Schloss Nymphenburg (detail from a miniature painting)

Fig 5
MAXIMILIAN VON GEER
The Badenburg at Schloss Nymphenburg (detail from a miniature painting)

Fig 7
MAXIMILLIAN VON GEER
View of the Sternberger See, Schloss Berg in the centre (detail from a miniature painting)

castles both at Starnberg and at Berg on the opposite bank. Let tutor Keysler speak:

> 'three leagues from Munich lies another electoral seat called Starenberg, where the court sometimes takes the particular diversion of water-hunting. A stag is forced into a lake in the neighbourhood, the hounds pursuing him and then followed by huntsmen in boats and their highnesses in a splendid barge which carries twenty-four brass guns.'

The colour plate, Fig 6, shows this 'splendid barge' which is a replica (built in 1669) of the Bucintoro in which the Doge annually travelled to wed the Adriatic. Not so the Wittelsbachs (whose colours of pale blue and silver or white enliven the sails and pennants); hunting was their sport. Fragments of this baroque extravaganza are preserved in Munich, and there is a model in the local museum at Starhemberg. Finally, we see the water-hunt in progress off the castle of Berg (Fig 7).

There is no room to show the remaining miniatures – the hunting lodge of Fürstenried, now uncomfortably close to an autobahn, Landshut and the castle of Trausnitz with its frescoes of the Italian Comedy, the Cascade in the gardens of Nymphenburg. Schleissheim, Lustheim and Nymphenburg are still as enticing as in Maximilian von Geer's bird's-eye views of the 1730s. The last word should be with Baron Pöllnitz: 'I spent my time so agreeably while I stay'd at *Munich*, that indeed I was very loth to quit a Place so charming.'

A miniature of a lady called Mrs Holland by Isaac Oliver, signed with monogram, *circa* 1593, 51mm
London £2,000($4,000). 17.XI.75

Right A miniature of a gentleman by Nicholas Hilliard, dated 1614, 55mm
Monte Carlo Fr75,000 (£8,928:$16,070). 23.VI.76
From the collection of the late Arturo Lopez-Willshaw

A miniature of a young nobleman, school of Isaac Oliver, *circa* 1610, 47mm
London £1,350($2,700). 17.XI.75
Formerly in the collection of the late Thomas Hugh Cobb

A double-sided marriage miniature by Alexander Cooper mounted in a Dutch enamel and gold case, *circa* 1645, 40mm
London £4,800($8,640). 5.VII.7
From the collection of the late Marcel Bury

PORTRAIT MINIATURES

A miniature of Sir Robert Wigram Bt by John Smart, signed and dated 1800, 75mm
London £4,000($7,200). 5.VII.76

Right A miniature of Charles X, King of France (1757–1836), by Jean-Baptiste Augustin, 93mm
Monte Carlo Fr31,000(£3,690:$6,642). 25.VI.76

A miniature of Agnes Mary Cockburn aged six years, by John Smart, signed and dated 1796, 76mm
London £4,200($8,400). 17.XI.75
From the collection of the late Henry Stafford Northcote, 3rd Earl of Iddesleigh

A miniature of a gentleman by Jean-Baptiste Augustin, signed and dated 1790, 65mm
Monte Carlo Fr32,000(£3,809:$6,856). 25.VI.76

A miniature of a young lady seated by a harpsichord by Etienne-Charles le Guay, signed, 85mm
Monte Carlo Fr21,000(£2,500:$4,500). 25.VI.76

A miniature of Emily, Countess of
Bellamont by Jeremiah Meyer, 64mm
Monte Carlo Fr12,000
(£1,428:$2,570). 23.VI.76
From the collection of the late Arturo
Lopez-Willshaw

A miniature of a gentleman by Lawrence
Crosse, signed with monogram, 83mm
London £1,200($2,400). 13.X.75

A miniature of a young officer by George
Engleheart, signed and dated 1804,
89mm
London £1,350($2,700). 17.XI.75
From the collection of the late Henry
Stafford Northcote, 3rd Earl of
Iddesleigh

A miniature of Marie-Thérèse-Charlotte, Duchesse of
Angoulême by Amélie d'Aubigny, *née* d'Autel,
signed *d'Autel*, 85mm
Monte Carlo Fr25,000(£2,976:$5,356). 25.VI.76
Marie-Thérèse-Charlotte was daughter of Louis XVI
and Marie-Antoinette. She was imprisoned with her
family but was liberated in 1799.

Silver and Pewter

A Commonwealth cup and cover, maker's mark A.F. in a shaped shield, London, 1653, height $5\frac{3}{4}$in
Monte Carlo Fr135,000(£15,000:$30,000). 1.XII.75
The Arms are those of Smith, perhaps for John Smith Esq of St Giles, Cripplegate, an Alderman of London

A late seventeenth-century silver-gilt beaker, apparently unmarked, height 3¼in, and a double-compartment spice box, maker's mark only, T.T. crowned, London, width 2¾in, both *circa* 1680
London £2,350($4,700). 27.XI.75
From the collection of G. Fullerton

A George III silver-gilt punch bowl, maker's mark of Andrew Fogelberg and Stephen Gilbert, London, 1789, diameter 11in
London £3,200($5,760). 29.IV.76
From the collection of Mrs E. A. Elgar
Now in the permanent collection of the Victoria and Albert Museum, London

Opposite page
Left
A Charles I tankard, maker's mark T.I. three annulets, a bird with a branch in its beak above, London, 1639, height 7¾in
London £6,800($12,240). 26.II.76
From the collection of Brigadier R. H. Keenlyside
The Arms are those of Newdigate of Arbury for Richard Newdigate Esq (died 1678).

Right
An American tankard, maker's mark of Paul Revere, Jnr, Boston, *circa* 1770, height 8½in
New York $45,000(£25,000). 27.IV.76
Formerly in the collection of the late J. P. Morgan

A pair of George II strawberry dishes, maker's mark of Paul de Lamerie, with another *en suite*, maker's mark of Sebastian and James Crespel, the pair diameter 9in, London 1734, the third diameter 9½in, London 1764
London £9,000($18,000). 16.X.75
From the collection of Charles Gore
The Arms are those of William IV, Prince of Orange and Anne, daughter of George II, whom he married on 25 March 1734

An early seventeenth-century Norwegian tankard, maker's mark of Jost Albertszenn of Bergen, *circa* 1610, height 8in
London £5,500($9,900). 15.VII.76
From the collection of the late 1st Baron Rochdale

A German silver-gilt coconut cup and cover, maker's mark a monogram, Augsburg, *circa* 1540, height 9¾in
New York $23,000(£12,777). 15.VI.76

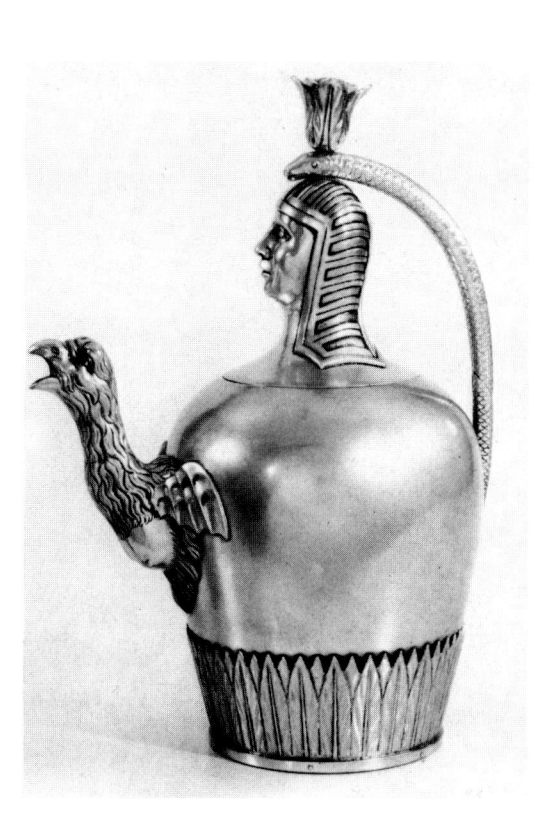

Above left
A late seventeenth-century German silver-gilt pilgrim bottle engraved on either side in the manner of Adriaen van Ostade, maker's mark of Johann Christoph Treffler, Augsburg, *circa* 1690, height 7¾in
London £8,000($16,000). 16.X.75

Above right
A German silver-gilt model of a leaping stag, maker's mark C.E. or C.F. (Rosenberg No. 366), Augsburg, *circa* 1600, height 12½in
New York $20,000(£10,000). 11.XI.75
From the collection of Mrs William Randolph Hearst, Snr

A nineteenth-century German parcel-gilt coffee pot (illustrated) and milk jug, maker's mark of Johann George Daniel Fournie, Berlin, *circa* 1800, height of coffee pot 8¾in
London £1,300($2,340). 15.VII.76

SILVER

A pair of Louis XV wine coolers, maker's mark of Edmé Pierre Balzac, Paris 1757/58 and 1759/60, height 9¾in. Monte Carlo Fr700,000(£83,333:$149,999). 23.VI.76
From the collection of the late Arturo Lopez-Willshaw

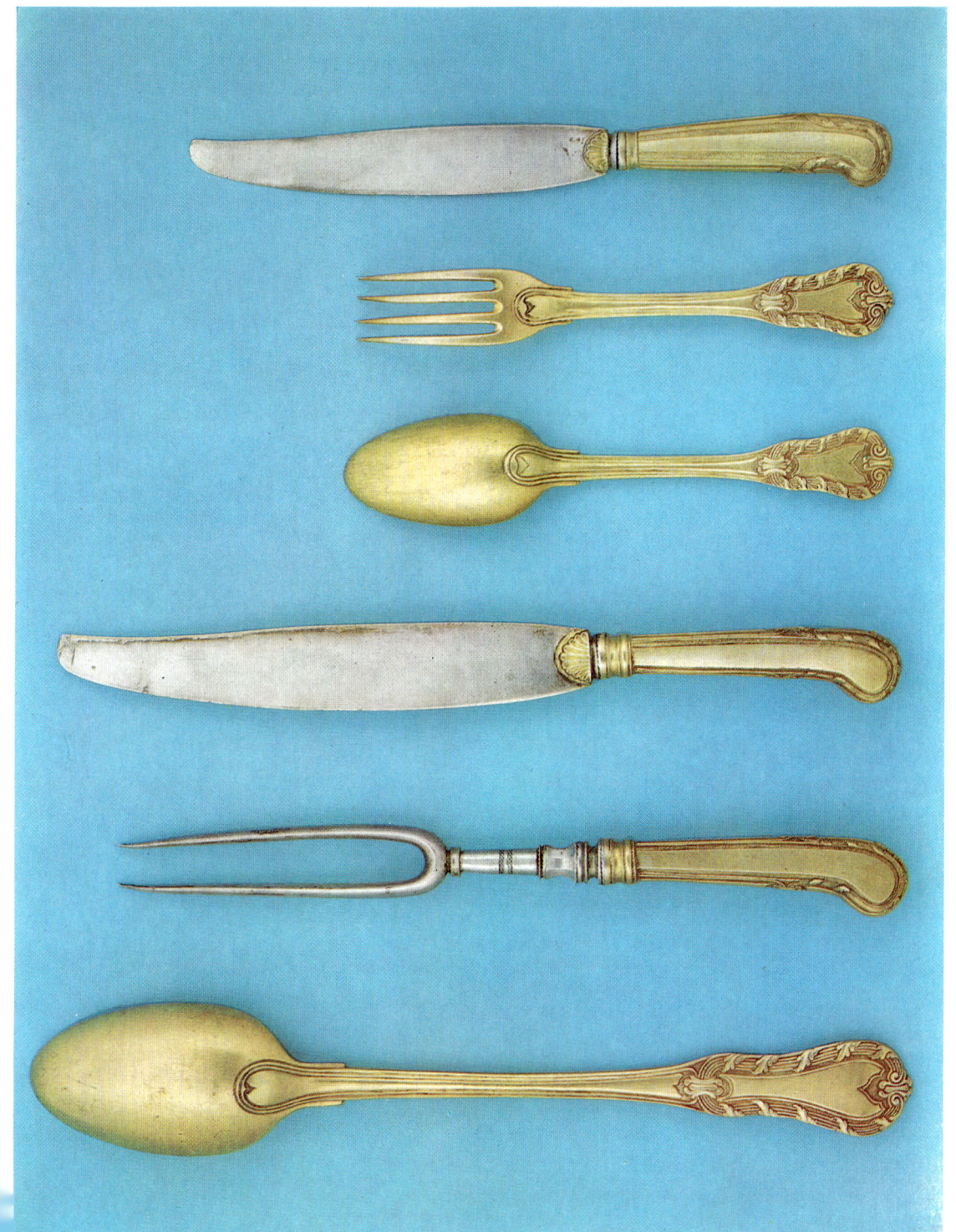

A silver-gilt travelling service in fitted case comprising seventy-eight pieces (six illustrated) engraved with the arms of the Duc de Cadaval, unmarked, Portugal *circa* 1750, the case 18¾in by 29½in Monte Carlo Fr160,000(£19,047:$34,285). 23.VI.76
From the collection of the late Arturo Lopez-Willshaw

SILVER

A Louis XIV silver-gilt bowl, maker's mark of
Claude Payne, Paris, 1686, diameter $4\frac{3}{4}$in
London £9,000($18,000). 16.X.75
From the collection of G. W. Alderman

Right
A Louis XIV *écuelle*, maker's mark crossed
fronds within an armorial shield, Dijon,
1675, diameter at lip $6\frac{3}{8}$in
New York $10,000(£5,555). 27.IV.76

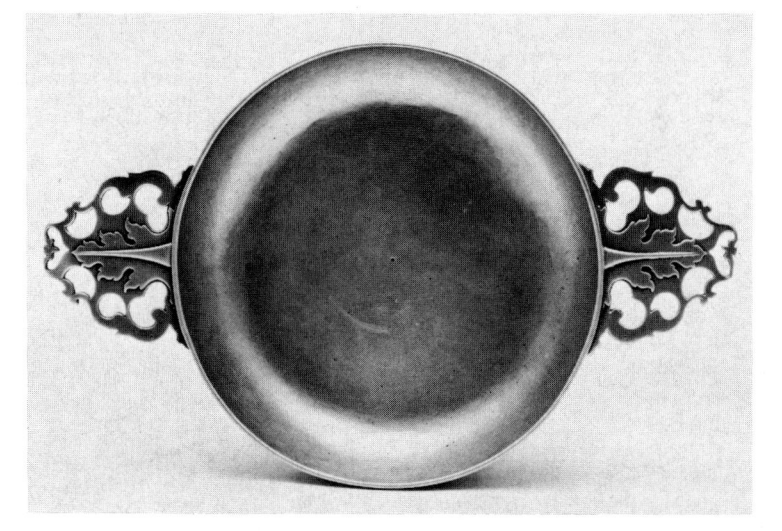

Left
A Louis XV caster, no apparent
maker's mark, Paris, 1737, height $9\frac{1}{2}$in
New York $17,000(£8,500). 11.XI.75
From the collection of the late Mrs
William Randolph Hearst, Snr

A pair of identical casters and other
pieces of silver appear in a painting
by François Desportes (1661-1743)
and are reminiscent of work by
Thomas Germain (1673-1748).

Right
A Louis XIV caster, maker's mark of
Charles Vassadel, Clermont-Ferrand
(Juridiction de Riom), *circa* 1670,
height 7in
New York $7,250(£4,028). 27.IV.76

Right
A sixteenth-century German silver-gilt buckle, unmarked, *circa* 1540, width 3½in
London £580 ($1,044). 26.II.76

Left
An early eighteenth-century Norwegian casket, maker's mark of Harmen Antoni Reimers of Bergen, *circa* 1715, width 2¼in
London £950($1,710). 26.II.76

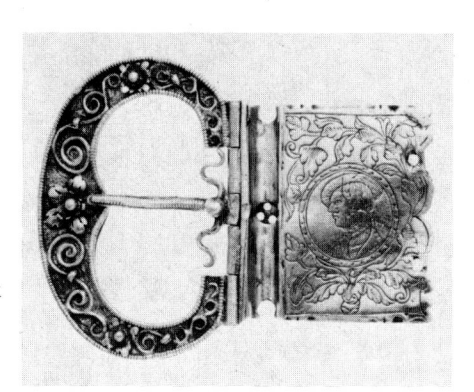

Left
A George III cream jug, maker's mark of Peter Podie, London, 1801, height 5½in
London £420($756). 26.II.76
From the collection of the late Dr Annie Parkes

Below
A William III wine taster, London, 1695, diameter 4¼in
London £800($1,440). 26.II.76

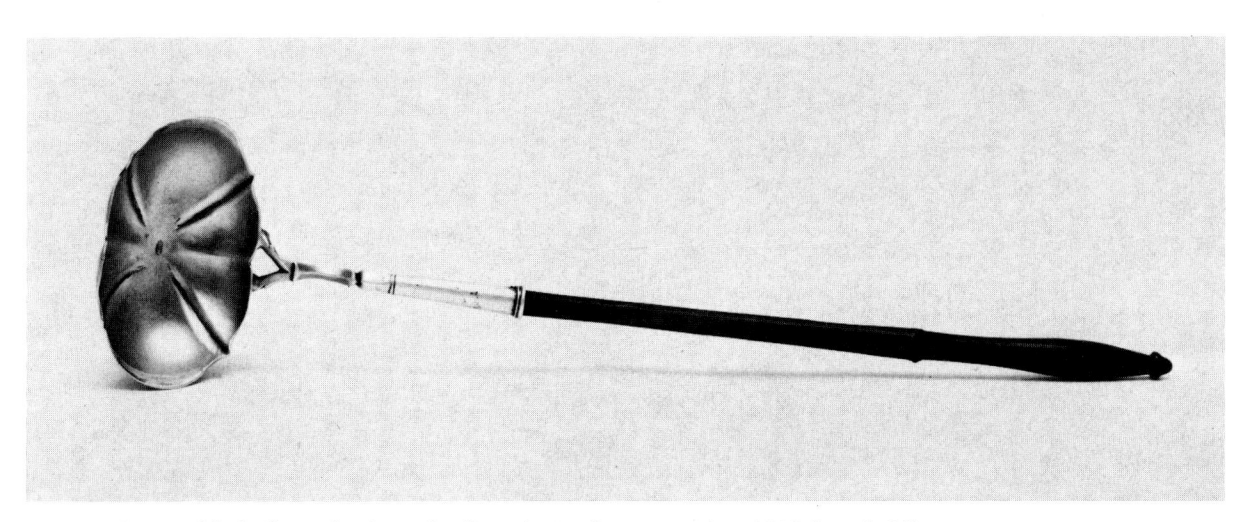

An American toddy ladle, maker's mark of Jacob Hurd, Boston, *circa* 1740, length 16in
New York $2,600(£1,300). 7.XI.75

288   SILVER

A Spanish silver-gilt sideboard dish, apparently unmarked, late sixteenth century, diameter 18½in
New York $14,000(£7,000). 11.XI.75
From the collection of the late Mrs William Randolph Hearst, Snr

A silver-gilt Italian ewer, apparently unmarked, probably Naples, early eighteenth century, height 13in
Monte Carlo Fr48,000(£5,714:$10,285). 24.VI.76

Two late sixteenth-century Spanish parcel-gilt ewers:
Left: with marks on base double struck, RAI only visible
Right: stamped *O. J. Bena venta*, and *ENCALADA*, Valladolid, both *circa* 1590, height of each 7in
Monte Carlo Fr75,000(£8,333:$16,666) and Fr80,000(£8,888:$17,776) respectively. 30.XI.75

A silver and frosted glass champagne jug, makers' mark of Nichols and Plinke, St Petersburg, *circa* 1885, height 15in
London £700($1,260). 22.IV.76

A silver-mounted glass squirrel claret jug, maker's mark of Alexander Crichton, London, 1882, height 10in
London £540($1,080). 11.XII.75

A pair of sugar nips, maker's mark of William Theobalds and Robert Atkinson, London, 1839, length 6in
London £145($261). 22.IV.76

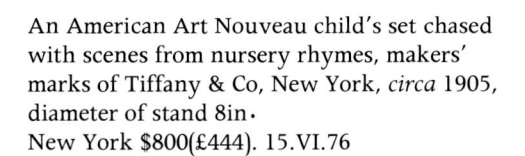

An American Art Nouveau child's set chased with scenes from nursery rhymes, makers' marks of Tiffany & Co, New York, *circa* 1905, diameter of stand 8in.
New York $800(£444). 15.VI.76

SILVER 291

A tea set, makers' mark of Omar Ramsden and Alwyn Carr, London, 1912-14
London £1,550($3,100). 18.XII.75

A breakfast set, maker's mark of John S. Hunt of Hunt & Roskell, London, 1849
London £2,800($5,600). 9.X.75

Fig 1 The Macready testimonial designed by Charles Grant, maker's mark of
Benjamin Smith III, London, 1841, height 30¾in
London £9,000($16,200). 22.IV.76

The inscription reads 'To William Charles Macready/in Commemoration of his management of the Theatre Royal Covent Garden/in the seasons 1837.8 and 1838 and 9,/when his personation of the characters, his restoration of the text,/and his illustration by the best intellectual aids/of the historical facts, and poetical creations,/of the plays of/Shakespeare,/ formed an epoch in theatrical annals,/alike honorable to his own genius,/and elevating in its influence upon public taste/this Testimonial/is presented/by the lovers of the National Drama.'

'Thou sheer, immaculate and silver fountain'![1]

John Culme

Reviewing the British Theatrical Loan Exhibition at Dudley House in 1933, *The Times* reporter remarked that it was intended 'to appeal mainly to that theatrical public which overlaps but does not entirely coincide with the public of art exhibitions'. We are told that the items shown, 'prints and sketches in costume . . . miniatures, snuff-box portraits, Battersea enamels, and Liverpool tiles, begin at once to add to their appeal to the eye a secondary appeal to minds tinged with theatrical and social history. . . .' The past season at Sotheby's has been, in a sense, the same, hinting 'by portrait . . . knick-knack . . . and all that lends actuality to the once lively, motley past'.[2] Be it a portrait of Basil Gill masquerading as a Samurai,[3] or a group of photographic studies from the archives of Messrs Bassano of the Edwardian *danseuse*, Gabrielle Ray,[4] the year has provided much of interest. Above all, however, it was the Macready testimonial (see Fig 1), last seen in public at Dudley House in 1933, which generated the greatest excitement. A monumental centrepiece of the early 1840s in frosted and burnished silver, it has recalled other connections between the silver-smiths' trade and the theatrical profession.

Apart from the Regency goldsmith, the extraordinary Thomas Hamlet who lost a fortune in building the Princess's Theatre in Oxford Street, perhaps the most intriguing figure in this field is the silversmith and dramatist Abraham Portal. As a former apprentice of Paul de Lamerie, he established his own business in Rose Street, Soho, in 1749, but as Arthur G. Grimwade has observed in his recently published *London Goldsmiths*, work bearing his mark is scarce (see Fig 2 for an example). *Olindo and Sophronia: a tragedy* was the first of his plays to be published, two editions appearing in 1758. In the preface to this work, Portal explained that 'the Author only sues for Fame in *Forma pauperis*. As he has been educated, and hitherto passed his Time, not in the learned and peaceful Retreats of *the Muses*, but in the rude and noisy Shop of *Vulcan*, his Performance is but the Effort of almost unassisted Nature; the Solace and Amusement of leisure Hours.' His ill-fated pastime was to claim a prominent part of his life.

By the end of 1762 Portal had moved to the Salmon & Pearl, 34 Ludgate Hill, where he went into partnership with Harry Gearing, trading as retail goldsmiths and

---

[1] *Richard II*, v.3.61. I am grateful to my colleague, David Battie, for suggesting this title.
[2] 22 February 1933 p 16e; 23 February 1933, p 15d.
[3] Sotheby's Belgravia, 30 September 1975, lot 158.
[4] Sotheby's Belgravia, 19 March 1976, lot 155.

Opposite page
Fig 3   A seven-piece tea and coffee service engraved with the arms of David Garrick, maker's mark of James Young and Orlando Jackson for Henry Shepherd, London, 1774.
London £1,000. 19.X.61, and subsequently sold in New York for $7,500. 20.III.70

Fig 2   A two-handled cup and cover, maker's mark of Abraham Portal, London, 1753/54, height 13in
London £680. 31.X.74
The inscription reads 'The Gift of her Royal Highness Princess Amelie to Thos. Ripley Esqr., Comptroller of his Majesty's board of Works.'

jewellers. This removal to a more prestigious position had its drawbacks, as *The Gentleman's Magazine* in 1763 indicated. It seems that a young, distressed Irishman, one John Freake, stepped into the shop and demanded of the senior partner £100, saying that unless he was satisfied both of them would die on the instant. Seeing the man was armed, 'Mr Portal amused the fellow with civil words till he got from behind the counter, when he made a push up stairs, and just got within the kitchen-door before the fellow could reach him.' Freake was later arrested and taken to Bow Street.

1778 was an unhappy year for Portal & Gearing. In February Portal's comic opera, *The Cady of Bagdad*, failed after but a single performance at the Drury Lane Theatre. *The St James's Chronicle* condemned the writing for its lewdness, concluding that 'it would be extremely hard to reproach, or to mark the Inattention of Performers in a Piece which no Abilities and Care could save from Disapprobation.'[5] Clearly Portal's talents as a playright were as slender as they were for business; Portal & Gearing were declared bankrupt later the same year. Presumably to recoup some of his losses, Portal published in 1781 a collection of poems, including 'Verses addressed to the Rev. Dr. L . . . . e, With a Present of a Gold-headed Cane', and 'A Morning Elegy',

> With silver hair, bright-flowing in the east,
>   And ruby-tinctur'd mantle lightly spread,
> With pearl-bestudded girdle bound her vest,
>   Aurora rises from her coral bed. . . .'[6]

In their review of this volume, *The Gentleman's Magazine* offered council: 'As Mr Portal's plays are all moral as well as entertaining, we wish them well, though we would not advise him to "leave a calling for this idle trade".' It was too late, however, and Portal is believed to have ended his career as box-keeper at the Theatre Royal, Drury Lane. He died in 1809.

[5] 19-21 February 1778, p 4a.
[6] *Poems*, London, 1781, pp 137-41, verse 4.

At a time when Abraham Portal's fortunes were declining, those of his contemporary, David Garrick, were drawing to a successful conclusion. The actor's farewell performance in 1776 was noted by *The Craftsman*, among other newspapers, with real regret: 'The play being ended, came the awful crisis. . . . The scene was too distressing to be described. . . . Behind [Garrick], and between every scene, stood groupes [sic] of mournful actors, whose tears spoke their sorrow. . . . Here he retired, crowned with never fading laurels, amidst the blended tears and acclamation of the most brilliant Theatre that ever was assembled. . . .'[7] Garrick had already had the distinction of being one of the very few English actors to be immortalised in silver. This was during 1771/72 when the London silversmith, William Vincent, produced a tea canister set with pierced and embossed panels of figures from a play.[8] A few years later, on 24 September 1774, Garrick settled his account with Henry Shepherd, the jeweller and toyman of Cornhill, for a tea and coffee service in the neo-Classical taste. Together with the receipt, this service, made in the workshops of James Young and Orlando Jackson, is now on view at the Victoria & Albert Museum (see Fig 3).

[7] Saturday, 15 June 1776, p 3d.
[8] Bristol City Art gallery; I am grateful to Charles Truman of the Department of Metalwork, Victoria & Albert Museum, for drawing my attention to this item.

Garrick's service, like Rossini's snuff-box,[9] being a privately purchased article, represents the rarest type of 'theatrical' silver. It is well known that by the end of the eighteenth century the presentation of plate to public figures had become a well-established custom. This was primarily due to the need to honour successful commanders in the war with France. Members of almost every class, from prime ministers to local officials and factory managers were recipients. The 'testimonial', an important part of the silversmith's output, reached a climax of popularity during the 1830s and 1840s. The success of Hunt & Roskell, Benjamin Smith & Co, and R. & S. Garrard & Co, all London manufacturing silversmiths, was based on the sale of these productions.

The Shakespearian actor, Charles J. Kean, was the recipient of two such testimonials. The first, presented in the Salon of the Drury Lane Theatre on 30 March 1838, consisted of a vase. According to *The Times*, it was 'one of the most beautiful and elaborate specimens of art that has been witnessed for a great length of time; it was manufactured by Messrs. Makepeace & Co., of Serle-street, Lincoln's-inn. . . . It is surmounted with a figure of Shakespeare in frosted silver. The handles, which are rustic and variegated with foliage, are frosted. They are very beautifully executed. The vase itself is of polished silver.'[10] The other, and more splendid of Kean's gifts was presented at the end of his career in 1862. Designed by H. H. Armstead, it was made in parcel-gilt by Hunt & Roskell and comprised a large vase with plinth, two five-light candelabra with plinths, four dessert stands, and two groups. It was the gift of Kean's fellow Etonians, including W. E. Gladstone, 'together with numerous friends and admirers among the public, as a tribute to the genius of a great actor, and in recognition of his unremitting efforts to improve the tone and elevate the character of the British Stage'.[11] The centrepieces were ornamented with portrait vignettes of Mr and Mrs Kean, while one of the groups, illustrative of *A Midsummer Night's Dream*, was a portrait model of Pattie Chapman as Oberon, with figures of Titania and Puck.

The finish of Kean's 1838 vase, frosted details set against a burnished ground, was an important feature of English silver at this period. Its dazzling effect, marvelled at by the public but rejected by some of the art critics, has rarely survived the polishing of a hundred years. The Macready testimonial is an exception; before its exhibition in 1933, a thoughtful member of the family sent it away to be frosted afresh. This was done by immersing the figures and other details in a weak solution of nitric acid, before washing and finally drying them with hot sawdust. It remains today much the same as it must have looked on its presentation in 1843.

William Charles Macready's testimonial, also dominated by a figure of Shakespeare, is applied with a figure of the recipient attended by various muses and cherubs. It had been manufactured in the workshops of Benjamin Smith, from designs and models by Charles Grant, a sometime employee of Elkington, Mason & Co of Birmingham. *The Times* expressed its opinion: 'The composition is remarkably fine and the combinations perfect. All the figures accord, harmonise, and concur to carry out the design and sentiment. The execution is equally good, and the likeness of Mr.

---

[9] Sotheby's, 25 April 1968, lot 82.
[10] 31 March 1838, p 6f.
[11] Hunt & Roskell, *Catalogue of Works of Art*, London, 1862, pp 13-14; a pair of the stands, and three plaques from the vase-plinth were sold at Sotheby's Belgravia, 29 March 1973, lot 337 and 1 May 1975, lot 181 respectively.

Fig 4   A portrait engraving of Charles William Macready from the frontispiece of *Macready's Reminiscences*, edited by Sir F. Pollock (London, 1875) and a detail from the Macready testimonial

Macready correct and full of spirit.'[12] (See Fig 4.) Its presentation was, however, doomed to delay, and it was nearly four years after the subscription was started that the actor finally received it at a meeting in St James's on 19 June 1843. The money had at first been lost when Hammersley's bank failed in 1839, and it was not until Charles Dickens, a close friend of Macready's, took matters into his own hands that the fund was started again. Writing to many prominent people, it seems that Dickens was largely responsible for the successful outcome. Even on the eve of the presentation we find Dickens writing to Bulwer Lytton that he had 'found two or three restless men, wandering in the depths of the Drury Lane scenery last night, and plundered them of as many Guineas. They had heard of the Testimonial in their infancy, and thought it a pleasant fiction.' After a further delay occasioned by the death of the Duke of Sussex, his brother, the Duke of Cambridge, agreed to conduct the proceedings. Macready was in a wretched condition of nerves on the day, and one spectator has reported that he looked 'almost miserable'.

Frosted silver was again in evidence when Mortimer & Hunt, succeeded by Hunt & Roskell, produced a cup and cover for Charles Kemble (see Fig 5). It had been commissioned for his retirement in 1840 by a group of friends and admirers 'as a testimony of their opinion that, by the high quality of his talents, he supported the reputation inseparable from his name in the annals of BRITISH DRAMA; enhanced it by their variety, and, by his conduct through a long and arduous career, raised the character of the profession which he adored'. To quote *The Literary World*, 'This superb vase has been executed in silver . . . from a model by Sir Francis Chantrey. . . . The design consists of a magnificent vase, in frost, or mat work. . . . The cover is surmounted with a figure of Mr. Charles Kemble, in the character of *Hamlet*: it is a good likeness, although only five inches in height. . . . The weight of the cup and pedestal is upwards of 700 ounces; and its cost £450. Its execution is alike honourable to the genius of Chantrey, and the taste of the manufacturers, whose work is characterized by highly artistical delicacy and finish.'[13] The ceremony took place on the stage of Covent Garden Theatre, Charles Matthews and Lucia Vestris being of the company.

[12] 20 June 1843, p 3e.
[13] 21 March 1840, pp 385-87.

As a footnote to the Kemble Cup, it is worth mentioning that at the International Exhibition of 1862, Hunt & Roskell showed various original models from their pattern room. One of these was of Charles Kemble 'in the character of Hamlet, by Chantrey, R.A.; . . . highly interesting, being the last model made by this eminent sculptor for a work in silver.'[14]

The fierce rivalry between London theatrical managements of the nineteenth century is legendary. For instance, when the Royal Italian Opera Company was formed during the 1840s at Covent Garden, they seriously threatened similar productions at Her Majesty's Theatre, then managed by Benjamin Lumley. Like Portal and Thomas Hamlet, Lumley was dogged by financial misfortune; when the new Italian Opera venture was launched, Lumley's friends showed their appreciation of his work by presenting to him a silver-gilt vase and plinth. Manufactured by Hunt & Roskell, it was decorated with 'Figures representing Melpomone, Thalia, Terpsichore, and Euterpe. Designed and modelled by Mr. Alfred Brown. . . .' Many years later, Lumley recalled that 'This handsome piece of plate was to me a great source of pride and solace amidst all my trials and anxieties. . . .'[15]

R. & S. Garrard & Co, perhaps Hunt & Roskell's nearest competitors, are well represented by the testimonial centrepiece they produced for the ballerina, Maria Taglioni, best remembered for her role in *La Sylphide*. 'The subject,' we are informed by *The Pictorial Times*, 'is "Diana visiting Endymion", and the artist Mr. Edmund Cotterell – the modeller of several of the Goodwood Cups, to which this bears in size and general appearance a very considerable resemblance. This is perhaps the best of Mr. Cotterell's works, which have hitherto been confined too closely to Arabs in the desert and Arab horses.'[16] (See p 301.) *The Illustrated London News* added that the centrepiece (Fig 6) 'consists of a group of three mythological figures, and two animals, partly taken from the ballet of "Endymion", in which Taglioni appeared in the season of 1845. . . . The whole is exquisitely designed: the figures are not portraits, but have the elegant Greek outline of features. . . . It has been executed in frosted silver, at the cost of 300 guineas. . . .' Some of Taglioni's costumes for *La Sylphide* had been designed by the Frenchman, Eugene Lami. This artist, who is distinguished for having devised the *tutu*, also worked for the retail silversmith, C. F. Hancock from Hunt & Roskell, for whom he produced several designs for silver at the time of the Great Exhibition in 1851.

No less remarkable for her success than Taglioni, Jenny Lind, the Swedish soprano, was wildly received when she came to London in the late 1840s. Her popularity had increased throughout her European tour, and on leaving Hamburg a group of admirers had given her a silver laurel wreath.[17] Once in England, Mlle Lind was showered with gifts, from one of Jennens & Bettridge's papier-mâché sewing cabinets,[18] to a silver skep-shaped honey pot for her birthday in 1848.[19] In appreciation of her help in raising money by charity performances for the Hospital for Consumption at Brompton, Mlle Lind was also given a salver manufactured by the Smith

---

[14] *Op cit.* 13, p 38.
[15] Benjamin Lumley, *Reminiscences of the Opera*, London, 1864, p. 197.
[16] 1846, p 197.
[17] *Memoir of Jenny Lind*, published by John Ollivier, London, 1847, p 17.
[18] 13 January 1849, p 32.
[19] Sotheby's 3 June 1969, lot 93.

Fig 6 An engraving of the Taglioni testimonial, designed for the manufacturers by Edmund Cotterell and produced by R. & S. Garrard & Co and now in the Musée des Arts Décoratifs. From *The Illustrated London News*, 19 September 1846

Fig 5 An engraving of the Kemble cup, manufactured from models by Sir Francis Chantrey in the workshops of Mortimer & Hunt. From *The Literary World*, 21 March 1840

& Co of the Macready testimonial. It was presented 'by a deputation of the committee: she expressed her thanks warmly – in good English – and her great pleasure that she had been the happy means of aiding a charity which she considered the best, as well as the most needed, of all the many charities of England.'[20] But we learn from her biographers that, 'in spite of her rooted antipathy to the presentation of testimonials, . . . Mdlle. Lind had not the heart to refuse that which was offered to her in the name of the recipients of her bounty at Brompton. . . .'[21]

[20] *The Art-Union*, 1848, p 286; the salver was sold at Sotheby's on 7 November 1968, lot 61.
[21] H. S. Holland & W. S. Rockstro, *Memoir of Jenny Lind*, London, 1891, vol II, pp 230–31.

Fig 7 *Left* A cigarette case, painted in enamels with a portrait of May Yohé. Maker's mark of George Heath for H. Lewis & Co, London, 1894/95. London £20 26.X.71.
Right A detail from a photograph of May Yohé sold with the previous item. An identifying feature is the ring worn on her right thumb

Jenny Lind's particular dislike of testimonials, especially, one suspects, of the large silver kind, was a feeling which became more general as the 1850s and 1860s passed. Although presentation centrepieces continued in production up till the First World War, the attitude towards silver objects became more relaxed. With such a change of emphasis, and the growing competition from foreign manufacturers, English silversmiths turned to inexpensive knick-knacks such as the animal pepperettes of the 1880s, when piglets and lyre-playing kittens became the rage. The less formal view of silver is apparent in a report of the silver wedding anniversary reception of the comic actor, J. L. Toole, and his wife. Each guest 'came with either a bouquet of flowers or a gift of silver plate, or both, and each might have wondered where the hostess would find room for another bouquet, or another less perishable souvenir; for quite early in the evening every sideboard, shelf, mantelpiece, table, seemed to be gay with flowers, or white with silver.'[22]

The silver industry, it is true, had lost its pre-eminence before the 1880s. But in the two decades before 1914, the manufacturer of plate and plated wares was, to a point, catering for the market in ephemera. Bon-bon dishes, pastry knives and the like, given as wedding presents at this date, still lie unused, boxed-up in bank vaults. In addition to theatre programmes or picture postcards of actresses, one London silversmith, George Heath, produced in 1894 a 'May Yohé' cigarette case (see Fig 7). The front of the case was painted in enamels with a portrait of Miss Yohé, an American actress. The daughter of a Pennsylvanian iron-moulder, she was born in 1869, made her first appearance in Chicago at the age of eighteen, and then in London in 1893 in the burlesque, *Little Christopher Columbus*. Her success in this piece was largely due to the skill with which the composer, Ivan Caryll, fitted her limited vocal powers with such songs as 'Oh, Honey, Ma Honey'. For this, as on the case, she was dressed in a plantation costume of straw hat, blouse, and striped shorts. She was pretty and her career short-lived; Miss Yohé married in 1894 Lord Henry Francis Clinton-Hope, subsequently the Eighth Duke of Newcastle-under-Lyme.

It might be said that the task of linking the writings of Abraham Portal, or the testimonial of W. C. Macready, with a little-known actress of the '90s is a frivolous one. Yet this connection has been made with a simple aim: 'to appeal to minds tinged with theatrical and social history. . . .'

[22] Joseph Hatton, *Reminiscences of J. L. Toole*, London, 1889, vol I, pp 70–71.

A centrepiece group, entitled *Arabs in the desert Tracking Travellers by their footmarks in the sand*, modelled by Edmund Cotterill, maker's mark of Robert Garrard II of R & S Garrard & Co, London, 1840, height 30½in
London £4,400($7,920).
22.IV.76

This centrepiece, an almost contemporary copy of the Goodwood Cup of 1839, was presented by Napoleon III to the Junior United Services Club in April 1855 'as a *souvenir* of his Majesty's having been an honorary member of the club during his residence in England'

A relief-cast Strasbourg tankard made by Isaac Faust, mid seventeenth century, height 7in
London £2,500($4,500). 16.III.76

A German pewter Passover dish, indecipherable maker's mark struck three times, eighteenth century, diameter 12⅞in
New York $1,400(£700). 2.XII.75

A north German flagon or *Roerken*, made by Jacob Hinrich Otto of Lubeck, mid eighteenth century, height 9in
London £1,050($1,890). 16.III.76

A north German flagon or *Roerken*, made by Hinrich Helmcke of Lubeck, dated 1653, height 8½in
London £980($1,960). 11.XII.75

A wriggled-work dish made by Sir John Fryers Bt, *circa* 1700, diameter 16½in
London £500($1,000). 11.XII.75

A flagon or *Roerken*, made by Hinrich Helmcke of Lubeck, dated 1656, height 8¼in
London £1,000($2,000). 11.XII.75

Arms, Armour and Militaria

A German close helmet, mid sixteenth century
London £1,350($2,430). 10.II.76

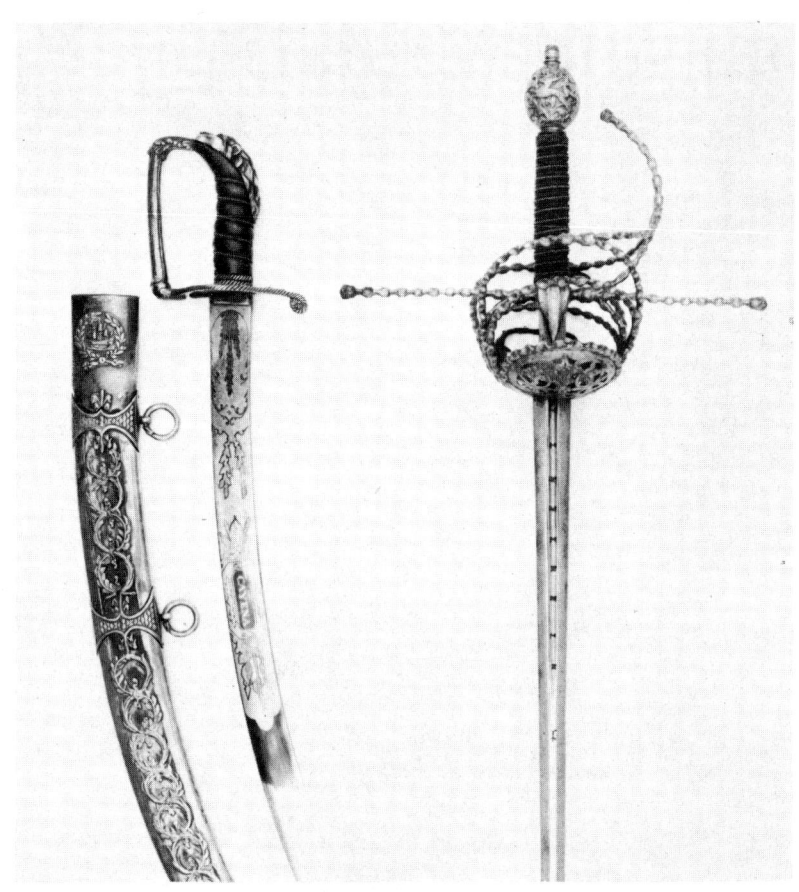

Far left
A silver-hilted naval officer's presentation sword, *circa* 1810, length 30¾in
London £1,200($2,160). 15.VI.76
From the collection of
Mrs D. M. Low
This sword was presented to Lieut George Forder by the King of Portugal as a result of his gallantry at the capture of Cayenne in 1809

Left
An Italian rapier, the blade of hexagonal section stamped with the Toledo Town mark, mid seventeenth century, length 54in overall
London £1,850($3,330). 15.VI.76

Below left
An Imperial Russian Garde-du-Corps helmet
London £700($1,260). 15.VI.76

Below right
An officer's shapska of the 16th Lancers
London £420($756). 15.VI.76

One of a pair of Silesian flintlock holster pistols, *circa* 1680, 19in
London £2,200($3,960). 18.V.76

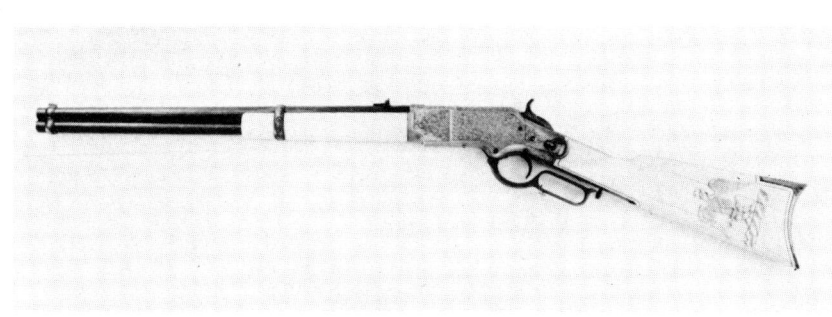

An ivory-stocked Winchester model 1866 lever-action carbine, *circa* 1869, barrel 20in
Los Angeles $30,000(£16,666). 7.III.76. From the collection of Walter B. Ford III. Formerly in the collections of William Locke and Richard Mellon

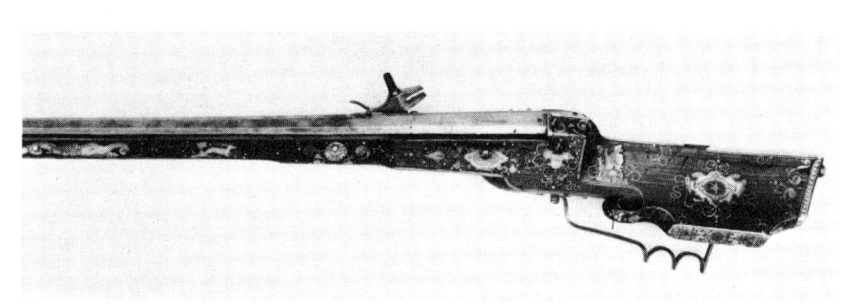

A German wheel-lock hunting rifle, *circa* 1600, 45¼in
London £2,574($5,148). 14.X.75

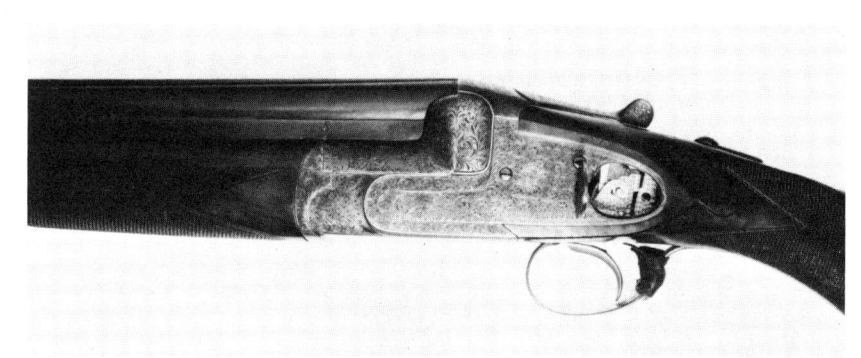

One of a pair of 12-bore double-barrelled over and under sporting guns by Westley Richards, serial nos. 18235/18236, length 45⅛in
London £5,600($10,080). 15.VI.76

One of a pair of Dutch rabinets signed *Cornelis Ouderogge, Fecit, Rotterdam* and dated *1670*, length 39¾in overall
London £4,200($7,560). 6.IV.76
From the collection of The Lord Vivian

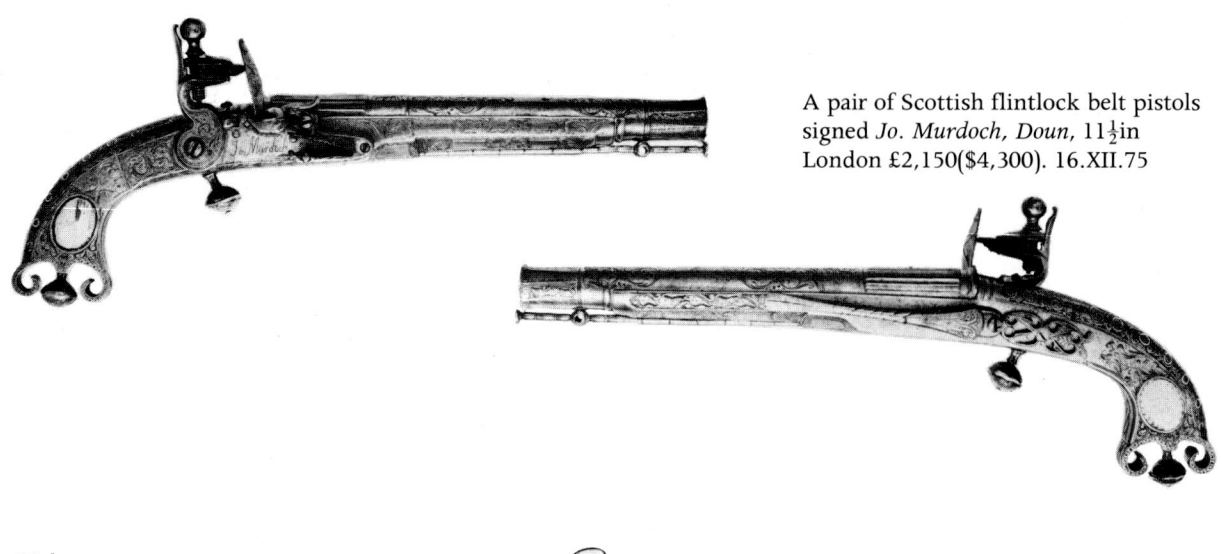

A pair of Scottish flintlock belt pistols signed *Jo. Murdoch, Doun*, 11½in
London £2,150($4,300). 16.XII.75

Right
A Colt single-action army revolver, serial no. 112737, originally owned by Bat Masterson, *circa* 1884, barrel 4¾in
Los Angeles $36,000(£19,999). 7.III.76
From the collection of Walter B. Ford III

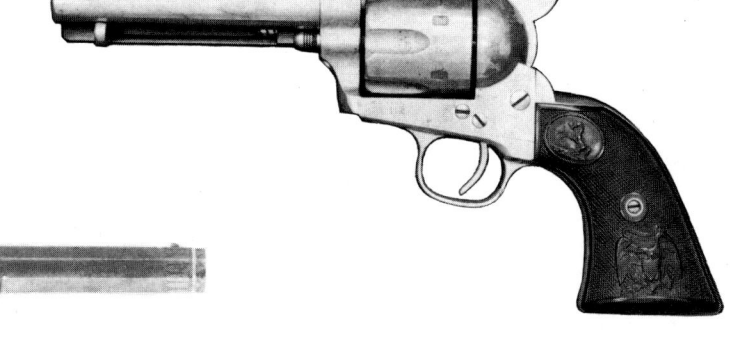

Left
A holster-model Colt Patterson revolver, serial no. 985, *circa* 1840, barrel 6in
Los Angeles $31,000(£17,222). 7.III.76
From the collection of Walter B. Ford III
Formerly in the collection of John S. Dumont

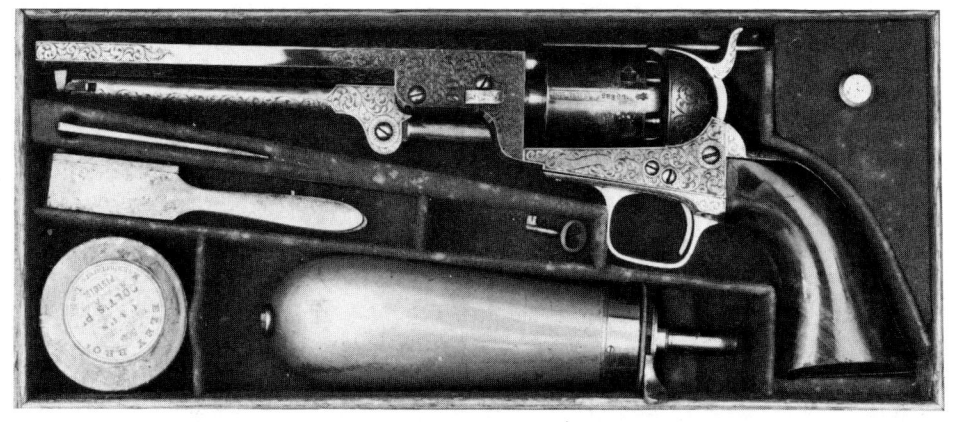

A Colt percussion cap Model 1851 navy revolver stamped *Address. Col. Colt. London*, inscribed *Edward Micklam, R.E.* and engraved with the arms of the Micklam family, 13in
London £5,400($9,720). 15.VI.76
From the collection of G. W. Earle

Coins and Medals

Silver penny, struck at Canterbury for Coenwulf, King of Mercia (796-821)
£1,600($2,880)

Silver penny, in the 'Roman style', struck for Coenwulf in London
£1,700($3,060)

Both pennies are outstanding examples of the Heptarchy coinages of Anglo-Saxon England and were part of the Delgany Hoard, found in Co. Wicklow in 1874. A portion of this hoard, which comprised the most significant group of Saxon pennies to appear at public auction for many years, was contained in the collection of Westminster School and sold in London on 26 and 27 May 1976

Eastern Celtic, base silver tetradrachm, *circa* first century AD £290($522)

Luxemburg, Henry VII (1288-1309), ½ gros £750($1,350)

Holland, Philip the Good as heir (1425-28), base gold chaise £750($1,350)

Burgundian Netherlands, Philip the Handsome, quadruple patard, 1489 £1,700($3,060)

From the collection of H.H. The Prince de Ligne sold in London on 17 and 18 June 1976

Carthage, tetradrachm, *circa* 410 BC, £3,000($5,400)

Rome, Augustus (27 BC-14 AD), denarius, £600($1,080)

Rome, Republican denarius of Pompeius Rufus, *circa* 54 BC, £980($1,764)

Anglo-Saxon, penny of Cuthred, King of Kent (789-807), £1,500($2,700)

Civil War period, sixpence of Charles Bristol mint, 1644, £310($558)

From the collection of Westminster School, London, sold in London on 26 and 27 May 1976

COINS AND MEDALS 309

USA dollar, 1795. London £4,000($7,200). 28.I.76

Transylvania, triple ducat of Joseph II, 1776
Zürich SF12,000(£2,182:$4,364). 26.XI.75

Chios, giglioto of Vicenzo
Giustiniani, 1562
London £850($1,700)
8.X.75

Ireland, James I, gold and enamel badge for the London Irish
Society, *circa* 1620. London £2,200($3,960). 15.VII.76

Anglo-Gallic, Edward III,
leopard d'or
London £1,800($3,240)
28.IV.76

Left and right
Rome, denarius of Julius Caesar and Mark Antony. London £520($1,040). 8.X.75

Centre Italy, bronze medal of Gianpaolo Lomazzo by Annibale Fontana, sixteenth century
Zürich SF3,100(£563:$1,126). 27.XI.75

Imperial Russia, Order of St Catherine the Great Martyr, a Royal presentation set of diamond insignia
London £8,500($17,000). 10.XII.75
This order, founded by Peter the Great in 1714 as a tribute to the courage of his wife during the Turkish War of 1711, was the highest Imperial Order reserved exclusively for women

Peninsular War, Military General Service medal, 1793-1814, with 11 battle clasps, awarded to Serjeant G. Kinch, 14th Light Dragoons
London £600($1,080). 25.VI.76

Italy, Sicily, Order of St Januarius, a gold and enamel badge, mid nineteenth century
London £1,400($2,520). 25.VI.76

Antiquities, Indian, Tibetan and Tribal Art

An Assyrian stone relief, probably from the Palace of Sennacherib, *circa* 700 BC, 39½in by 18in
London £14,000($25,200). 12.VII.76

312 ANTIQUITIES

An Achaemenid silver dish with an inscription of Artaxerxes I, fifth century BC, diameter 11¾in
London £12,000($24,000). 10.XI.75
Formerly in the Peter Adam collection

An Achaemenid glass bowl, *circa* fifth century BC, diameter 6¾in
London £62,000($111,600). 12.VII.76

Above
An Iranian bronze axehead, second millennium BC, length 7½in
London £6,000($12,000). 10.XI.75
Formerly in the Peter Adam collection

Above right
One of a pair of Luristan bronze harness rings, *circa* 1000-650 BC, diameter 4¼in
London £3,800($7,600). 10.XI.75
Formerly in the Peter Adam collection

Right
An Urartian bronze belt terminal, *circa* seventh century BC, length 3⅜in
London £4,500($8,100). 12.VII.76

Left
A Neolithic clay female figure, possibly from Hacilar, Anatolia, *circa* 6000-5000 BC, height 5in
New York $9,200(£4,600). 20.XI.75
From the collection of Jay C. Leff

Below
A Mesopotamian black stone vessel in the form of a reclining lion with a cuneiform dedicatory inscription, *circa* 1955-32 BC, length 4¾in
London £5,200($9,360). 12.VII.76

A Hellenistic marble head of a woman, Alexandria, third century BC, height 14½in
London £23,000($41,400). 13.VII.76
From the collection of Mrs V. R. Campbell

An Iranian bronze ram, southwest Caspian area, *circa* late second millennium BC, height $4\frac{7}{8}$in
New York $30,000(£15,000). 20.XI.75
From the collection of Jay C. Leff

A Mayan polychromed pottery vase, Placeres region, Campeche, 600-900 AD, height 6½in
New York $21,000(£10,500). 11.X.75
From the collection of Jay C. Leff

318 PRE-COLUMBIAN ART

Left
A Veracruz pottery pensive figure, probably Early Classic, *circa* 250-550 AD, height 10⅝in
$10,000(£5,000)

Right
A Colima pottery shark jar, 100 BC-250 AD, length 17⅛in
$4,200(£2,100)

A Mayan cylindrical pottery censor stand, Palenque region, Chiapas, 600-900 AD, height 32in
$12,000(£6,000)

A monumental Peruvian pottery effigy jar, early Nazca, 100 BC-200 AD, height 34½in
$16,000(£8,000)

The objects illustrated on this page are from the collection of Jay C. Leff sold in New York on 11 October 1975

TRIBAL ART 319

Left
A Marquesas Islands stone poi pestle
New York $8,000(£4,000). 10.X.75
From the collection of Jay C. Leff

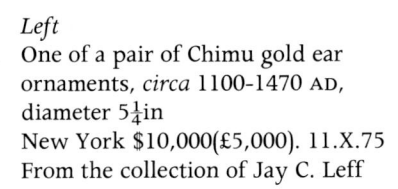

Left
One of a pair of Chimu gold ear ornaments, *circa* 1100-1470 AD, diameter 5¼in
New York $10,000(£5,000). 11.X.75
From the collection of Jay C. Leff

Below
A Fang wood female reliquary figure, height 15in
London £8,500($15,300). 12.VII.76

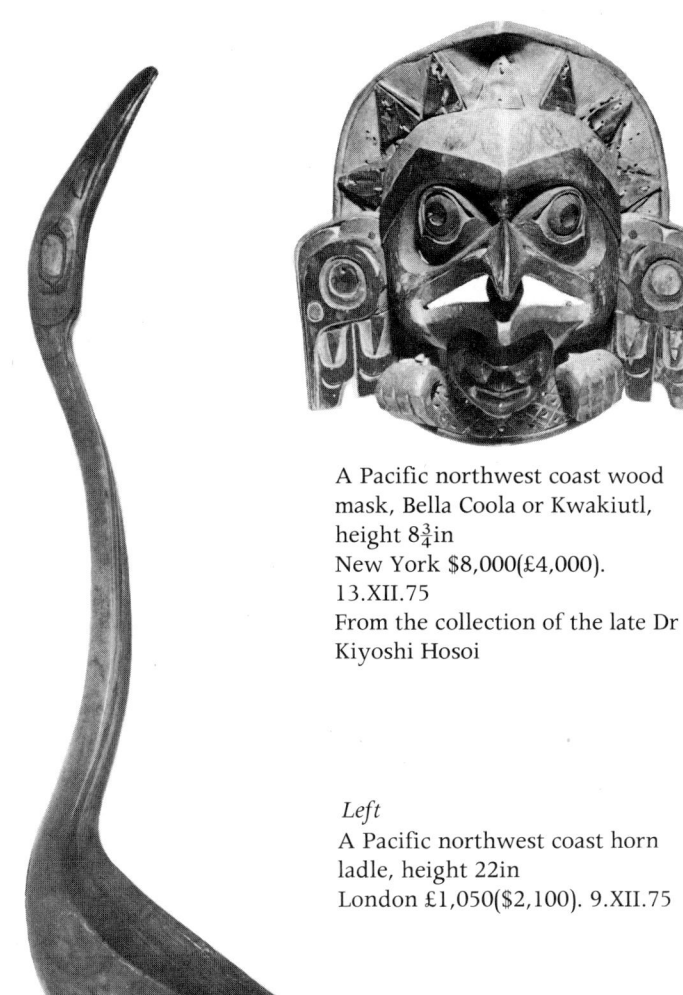

A Pacific northwest coast wood mask, Bella Coola or Kwakiutl, height 8¾in
New York $8,000(£4,000). 13.XII.75
From the collection of the late Dr Kiyoshi Hosoi

Left
A Pacific northwest coast horn ladle, height 22in
London £1,050($2,100). 9.XII.75

320 TIBETAN ART

A Tibetan silk embroidered and appliqued tanka depicting the Dharmapala Sridevi, *circa* nineteenth century, 11ft 6in by 7ft 1½in
London £5,000($9,000). 12.VII.76

A pair of Chola bronze figures of Siva and Parvati, late eleventh century, heights 21¾in and 17¼in
New York $60,000(£30,000). 19.XI.75
From the collection of Jay C. Leff

A Sassanian glass beaker, *circa* fifth-sixth century AD, height 7½in
London £18,000($32,400). 12.IV.76

Islamic Works of Art

A Maghribi Qur'an section, Andalucia or North Africa,
thirteenth/fourteenth century, 13in by 10in
London £13,000($23,400). 14.IV.76

324 ISLAMIC POTTERY

Above left
An Iranian turquoise-glazed pottery pitcher, twelfth or thirteenth century, height $12\frac{1}{4}$in
London £3,800($6,840). 12.IV.76

Above right
A Gurgan lustre pottery albarello, thirteenth century, height $8\frac{7}{8}$in
London £5,200($9,360). 12.IV.76

Left
An Isnik pottery dish, late sixteenth century, diameter $13\frac{3}{4}$in
London £2,100($3,780). 12.IV.76

Opposite page
A Seljuk *lakabi* albarello, Mesopotamia (Rakka) or Iran, late twelfth century, height $7\frac{1}{4}$in
New York $26,000(£13,000). 20.XI.75
From the collection of the late Ruth K. Henschel

ISLAMIC POTTERY 325

Fig 1   An eighteenth-century Shiraz mille-fleurs prayer rug, 5ft 4in by 3ft 8in
London £17,000($30,600). 14.IV.76

Islamic Week Sale of Carpets

Donald King

For several centuries now, England has been a good place to see Oriental carpets. The story is often told of how Cardinal Wolsey solicited a gift of scores of Damascene carpets from the Signoria of Venice in exchange for trade concessions to the Venetian merchants and the palace inventories of both Wolsey and Henry VIII list literally hundreds of Turkish carpets. From that time forward, innumerable English worthies have had themselves depicted in their portraits standing on Oriental carpets, which were both prized possessions and conspicuous signs of wealth. The great English country houses such as Boughton, Hardwick and Knole can still show some of the fine carpets with which they were furnished two, three or even four centuries ago. And when in the nineteenth century, large-scale imports of Oriental carpets made them available to a much wider segment of Western society, England became, and still remains, the main distribution centre for the European market.

Today London is probably the best place in the world for studying carpets. Not only is there one of the world's most comprehensive carpet collections at the Victoria & Albert Museum, with several hundred rugs of every kind permanently available for examination, but there is also a vast and constantly changing stock to be seen in the trade. New carpets continue to arrive in large numbers from the East, while antique and semi-antique pieces flow in from European and American collections, making London the hub and turntable of international commerce in this field. Interesting examples are to be found in the shops of the many specialist dealers and many others can be seen passing through the salerooms week by week. Anyone who aspires to know something of carpets or to form a collection of their own, however modest, is wise to keep a close eye on this constant traffic. For although there are plenty of books on the subject, some of which (like Cecil Edwards's *The Persian Carpet*) are the distillation of long years of experience in the East, there can be no substitute for personal study of large numbers of rugs. Only in this way can one learn to distinguish real quality in a carpet, to recognise the old carpet which has been given a new and spurious lease of life by restoration, and to discern the innumerable later reproductions of the old classic patterns.

An excellent opportunity for some advanced study in this field was provided by Sotheby's sale of Islamic rugs and carpets on 14 April 1976. Although rugs are included in the furniture sales almost every week, this was Sotheby's first top-class sale devoted solely to carpets since the two-part Kevorkian sale in 1969-70 and it was deemed sufficiently important to be given the accolade of an evening performance. Timed to coincide with the Islamic Festival currently running in London, it naturally attracted a great deal of attention. The period since the Kevorkian sale has seen the upward revaluation of oil, greatly strengthening the resources of Near Eastern buyers, and the corresponding depreciation of sterling, so that considerable advances in prices were to be expected. This expectation was immediately borne out by the first two lots in the present sale, both of which had also figured in the Kevorkian dispersal. The first, a late eighteenth-century mille-fleurs prayer rug (Fig 1) of a type attributed to Shiraz, or more generally to the province of Fars in southern Persia, had a distinguished provenance from the Marquand, Benguiat and Kevorkian collections; related pieces from the late Joseph McMullan's collection are in the Metropolitan Museum and the Art Institute, Chicago. This pretty and colourful rug which sold for £2,600 in the 1969 Kevorkian sale, this time fetched a price of £17,000. The price must be accounted rather high for such a rug, but was exactly in line with the Sotheby forecast. The second (Fig 2), was a fine, large and complete example, twenty-seven feet long, of the ever-popular garden carpets, presenting a bird's-eye view of a Persian garden, its straight canals with rippling water and fish, its trees and flowering plants in rectangular beds. There are similar carpets in museums at Berlin and elsewhere; they are probably of the late eighteenth century, or perhaps even later, and are generally attributed to Kurdistan or the north-western extremity of Persia. The present example, sold for £3,700 in the 1969 Kevorkian sale, fetched £25,000 this time, well above the forecast price.

The star of the show turned out, as expected, to be a complete carpet of moderate size belonging to the rare and distinguished family of Persian shrub carpets or tree carpets (Fig 3). This is a very near relative of a famous carpet now known only from fragments, one of which belonged to Professor Sarre, while others are in the museums of Paris and Boston; both carpets have an elegantly-flowing foliate lattice pattern, enclosing naturalistically-drawn flowering plants and trees of extraordinary variety. Another near relative, in the Metropolitan Museum, lacks the lattice, but has similar naturalistic plants and an almost identical border. This border and various other features link the small family of shrub carpets very closely with the larger family of Persian vase carpets and both are generally attributed to the same centre, though this has been variously identified by different authorities. The attribution usually favoured is that to Kirman in southern Persia. Arthur Upham Pope's attribution to Joshaghan, near Isfahan, in central Persia, is generally discredited, but still finds occasional echoes today thanks to its prominence in that great work of reference, the *Survey of Persian Art*; incidentally, lot 47 of the sale illustrated the type of rectilinear floral lattice which has remained current at Joshaghan until the present time and has been cited in argument both for and against Pope's attribution. The sale catalogue assigned Fig 3 to the sixteenth century, a dating which may well be judged a shade optimistic by some critics. None the less it is unquestionably an extremely important carpet and one of international stature, as was amply acknowledged by a price of £62,000.

In some ways more stately and impressive than the shrub carpet, though less rare, were two strikingly similar carpets (Figs 4 and 5), both measuring about sixteen feet by seven, with handsome patterns of curving stems, leaves, great palmettes and cloud-bands. These carpets belong to a type, frequently depicted in European

Fig 2 Detail from a late eighteenth-century Persian garden carpet, 27ft by 8ft 9in
London £25,000($45,000). 14.IV.76

paintings of the seventeenth century, which is generally attributed to Herat, formerly in eastern Persia, now in Afghanistan. Actually Herat is not now, and perhaps never was, a carpet-weaving centre and it might be preferable to attribute these carpets to Khorassan, the province of which Herat was the capital, but in fact the so-called Herat patterns were woven in various parts of Persia and in India, too, so that it is difficult to determine the origin of individual specimens. Fig 5, a particularly well known example formerly in the Marquand and Benguiat collections, which had figured in several exhibitions in New York, fetched £30,000. Fig 4, less well known, but in

Fig 3 A sixteenth-century north Persian shrub carpet, 11ft 6in by 9ft 5in
London £62,000($111,600). 14.IV.76
From the collection of Grace, Countess of Dudley

ISLAMIC WEEK SALE OF CARPETS

Fig 6   An early nineteenth-century Herez silk carpet, 15ft by 11ft
London £18,000($32,400). 14.IV.76

Fig 5 *Opposite page*
A detail from a sixteenth/seventeenth-century Herat carpet, 16ft by 7ft 1in
London £30,000($54,000). 14.IV.76

Fig 4 A detail from a sixteenth/seventeenth-century Herat carpet, 16ft 2in by 7ft 1in
London £40,000($72,000). 14.IV.76
From the collection of Grace, Countess of Dudley

rather fresher condition, was knocked down at £40,000. The sale also included several other carpets in this style, though less fine in quality and condition.

Another extremely handsome design generally assigned to eastern Persia or Herat is that of the large animal carpet, depicting tigers, leopards, deer and other creatures interspersed among the curving stems, palmettes and cloud-bands, and having a long poetical inscription in the inner guard stripe. This is the pattern of a very famous pair of sixteenth-century carpets which are said to have been given by Peter the Great of Russia to the Emperor Leopold I of Austria; one of the pair remains in the Austrian Museum of Applied Art in Vienna, while the other is in the Metropolitan Museum. This carpet was clearly a later copy of this pattern, remarkably accurate, but not very pleasing in colour. It fetched £13,500, a good price, though less than the estimate.

Among the later Persian rugs, one which sold exceptionally well was a sample piece with a design almost identical to that of a carpet in the Metropolitan Museum which has an inscription recording that it was made at Garus in Kurdistan in 1794. The price of £4,620 realised by this sample, less than six feet square, no doubt reflected the fact that it is illustrated and discussed in one of the standard books, Erdmann's *Seven Hundred Years of Oriental Carpets*. Other good prices among the later Persian pieces were £18,000 for Fig 6, a colourful nineteenth-century Herez silk carpet depicting a tree inhabited by demons and monsters, and £9,000 for a vast nineteenth-century Kirman carpet with a field subdivided by compartments and prayer niches filled with intricate floral patterns.

A group of Caucasian carpets, of various types and dates, proved popular and most of them comfortably exceeded their estimates. The star performer here was a handsome dragon carpet (Fig. 7), with unusually well-defined dragons and other creatures in a lattice of broad leaves. This carpet, assigned to the seventeenth century, had had some restoration but was otherwise in very good condition with fresh, bright colours. It sold for £22,000, roughly twice the estimate. A large fragment of a seventeenth- or eighteenth-century Caucasian carpet, with huge, boldly-stylised palmettes, flowers and leaves, also did well at £9,000. Nineteenth-century Caucasian rugs, with their powerfully-simplified patterns, likewise attracted excellent prices. A small group of Cairene rugs of the sixteenth and seventeenth centuries were distinguished by their rarity rather than their condition which, as is often the case with these rugs, left a good deal to be desired. The top price here, £6,160, went to a rug with a geometrical pattern of octagons and stars, probably dating from the first half of the sixteenth century and hence the oldest rug in the sale, but rather extensively reknotted at a later date.

More than a score of Turkish rugs offered a wide range of types, though not all were of the highest quality. The best result among these Turkish pieces was a price of £12,000 for a nineteenth-century silk Hereke carpet, with a medallion pattern in the Persian style, in soft tones of ivory and rose. The Turkish prayer rugs were a mixed bag, including some later copies of earlier styles. The surprise here was a small early nineteenth-century Melas prayer rug, extremely bright and new-looking, which fetched £4,000, roughly doubling its estimate. An attractive Ghiordes prayer rug fetched £3,800. Other prayer rugs were rather more modestly priced ranging right down to a little Mudjur at £240.

To sum up, it seems that, with a few exceptions, the level of prices was extremely healthy and very much in line with expectations. Early pieces of exceptional rarity or very fine quality, in a good state of preservation, commanded extremely high prices, as had been foreseen. The outstanding early Persian carpets, Figs 3, 4 and 5, were in the £30,000-£70,000 range, as estimated. Slightly less important Persian, Caucasian and Turkish carpets, Figs 1, 2, 6, and 7, were in the range £10,000-£30,000, again as estimated. Early pieces in poor or over-restored condition, on the other hand, failed to attract much enthusiasm, while later copies of early patterns were clearly recognised for what they were. It was an instructive sale, including a number of interesting problem pieces, and one had the impression throughout that the prices paid corresponded to very accurate assessments of the quality and the condition of the individual items. Evidently this is both a very active and a very discriminating market, in which the casual buyer is unlikely to find many unconsidered bargains.

Fig 7　A seventeenth-century Kuba dragon carpet, 10ft 8in by 5ft 7in London £22,000($39,600). 14.IV.76

336 ISLAMIC CARPETS

A Herez silk rug, 5ft 5in by 3ft 11in
New York $31,000(£15,500). 27.IX.75

A detail from a Herez silk carpet, signed and dated, 11ft 9in by 9ft 8in
New York $44,000(£24,474). 10.1.76

338 ISLAMIC ARMS AND ARMOUR

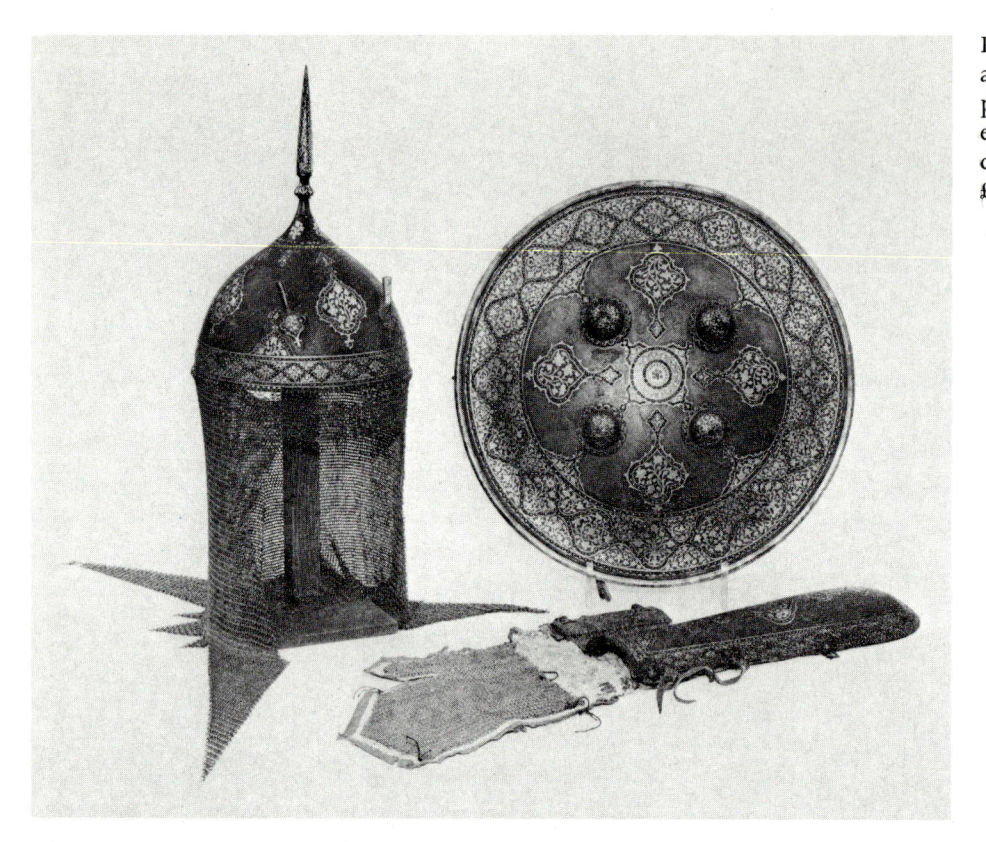

Part of a suit of Persian armour decorated with pieces of turquoise, late eighteenth century, diameter of shield 15¾in £6,000($10,800)

From top to bottom below
An Indian dagger, the hilt with ivory grips and velvet-covered scabbard, eighteenth or nineteenth century, length 14½in £900($1,620)
An Indian khanjar with crystal hilt and brocade-covered scabbard, eighteenth century, length 13¾in £1,200($2,160)
An Indo-Persian peshkabz with crystal hilt and brocade-covered scabbard, eighteenth century, length 19⅛in £1,500($2,700)

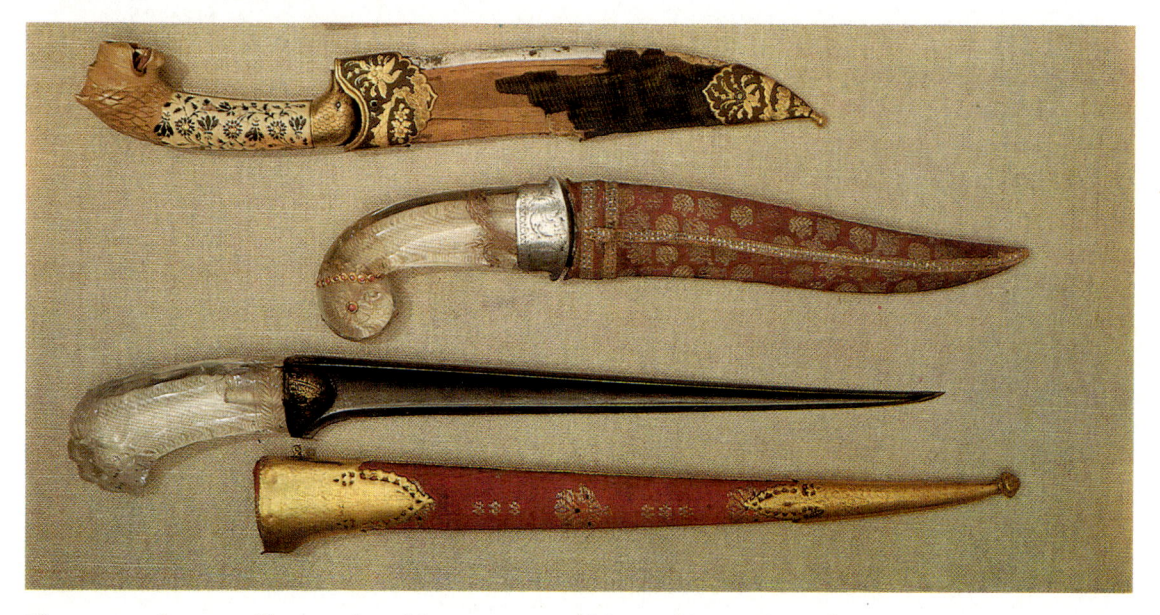

The arms and armour illustrated on this page were sold in London on 12 April 1976

A Qajar gold Qalian bowl, mid-nineteenth century, height 2½in London £14,000($25,200). 12.IV.76

A Qajar enamelled copper rose water set, *circa* 1880, height of flagons 18¾in and 12¼in, diameter of basin 10¼in London £40,000($72,000). 12.IV.76

A portrait of a courtesan, Qajar,
late eighteenth century,
55in by 30¼in
London £33,000($66,000).
9.XII.75
From the collection of Lord
Strathcona and Mount Royal

A portrait of a young lady, Qajar, *circa* 1820, 65in by 36in London £48,000($86,400). 13.IV.76

Left
A Persian lacquer mirror-case executed by Muhammad 'Ali Ashraf, signed and dated 1169AH/1756AD, 8¼in by 5¾in
London £10,000($18,000). 14.IV.76

A Qajar lacquer pen-box attributed to Nasr Allah Imami, mid-nineteenth century, length 9¼in
New York $3,700(£1,850). 20.XI.75

A Persian lacquer pen-box, Qajar, *circa* 1830, length 9¾in
London £2,200($3,960). 14.IV.76

Chinese Ceramics and Works of Art

An archaic bronze *fang-ting*, eleventh century BC, $8\frac{1}{8}$in by $6\frac{1}{8}$in
New York $85,000(£47,222). 20.III.76
From the collection of Mr Fred C. Snider

A white marble stele, Northern Ch'i Dynasty, height 24½in
London £27,000($54,000). 9.XII.75

A double-sided bronze pole finial, Shang/early Western Chou Dynasty, 5⅞in by 4in
London £80,000($144,000). 6.IV.76

A green-glazed stoneware caryatid lamp, late sixth century, 8¼in by 6¾in
London £34,000($61,200). 6.VII.76

CHINESE CERAMICS 347

A blue-glazed pottery figure,
T'ang Dynasty, height 14in
London £36,000($64,800). 6.IV.76

A purple-glazed Chün-yao narcissus bowl, Sung Dynasty, 3in by 8¼in Hong Kong £38,000($76,000). 17.XI.75

CHINESE CERAMICS 349

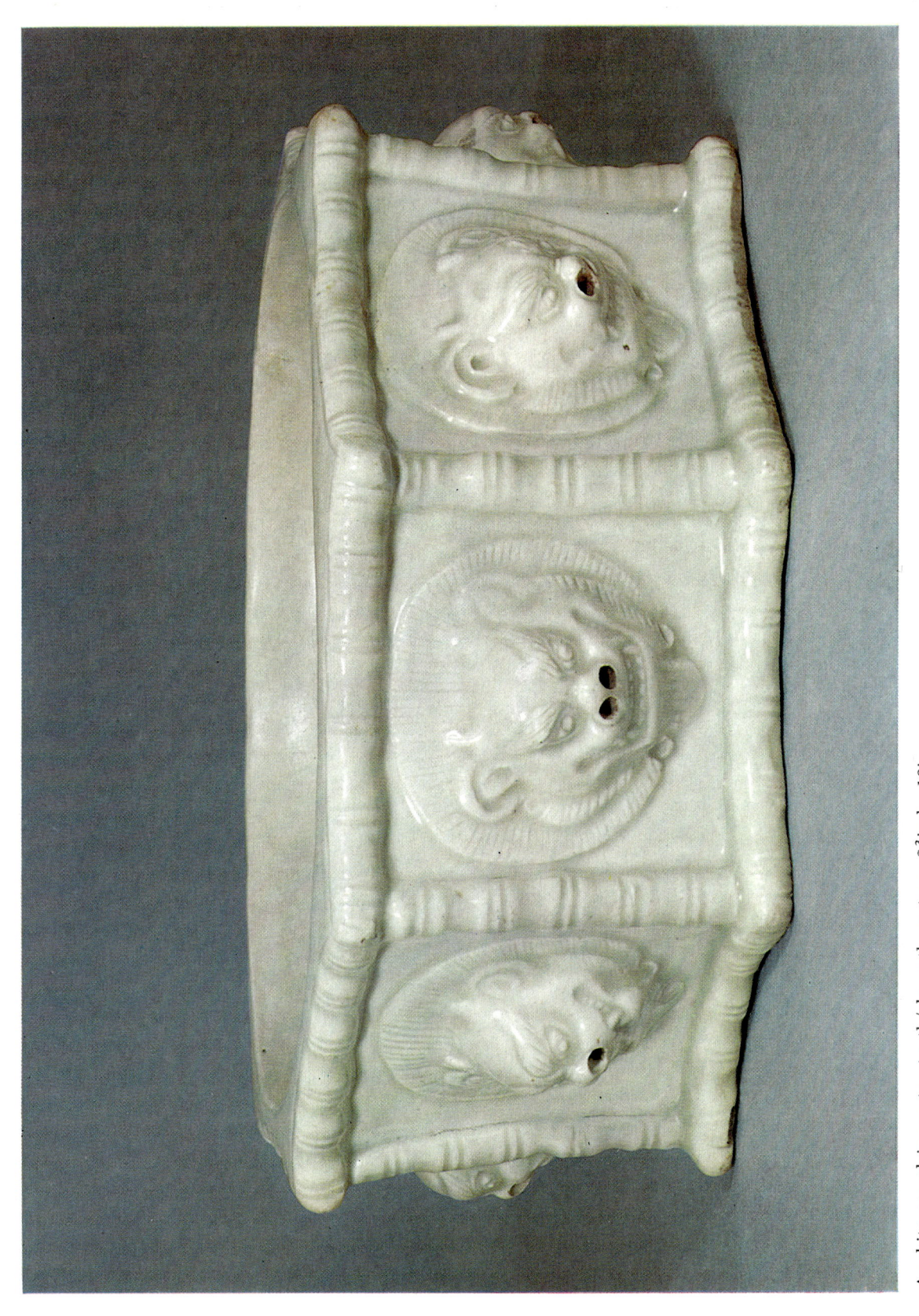

A white porcelain mortar, tenth/eleventh century, 3¾in by 10in London £17,000($30,600). 6.VII.76

A Ming blue and white dish, early fifteenth century, diameter 17¼in
Los Angeles $100,000(£55,555). 11.III.76

An early Ming blue and white dish, six character mark and period of Hsüan Tê, diameter $7\frac{7}{8}$in
Los Angeles $100,000(£55,555). 11.III.76

An early fifteenth-century saucer dish, six character mark of Hsüan Tê written in a line below the lip in pale underglaze-blue, and of the period, diameter 11¾in
London £53,000($95,400). 6.VII.76

An underglaze-red decorated basin, late fourteenth century, diameter 16½in
London £125,000($250,000). 9.XII.75

354 CHINESE CERAMICS

An engraved blue-ground dragon bowl, six character mark and period of Chia Ching, diameter 11⅛in Hong Kong £51,000($91,800). 12.V.76

CHINESE CERAMICS 355

A Yüan copper-red and blue glazed bowl moulded with dragons, fourteenth century, diameter $7\frac{7}{8}$ in London £52,000($93,600). 6.VII.76

CHINESE CERAMICS

An early Ming slip-decorated blue-ground bowl, six character mark and period of Hsüan Tê, diameter 6in
London £31,000($55,800). 6.VII.76

A Ming polychrome jar, six character mark and period of Chia Ching, height 15½in
New York $260,000(£144,444). 20.III.76
From the collection of Mr and Mrs A. Douglas Oliver

A Ming polychrome wine ewer and cover, six character mark and period of Wan Li, the English silver mounts *circa* 1680, height 9¾in
London £48,000($86,400). 6.IV.76
From the collection of Robert Bourne

A Ming *tou ts'ai* winecup, six character mark of Ch'êng Hua within a double square, and of the period, diameter $2\frac{7}{8}$in London £44,000($79,200). 6.VII.76

A Ming red and yellow dragon jar, six character mark and period of Chia Ching, height $5\frac{1}{2}$ in Hong Kong £30,000($54,000). 12.V.76

CHINESE CERAMICS 361

An imperial yellow-ground *famille rose* bowl, four character mark *k'ang hsi yü chih* in pink enamel within a double square and of the period of K'ang Hsi, 2¼in by 4¼in
Hong Kong £28,500($57,000). 17.XI.75

An imperial ruby-ground censer, four character mark *k'ang hsi yü chih* in blue enamel within a double circle and of the period, 2½in by 6⅛in
London £48,000($86,400). 6.VII.76

362 CHINESE CERAMICS

A pair of octagonal *famille rose* dishes, Yung Chêng, diameter 13in
London £4,200($7,560). 24.II.76

An imperial carved copper-red *mei p'ing*, six character mark and period of Yung Chêng, height 11in
New York $30,000(£15,000). 25.X.75
From the collection of the late Geraldine Rockefeller Dodge

CHINESE PAINTINGS

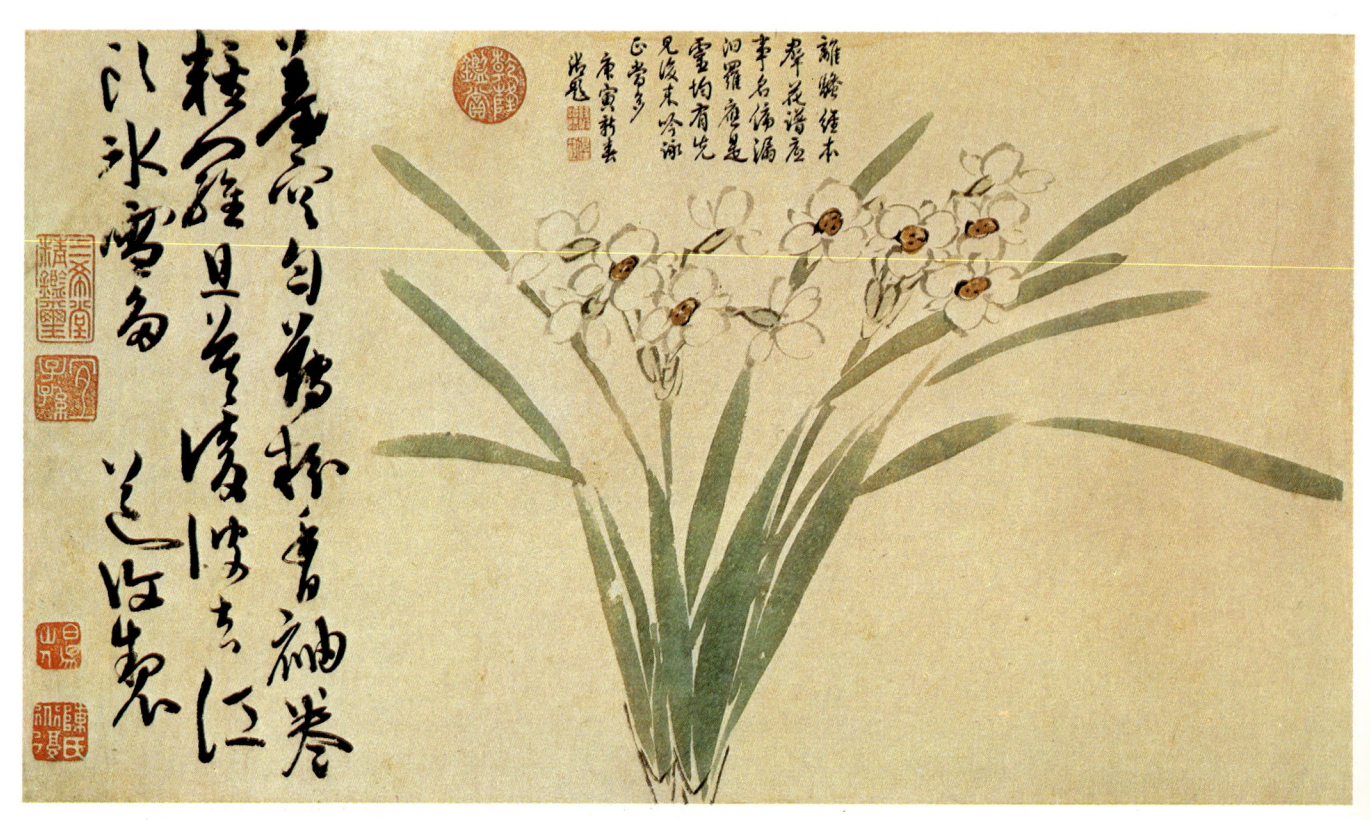

A detail from a handscroll of flowers by Ch'ên Shun (1483-1544), 11¼in by 130in
New York $30,000(£16,666). 22.IV.76

A detail from a handscroll of mountains and rivers in the style of Huang Kung-wang by Chao Tso, *circa* 1600-1630, 9⅝in by 248in
New York $22,000(£12,222). 22.IV.76
Both these are from the Lok Tsai Hsien Collection

Japanese Ceramics and Works of Art

An early Kakiemon bottle,
late seventeenth century,
286mm
London £20,000
($36,000). 2.VI.76
From the collection of
Richard de la Mare

366 JAPANESE CERAMICS

A Kakiemon bowl moulded on the interior with the 'Three Friends', late seventeenth century/early eighteenth century, 192mm
London £8,500($15,300). 2.VI.76

A Kakiemon bowl bearing the Dresden Johanneum mark, N:3, late seventeenth century, 243mm
London £42,000($76,600). 2.VI.76

The pieces of porcelain on this page are from the collection of Richard de la Mare

A Kakiemon jar, late seventeenth century, 264mm
London £16,500($29,700). 2.VI.76
From the collection of Richard de la Mare

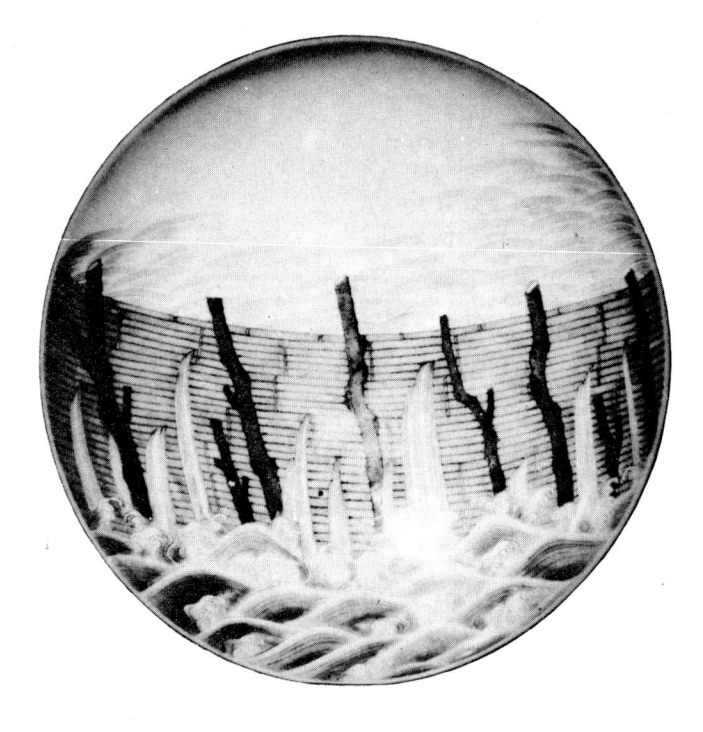

An Ao-Nabeshima dish in underglaze blue, early
eighteenth century, 198mm
London £3,600($6,480). 2.VI.76

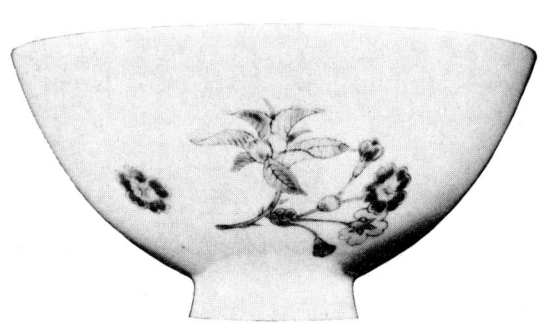

A Kakiemon cup, early eighteenth century, 109mm
London £3,400($6,120). 2.VI.76

A Kakiemon bowl in *rouge-de-fer* and enamel, late
seventeenth century, 180mm
London £4,800($8,640). 2.VI.76

All the pieces of porcelain illustrated on this page are from
the collection of Richard de la Mare

Right
A Kakiemon dish in *rouge-de-fer* and blue, green and yellow enamels, late seventeenth century, 305mm
London £5,200($9,360). 2.VI.76
From the collection of Richard de la Mare

Below right
A Kakiemon jar in iron-red and blue and green enamels, second half of the seventeenth century, 202mm
London £9,500($17,100). 2.VI.76
From the collection of Richard de la Mare

Below left
A Ko-Kutani bottle, late seventeenth century, 248mm
London £10,500($18,900). 18.II.76

JAPANESE NETSUKE

UNSHO HAKURYU I
An ivory group of a
tigress and cub,
London £2,450($4,410).
23.VI.76

TOMOKAZU: A wooden
group of turtles
New York $1,800(£900).
18.XI.75

TETSUGENDO KYUSAI
An ivory group
of two monkeys
London £2,000($3,600).
23.VI.76

GANBUN: A boxwood
study of a group
of mushrooms,
Los Angeles $5,500
(£3,055). 9.VI.76

MORITA SOKO: A wooden
group of herbs and leaves
London £2,100($3,780).
23.VI.76

TOYOMASA: A wooden
study of a tiger,
London £3,800($6,840).
23.VI.76

Far left
TOKOKU: A group of Shoki and Oni
London £2,300($4,600). 29.X.75

Left
IKKOSAI TOUN: An ivory group
of a Kirin and young
London £6,800($12,240).
23.VI.76

Below
OTOMAN: A study of a tiger
London £1,600($3,200).
29.X.75

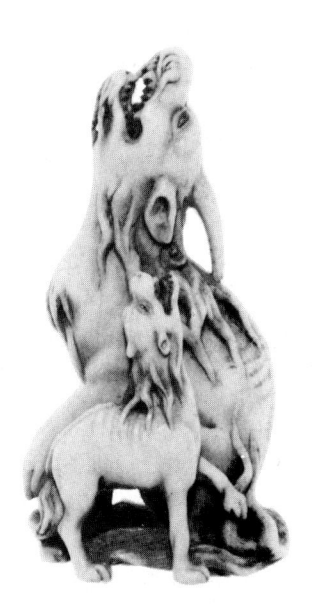

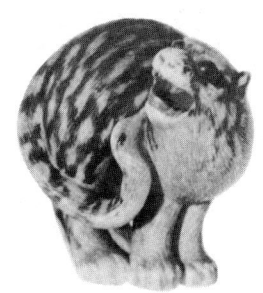

JAPANESE INRO AND IVORY 371

SHOYO
A gold-lacquer and metal three case *inro*
London £2,000($3,600). 23.VI.76

KAIGYOKUDO MASATERU
A boxwood *tabako-ire* in the form of a human skull
London £3,200($5,760). 23.VI.76

Left
An ivory elephant, 65mm
£230($414)

Right
A gold lacquer and shibayama three-case *inro*, 114mm
£1,500($2,700)

Both these objects are from the Hood collection sold in London on 29 April 1976

Opposite page
Left
A Shinto *tachi* after Bishu Nagayoshi with silver *tsuba* signed *Hitotsuyanagi Tomoyoshi*
New York $7,250(£3,625). 19.XI.75
From the collection of Jay C. Leff

Centre
A Shinto *katana* blade in *shirasaya*, 723mm
London £3,000($6,000). 12.XI.75

Left
A lacquer box and stand, late nineteenth century, height 190mm
London £3,500($6,300). 29.IV.76

Below
A gold-lacquer *kodansu*, nineteenth century, 170mm by 107mm
New York $3,400(£1,700). 18.XI.75

JAPANESE ARMS AND ARMOUR 373

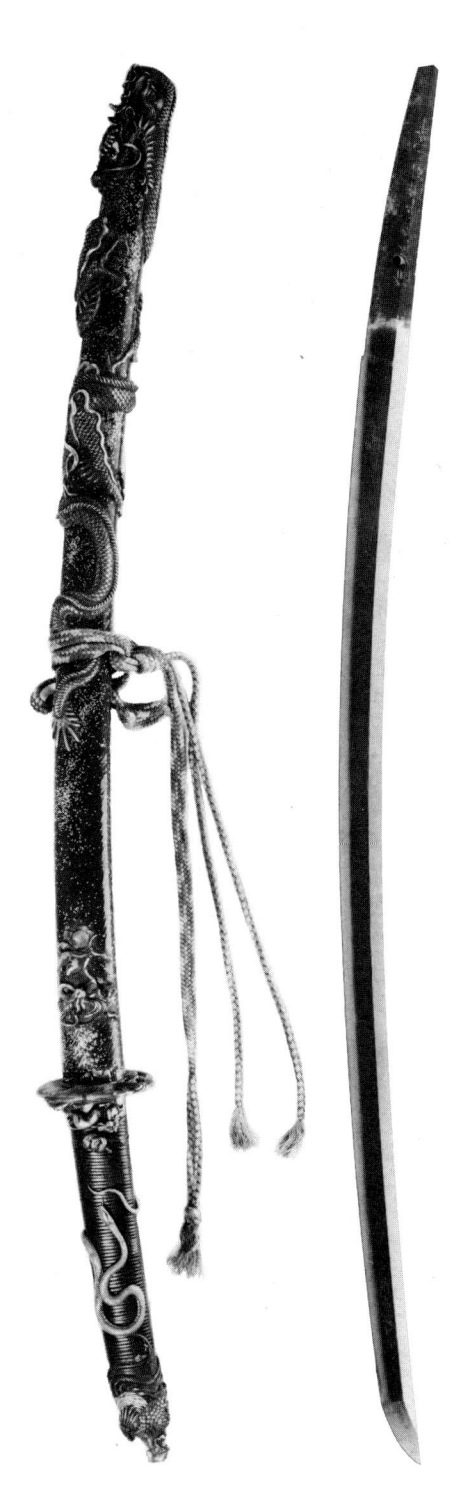

Right
A *Midori-fukaki-odoshi tachi-do*, including a sixty-two plate *Koshozan-suji no kabuto*, early nineteenth century and earlier
New York $8,500(£4,250). 19.XI.75

A Haniwa ceramic figure of a warrior, late Tumuli period
(fourth-sixth century), height 768mm
Los Angeles $1,000(£500). 14.X.75
From the collection of the late Dr Kiyoshi Hosoi

A late Heian wood figure of Kichijo-ten,
height 800mm
New York $5,400(£2,700). 19.XI.75

EISHOSAI CHOKI
Oban: A half-length portrait of a courtesan
Colour print, signed
New York $19,000(£10,555). 4.III.76
From the collection of the late Louis W. Black

ANDO HIROSHIGE
Otanzaku: *Bow Moon*
Colour print, signed. One from the series 'The twenty-eight views of the Moon'
New York $6,800(£3,777). 4.III.76
From the collection of the late Louis W. Black

SUGIMURA JIHEI
Oban yoko-e: A *samurai* converses with a courtesan
Print, hand coloured
New York $17,000(£9,444). 4.III.76
From the collection of the late Louis W. Black

HOKUTEI JOREN
A snow scene of Kan U and his companion
Painting in diptych form, each panel 420mm by 385mm
London £740($1,332). 12.V.76

European Ceramics

387 ENGLISH POTTERY
388 ENGLISH PORCELAIN
392 CONTINENTAL POTTERY
395 CONTINENTAL PORCELAIN
402 NINETEENTH- AND TWENTIETH-CENTURY CERAMICS

A Ralph Wood equestrian group, probably depicting King William III as a Roman emperor, *circa* 1770-75, height 15½in
London £5,750($11,500). 30.IX.75
From the collection of the late Constance, Viscountess Mackintosh

Fig 3   A Wedgwood encaustic decorated black basalt plaque, *circa* 1770, 8in by 10in
New York $4,000(£2,222). 6.IV 76

The design of this plaque is taken directly from Sir William Hamilton's *Antiquities*, vol II, p.35, published in Naples in 1767

The Milton Milestone Collection of early Wedgwood

Bruce Tattersall

Important auctions of Wedgwood are rare events in the saleroom. Even rarer are sales in which the majority of the lots are of major significance and bear that mark which is the talisman of the collector – the magic symbols of Wedgwood & Bentley. The Milton Milestone collection sales at Sotheby Parke Bernet, New York, on 16 December 1975 and 6 April 1976 were two such events. Indeed, it could be argued that such a rich variety of their wares has not appeared before the buying public since those twelve days in December 1781, when in the words of that catalogue 'Mr. Wedgwood having had the Misfortune to lose his much-lamented *Friend* and *Partner* Mr. BENTLEY, has found it necessary . . . to dispose of their joint Stock by PUBLIC AUCTION.'

It would be possible, but excessively tedious, to discuss almost all the three hundred and fifty-one lots in considerable detail, for they all play their part in the history of Wedgwood at its most inventive, significant and *avant-garde* period. However, a selection must be made which will illuminate the almost unbelievable variety of wares which emerged from Etruria in the short period between its foundation in 1769 and Wedgwood's own death in 1795, and which will also indicate the role that he and his partner Thomas Bentley played in the revival of what they considered the 'true antique style', which today we call neo-Classicism.

To begin with a crime, that of *lèse majesté*, Fig 1 was catalogued as the Duke of Marlborough and condemned to the outer darkness of 'after 1787'. Scarcely ever has such an injustice been inflicted upon the true subject of this fine black basalt bust which is, in fact, His Majesty George II. It should be added, however, that this case of mistaken identity was no fault of the auctioneers as this bust has been wrongly recorded for some time. It was one of the earliest ever to be manufactured by the partnership, thus is usually unmarked, and consequently disregarded. It appeared initially in the first Wedgwood & Bentley catalogue of 1773 as no. 4 in class XII: 'George II a fine Bust from an Ivory in the Possession of Mr. Ranby carved by Mr. Rysbrack, with the Pedestal, 10 inches.' The original ivory was a smaller version of the lifesize, marble bust in the Victoria & Albert Museum. This is signed and dated 1760.

Wedgwood's connexion with Rysbrack, as with several other sculptors, was only indirect. He either borrowed pieces from their owners, like Mr Ranby, or he had recourse to the reproductions sold in plaster shops owned by such worthies as Mary Landres, John Cheere, Hoskins & Grant or John Flaxman, senior, with whose son Wedgwood would have had a close, direct working relationship. It is to the work of

Fig 1 *Left* A Wedgwood black basalt bust of King George II, *circa* 1773, height 9¾in
New York $400(£222). 6.IV.76

Fig 5 *Far left* A Wedgwood & Bentley black basalt triton candlestick, *circa* 1768-80, impressed *Wedgwood & Bentley* mark, height 10¾in
New York $1,700(£850). 16.XII.75

this son, John Flaxman, junior (1755-1826), that we must now turn. During his stay in Rome from 1787 to 1794, Flaxman was in charge of an extempory academy of sculptors who made sketches and wax reliefs for Wedgwood to be reproduced in jasper. Included in this group were John de Vaere, Angelo Delmozzoni and Camillo Pacetti. A blue and white jasper plaque in the sale, depicting the infant Achilles mounted on the centaur, Chiron, is usually attributed to Pacetti on the strength of the surviving wax originals which he made of the Achilles series. However the Wedgwood Museum possesses a drawing by Flaxman of this subject (Fig 2) and it should be acknowledged that the original idea for the composition was his, as the design has undergone a subtle transformation. The classical marble dish in the Capitoline Museum, whence the original inspiration came, depicts the youthful Achilles mounted upon a female centaur who has been translated into the male Chiron in the Flaxman version. This is both more correct classically (Chiron was Achilles' tutor who fed the young hero on the hearts of lions), as well as being less sexually overt. Wedgwood was much concerned about the prudery of his clientele as a letter he wrote to Flaxman in February 1790, mentioning the Achilles series, shows:

> 'There is one objection which I am afraid is insurmountable and that is the nakedness of the figures . . . indeed the nude is so general in the works of the ancients, that it will be very difficult to avoid the introduction of naked figures. On the other hand it is absolutely necessary to do so, for none either male or female of the present generation, will take or apply them as furniture if the figures are naked.'

Fig 2   Flaxman's sketch for Wedgwood's blue and white jasper plaque
depicting Achilles hunting on Chiron, *circa* 1787-90
In the collection of the Wedgwood Museum

By 1790 Wedgwood was supplying not only a less sanguine generation but also the 'middling classes' whose delicate sensibilities required more chaste designs. Yet when he produced such items as the black basalt plaque illustrated in Fig 3, Wedgwood was making *objets d'art* for a more select aristocratic market: those who in the mid eighteenth century had adopted the Etruscan style as expounded in the four volumes of Sir William Hamilton's *Antiquities*.[1] This style was a far more exact, full-blooded classical one than that of the 1780s which was rather a manifestation of the late Rococo and less serious in its intent: a dainty minuette compared with the base notes of true classicism. Such plaques as these were made for the delectation of connoisseurs who could marvel knowledgeably at Wedgwood & Bentley's 'rediscovery' of the ancient method of 'encaustic' painting and upon the accuracy of the style of the classical figures so depicted. For such a sophisticated market nudity was obviously permissible, due partly to a desire for verisimilitude to the original and partly to a more tolerant attitude among customers. This androgynous Cupid is one of Wedgwood's 'Encaustic Pictures' which are mentioned in letters to Bentley as early as 1771. They appear to have been made for chimney pieces and decorated in London under Bentley's supervision, (the tablets themselves being made in the Potteries by a craftsman who had been diverted from the more mundane task of making fish-drainers!) Despite their popularity they are today some of the rarest surviving productions of Etruria. Even at the 1781 sale one fetched the second highest price of the whole twelve days.

[1] Coincidentally, a set of Sir William Hamilton's *Antiquities*, was sold at Sotheby's in London on 10 November 1975.

Wedgwood's encaustic ware was the second attempt to 'captivate nay ravish' the aristocracy by a re-interpretation of the antique. His first attempt was to make vases in a classical style, for which the demand became so great that Mr Cox, Wedgwood's London agent, became 'as mad as a March Hare for Etruscan vases'. At the Milestone sale a similar insanity seems to have affected the buyers of both the early black basalt vases and the contemporary variegated pieces. Of the latter a single vase and two pairs (see Fig 4) show to advantage the effect which was desired by using these vases as *garnitures de cheminée* as indicated in the Wedgwood & Bentley catalogues: 'They are generally sold in *Pairs* or Sets of *Three, Five* or *Seven Pieces*. The sets of five Pieces sell from about Two Guineas to Five or Six Guineas a Set.' The outside pair in Fig 4 probably date from early in the partnership before 1772 when Sir William Hamilton magisterially banished 'this offensive Gilding', which admonition Wedgwood obeyed, though not without qualms:

'I do not find it an easy matter to make a Vase with the coloring so natural, varied, pleasing & *unpot-like* & the shape so delicate, as to make it seem worth a great deal of money, without additional trappings of handles, ornaments and Gilding.'

The origin of these vases was most 'unpot-like' being a classical porphory vase in the Capitoline Museum in Rome. The other pair (in the centre front) are even earlier and probably date from the period in which Wedgwood was experimenting with his solid agate bodies and enduring difficulties with inexperienced workmen suffering from 'unhandiness and want of ideas'. These squat vases seem to be rather unclassical in form, similar to the decorative finials on furniture and clocks. One is tempted to speculate that Wedgwood is referring to items very like this pair when he writes to his wife Sarah early in 1769:

'Some of the ladys say the same thing that occurred to you & me about the sugar dish vases – that they are like the things on the tops of Clock Cases, or Bed Heads. They certainly are not Antique and that is fault enough to D(am)n them with most of our customers.'

The central vase in Fig 4 is one of the most elegant of Wedgwood & Bentley's classical creations. With its stately winged caryatids bearing swags of drapery in each hand it possesses all the points in Sir William Chambers's definition of urns: 'The character of urns is simplicity, to have covers, but no handles, nor spouts, they are monumental.'

Similar pieces known as 'Caryatic' vases were made by Boulton and Fothergill at Soho. Here the ladies are employed in supporting the candle-holders in a rather inelegant manner while the swags around the belly of the vases are supported by willpower alone! These vases were made at Soho before 1771 and the Wedgwood examples are probably contemporary. At this time there was much interchange of both models and ideas between Etruria and Soho. Chambers himself was suggesting designs to both establishments. For instance, he loaned his figure of Triton (Fig 5 is an example) to both. So it is highly probable that the design for this particular urn is his. This attribution is strengthened by its similarity to designs in his 'Treatise on Civil Architecture' in which 'Persians and Caryatids' are given a chapter to themselves.

THE MILTON MILESTONE COLLECTION OF EARLY WEDGWOOD

Fig 4

Centre above
A Wedgwood & Bentley variegated vase, *circa* 1772-80, impressed Wedgwood & Bentley marks, height 10½in, $3,500(£1,750).

Left and right
A pair of Wedgwood & Bentley variegated vases and covers, *circa* 1769-72, impressed Wedgwood & Bentley marks, height 9¼in, $6,000(£3,000)

Centre below
A pair of Wedgwood & Bentley porphyry chimney ornaments, *circa* 1769-80, impressed Wedgwood & Bentley marks, height 5½in, $3,100(£1,550)

The pottery illustrated on this page was sold in New York on 16 December 1975

384 THE MILTON MILESTONE COLLECTION OF EARLY WEDGWOOD

Fig 6 *Left* A Wedgwood & Bentley black basalt 'fish tail' ewer, *circa* 1770-80, impressed *WEDGWOOD & BENTLEY ETRURIA* wafer mark, height 12½in
New York $4,000(£2,222). 6.IV.76

Fig 7 A pair of Wedgwood & Bentley variegated vases, *circa* 1770-80, impressed *WEDGWOOD & BENTLEY ETRURIA* wafer marks, height 8¼in
New York $2,700(£1,350). 16.XII.75

Fig 9 *Right* Two Wedgwood blue and white jasper bamboo vases, *circa* 1785, impressed *WEDGWOOD* mark and letter S, heights 10½in and 10⅜in
New York $3,200(£1,600) and $1,100(£550). 16.XII.75

Fig 8 A Wedgwood black basalt bulb pot and cover, *circa* 1780, impressed Wedgwood mark and an S scroll, length 6⅛in
New York $1,200(£666). 6.IV.76

The black basalt vases, though not so numerous, were equally fine. The ewer (Fig 6) from Stella's book on vases in the Louvre could at a pinch, by Chambers's definition, be called a useful article which rather perturbed Wedgwood. The partnership with Bentley was to produce 'ornamental earthenware' but there was also his partnership with a cousin to produce 'useful' ware. Where did such an item belong and to which partnership should the profits accrue? This question was worrying Bentley in late 1770, but Wedgwood had the answer:

'With respect to the difference between *Useful Ware* & *Ornamental* I do not find any inclination in myself to be over nice in drawing the line. You know I never had any idea that *Ornamental Ware* should not be of "Some use". . . . I could have wish'd therefore that you had not repeated this idea so often, & asked me if my partnership with T.W [Thomas Wedgwood] would exclude our making Stella's Ewers.'

Although the reputation of the partnership has been rightly established upon its classical ware, other styles were attempted in both variegated ware and black basalt. Fig 7 shows just such a venture in a pair of vases very much in the Sèvres Rococo style which Wedgwood had pursued before his conversion to all things Etruscan. Nor was Chinoiserie forgotten either, with black basalt pieces emerging from Etruria towards the end of the partnership. An oven book indicates that '6 black cane vine pots with two cups' were produced on Thursday, 25 November 1780, the very month of Bentley's death. A similar piece (Fig 8), marked 'Wedgwood', appeared in the sale which must imply that it was manufactured very soon afterwards. Such an early date is something of a surprise, for it would seem that such wares should belong to the second phase of Chinoiserie, that of Nash and the Brighton Pavilion, where the main staircase has bamboo balustrades made of cast iron. Despite a similar whimsical quality, bordering on the perverse, Fig 8 was executed some decades earlier. Its inspiration may lie in Chambers's books describing his Chinese travels. An even more ebullient interpretation of this theme also presents itself in the blue and white jasper vases illustrated in Fig 9.

These flamboyant receptacles must date from the mid 1780s and are consequently some of the earliest pieces of jasper to have been produced in the round. Until about 1783 Wedgwood could only make jasper into flat objects such as plaques and cameos, but about then, despite firing problems, a trickle of jasper vases and teaware begins to appear and by the publication of the 1786 catalogue, a large range is available.

From that same decade, as evidence of his progress, came two of the most triumphant pieces of ceramic art in the whole history of Etruria. They are a pair of candelabra depicting Minerva and Diana (Fig 10). The quality of the jasper ware and the meticulous detail of the modelling are incomparable, but what is most striking about them is their style which is far more lively than the restrained monumentality of Flaxman and his atelier. The delight in complex intersecting planes of drapery and the mastery of anatomy puts these works above the skills of even the most competent modeller. The detail has a suavity which convinces the observer that this is the work of a very fine sculptor indeed. All the visual and circumstantial evidence excitingly points to one elusive man, Henry Webber.

Fig 10 A pair of Wedgwood blue and white jasper candelabra modelled as Diana and Minerva, late eighteenth century, height 13¾in
New York $4,250(£2,125). 16.XII.75

Webber (1781-1826) was a pupil of the sculptor John Bacon, whose fluid style he adopted and made even more lively. In 1782 he entered into a contract to work for Wedgwood at Etruria upon the recommendation of Sir Joshua Reynolds and Sir William Chambers. Wedgwood eventually sent him to Rome, whence he sent back various designs. Wedgwood also bought from him several models and a sketch book which tantalisingly contained drawings of 'four statues', alas unspecified. While in Bacon's studio Webber must have been occupied with the Chatham monument in Westminster Abbey. On this there is a seated figure of Britannia which must be the prototype for this Minerva. The pose is identical as are many of the trappings, helmet, breastplate, shield. Only the attributes and the scale have been altered; Britannia is over lifesize, Minerva a mere fourteen inches high. Yet she and her companion have lost nothing by this translation and can reasonably claim to be the zenith of the Wedgwood's achievements in jasper; the combination of the work of a fine sculptor and a ceramic body which could produce the effect of finely chiselled marble. They make a poignant memorial to the achievements of a man, who through his experiments, his business acumen and his superlative ware succeeded in his self-stated aim to 'astonish all the world at once'.

Collections such as the Milton Milestone give today's collector a chance to share in that astonishment and to wonder about an age in which the stuff of classicism seemed to breathe anew. In the lines of Wordsworth to

> 'Have glimpses that would make me less forlorn
> Have sight of Proteus rising from the sea
> Or hear old Triton blow his wreathèd horn.'

ENGLISH POTTERY

An Astbury-Whieldon-type teapot and cover decorated with sportsmen and dogs, *circa* 1750-60, height 4¾in
London £1,050($1,890).
22.VI.76

A Lambeth 'Playing Cards' plate, *circa* 1750, diameter 8¾in
London £850($1,530). 22.VI.76

A London delft plate, *circa* 1740, diameter 9in
London £480($864). 17.II.76
From the collection of Mrs B. Barrington

One of a pair of Prattware teapots, *circa* 1785-90, height 8½in
London £400($800). 30.IX.75
From the collection of the late Constance, Viscountess Mackintosh

ENGLISH PORCELAIN

A pair of Bow monkey sweetmeat figures, the female with incised *T* mark, *circa* 1755-60, height 6in
London £1,450($2,900).
16.XII.75
From the collection of G. M. Cavendish

Far left
One of a pair of Champion's Bristol figures of a shepherd and shepherdess, *circa* 1775, height 7in
London £900($1,800). 30.IX.75

Left
One of a pair of Bristol allegorical figures of Autumn and Winter, modelled by Pierre Stephan, *circa* 1773-74, height 10¾in
London £940($1,692). 25.V.76

ENGLISH PORCELAIN

A blue and white bowl and cover after a Chinese original, probably Lund's Bristol, *circa* 1750, diameter 4½in
London £1,300($2,340). 27.IV.76

An early Worcester cream jug, *circa* 1755, height 4in
London £660($1,188). 25.V.76
From the collection of the late J. W. Goldsmith

A Worcester mug, *circa* 1755, height 3¼in
London £1,300($2,340). 30.III.76
From the collection of Anthony Tuke

Left
A Chelsea figure of a drunken peasant modelled by Joseph Willems, red anchor period, height 5in, $2,600(£1,300)

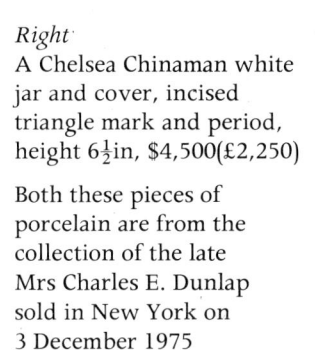

Right
A Chelsea Chinaman white jar and cover, incised triangle mark and period, height 6½in, $4,500(£2,250)

Both these pieces of porcelain are from the collection of the late Mrs Charles E. Dunlap sold in New York on 3 December 1975

A Chelsea group of 'The Music Lesson', gold anchor mark and period, height 15½in
New York $11,000(£5,500). 3.XII.75
From the collection of the late Mrs Charles E. Dunlap

Another version of this group is in the Schreiber Collection at the Victoria and Albert Museum. The model is traditionally attributed to L. F. Roubiliac after a painting by François Boucher entitled *L'Agréable Leçon*

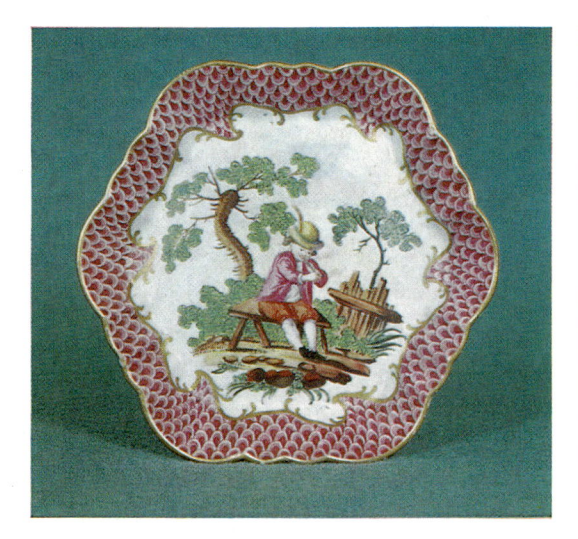

Top left A Worcester pink-scale teapot stand, probably painted in the atelier of James Giles with a scene after Teniers, 1770-75, diameter 6in, £4,600($8,280)
Top right An early Worcester wine funnel, 1752-53, height 5¼in, £4,400($7,920)
Centre right A Worcester teabowl, coffee cup and saucer after a Chinese original, the coffee cup with crescent mark in purple, 1770-75, £700($1,260)
Bottom right A Worcester yellow-bordered bowl, probably painted in London, crossed swords and 9 marks in underglaze-blue, 1770-75, diameter 6¾in, £1,400($2,520)
From the collection of Anthony Tuke sold in London on 30 March 1976

Bottom left One of a pair of Worcester pink-scale vases, *circa* 1770-75, height 7½in, $19,000(£9,500)
From the collection of the late Mrs Charles E. Dunlap sold in New York on 3 December 1975

Right
An Angarano plate, late seventeenth century, diameter 15¾in
Florence L1,900,000(£1,266:$2,279). 8.IV.76

Below
One of a pair of Dutch Delft wild boars, eighteenth century
Amsterdam Fl27,000(£5,000:$10,000). 16.IX.75

Below left
An Urbino Gubbio-lustred plate painted by Francesco Xanto Avelli with an episode from Virgil's *Aeneid*, showing Metabus passing his daughter across the River Amasenus tied to a spear to preserve her from the Volscians, 1534, diameter 10¼in
London £8,800($15,840). 16.III.76

Below right
A Hispano-Moresque wet drug jar, late fifteenth century, height 8¾in
London £1,386($2,772). 21.X.75

A Florentine drug jar decorated in Valencian style with a coat-of-arms azure, a cross *botonnée* or, on two sides, late fifteenth century, height 10in
London £12,500($22,500). 16.III.76
Formerly in the Emile Dreyfus and Fischer collections

A Castelli plate painted with a scene depicting a lion-hunt derived from an engraving by Antonio Tempesta, *circa* 1665, diameter 8¾in
Florence L3,400,000(£2,266:$4,078). 8.IV.76

One of a pair of Dutch Delft plaques, early eighteenth century, diameter 10in
London £3,400($6,120). 11.V.76

An Angarano plate, late seventeenth century, diameter 15¼in
Florence L4,000,000(£2,666:$4,798). 8.IV.76

A pewter-mounted Nuremberg hausmaler-decorated jug painted by Abraham Helmhack and signed with his monogram *AH*, *circa* 1690, height 7⅞in
New York $12,000(£6,666). 12.V.76

CONTINENTAL PORCELAIN

A Meissen *Commedia dell'Arte* gold-mounted double snuffbox, possibly painted by Johann Martin Heinrici, circa 1750, width 3½in
New York $22,000(£11,000). 3.XII.75
From the collection of the late Mrs Charles E. Dunlap

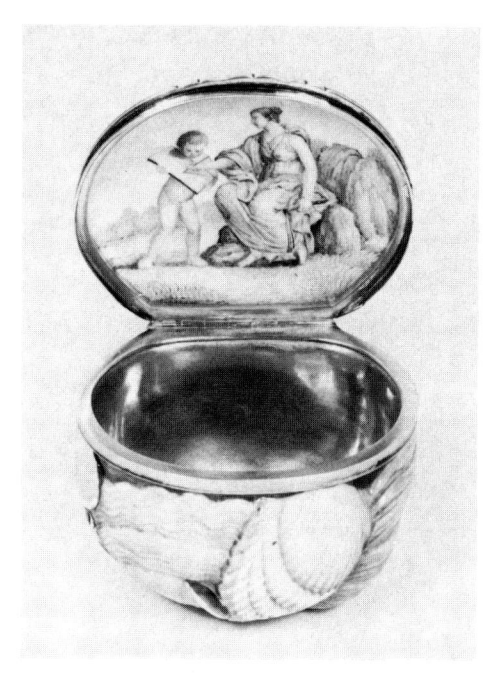

A Capodimonte conchological snuff box, the lid and base modelled by G. Gricci, the inside of the lid probably painted by Giuseppe della Torre, *circa* 1750, width 3in
London £4,000($7,200). 13.VII.76

Meissen yellow-ground cream jug, crossed swords in underglaze-blue, *circa* 1735, height 2¼in
London £1,980($3,960). 21.X.75
From the collection of Mrs Stella Pitt-Rivers

A Capodimonte cup and saucer, fleur-de-lys mark in blue, *circa* 1750
London £3,600($6,480). 16.III.76
From the collection of R. Spencer C. Copeland

CONTINENTAL PORCELAIN

A Capodimonte figure modelled by Giuseppe Gricci, impressed fleur-de-lys mark with the numerals 43, *circa* 1745, height 6¼in
London £16,000($28,800). 13.VII.76

A pair of Mennecy chinoiserie figures, *circa* 1735-40, height 6½in
London £15,000($27,000). 13.VII.76

Other chinoiserie figures by the same modeller are to be found in the Musée des Arts Décoratifs, Paris, and in the Linsky Collection

A Capodimonte *Commedia dell'Arte* group modelled by Giuseppe Gricci with Harlequin seated on two sheep-milk cheeses (*pecorini*), playing the Neapolitan card game of *scopa* with Pulcinella, watched by Pantaloon, traces of fleur-de-lys marks in blue, *circa* 1750, height 6in
London £32,000($57,600). 13.VII.76

One of the only two examples recorded of what is generally agreed to be one of the masterpieces of Italian porcelain, 'the apex of perfection' as Stazzi has remarked. The other example is in the Blöhm Collection on loan to the Hamburg Museum and is very similar in colouring. This model should be compared to Gricci's other group of three Italian Comedy figures, all standing, of which a white example is in the Theatrical Museum at La Scala, Milan

Left
One of a pair of Mennecy rearing horses, one with incised DV mark, *circa* 1750, height 4⅞in
New York $6,000(£3,000). 3.XII.75
From the collection of the late Mrs Charles E. Dunlap

Right
A Meissen figure of a dancing peasant by J. J. Kaendler, *circa* 1740, height 6¾in
London £1,600($3,200). 16.XII.75
From the collection of Humphrey W. Cook

A pair of Nymphenburg *Commedia dell'Arte* figures modelled by Franz Anton Bustelli, impressed shield marks, *circa* 1760, height 7⅞in
New York $32,500(£16,250). 3.XII.75
From the collection of the late Mrs Charles E. Dunlap

CONTINENTAL PORCELAIN 399

A pair of early Höchst figures of dancers modelled by Johann Friedrich Lück, wheel marks in red, *circa* 1758, height 6¾in
New York $7,500(£3,750). 3.XII.75
From the collection of the late Mrs Charles E. Dunlap

A Meissen pagoda figure probably intended as a pastille burner, 1730-40, height 4¼in
London £1,200($2,400). 21.X.75

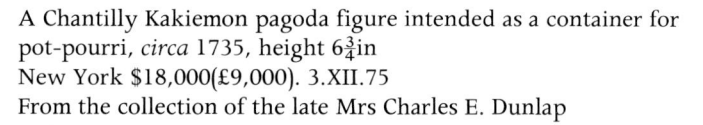

A Chantilly Kakiemon pagoda figure intended as a container for pot-pourri, *circa* 1735, height 6¾in
New York $18,000(£9,000). 3.XII.75
From the collection of the late Mrs Charles E. Dunlap

A Ludwigsburg figure of a cockatoo modelled by Jean-Jacob Louis, crowned interlaced C's mark in underglaze-blue, incised numeral 59, an L within an incised cartouche, and 3M within a cartouche, *circa* 1762, height 11¾in.
New York $26,000(£13,000). 3.XII.75

An early Meissen chinoiserie arbour figure modelled by Georg Fritzsche, early crossed swords mark in underglaze-blue, *circa* 1728, height 9¾in.
New York $27,500(£13,750). 3.XII.75

The porcelain on these pages is from the collection of the late Mrs Charles E. Dunlap

A pair of Meissen figures of bitterns, modelled by J. Kaendler, crossed swords mark in underglaze-blue, *circa* 1753, height 14½in
New York $50,000(£25,000). 3.XII.75

From left to right
A Mintons *vase à elephants* painted by A. Boullemier, signed, impressed Mintons and indistinct date code, *circa* 1900, height 11¾in
London £480($960). 18.XII.75

A Mintons vase *vaisseau à mât*, printed crowned globe, impressed Mintons and date code for 1925, height 17½in
London £1,300($2,600). 18.XII.75

A Mintons *vase à elephants*, printed crowned globe, impressed Mintons, *circa* 1900, height 11¾in
London £400($800). 18.XII.75

One of a pair of Minton blue-ground pâte-sur-pâte vases decorated by Marc Louis Solon, signed *L Solon* or with monogram, impressed Minton, possible date code for 1872, height 15¾in
London £3,300($6,600). 18.XII.75

A Royal Worcester mermaid and nautilus vase designed by James Hadley, printed and impressed crowned circle marks, impressed 592, date code for 1877, height 15in
London £450($810). 15.VII.76

NINETEENTH- AND TWENTIETH-CENTURY CERAMICS 403

Left A Soviet Russian figure of a sailor, painted hammer and sickle, *43/3* and dated 1922, height 7¼in
London £120($216). 5.II.76

Right An Ernst Barlach, Schwarzburger figure of a walking nun, impressed running fox, *U 10*, 1909–13, height 10in
London £420($756). 5.II.76

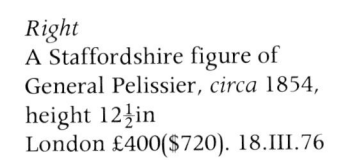

Right
A Staffordshire figure of General Pelissier, *circa* 1854, height 12½in
London £400($720). 18.III.76

Left
A Royal Worcester figure of a soldier from the Royal Worcestershire regiment, printed crowned circle, shape number 2591, Rd.No.645890, date code for 1915, height 6in
London £120($216). 29.I.76

Right
A stoneware spirit flask modelled as Daniel O'Connell, impressed *Denby and Condor Park, Bournes Potteries Derbyshire*, circa 1835, height 8in
London £120($216). 18.III.76

ORIENTAL CERAMICS AND ENGLISH STUDIO POTTERY

From left to right
A William Staite-Murray stoneware baluster vase, *circa* 1934, height 15¼in £380($684)
A Michael Cardew slipware bowl, impressed *MC and WP* for Winchcombe Pottery, label reading *3382 Cardew Bowl 1½Gns, circa* 1930, diameter 13¾in £320($576)
A William Staite-Murray stoneware bowl, *circa* 1930, height 5¾in £210($378)
A Charles Vyse *Tz'u Chou* stoneware vase, incised *CV* and dated 1929, height 12in £140($252)
A Michael Cardew slipware bowl, impressed *MC and WP, circa* 1930, diameter 10½in £170($306)
Firecircle. A William Staite-Murray stoneware vase, *circa* 1935, height 16¾in £260($468)

From left to right
A Ruskin high-fired jar and cover, impressed *Ruskin, circa* 1905, height 8¼in £540($972)
A Royal Doulton *Chang* vase, printed lion and crown mark and Flambe, date code for 1929, height 7¼in £250($450)
A William de Morgan *Isnik* vase painted by *Miss Babb*, impressed *De Morgan Merton Abbey, JB* monogram, 1882-88, height 7½in £600($1,080)
A William de Morgan lustre *jardinière* by Fred Passenger, signed with initials *FP, circa* 1900, height 7¾in £410($738)

This pottery was sold in London on 1 April 1976

Oriental ceramics and English studio pottery

Ian Bennett

'Sometime in early 1919, I was living with Soetsu Yanagi (the founder of the Japanese folkcraft movement) at Abiko, a village some twenty-five miles north-east of Tokyo. . . . One day a letter arrived in rather clear and bold handwriting, which impressed me by its look and still more by its content; it also impressed Yanagi. It told of a young man, about twenty-four, who as a lad had intended to become an artist. But he had changed his mind and decided to take up pottery as his profession. . . . He wrote asking whether he could come up and meet me at Abiko. . . . He came some days later, and the first moment I saw him, I felt that here was someone I would like.'

Thus Bernard Leach, in his recently published monograph on his Japanese friend, has described his first meeting with Shoji Hamada, a meeting which, in time, was to have a profound effect upon ceramics both in Japan and the Western world. The Leach-Hamada influence created a distinct aesthetic approach to pottery, and although the major impact was upon individual studio potters, art potteries and even some of the major industrial factories, particularly those in Scandinavia, reacted to their work.

On 24 August 1920, Leach and Hamada arrived at St Ives, the latter remaining until 1923. They founded a pottery which still exists today. Over the next ten years, Leach was to be host to a number of distinguished Japanese potters – Hamada himself, his sons Shinsaku and Atsuya, Kenkichi Tomimoto, Tsuneyoshi Matsubayashi and Kanjiro Kawai – and to teach a group of exceptional students: Michael Cardew, Norah Braden and Katherine Pleydell-Bouverie. In the decade 1920 to 1930, the Leach pottery changed the concept of the potter's role in society, and if it has done little of great interest since (although an outstanding recent visitor was Ichigawa Ichino, an hereditary member of the Tamba family of potters), its work during that period ensures it a permanent and important place in ceramic history.

The intellectual content of Leach and Hamada's pottery was dominated by the idea of *Mingei*, a Japanese word coined by Yanagi and meaning 'art of the people'. The essence of this philosophy is that the artist should subvert his own ego to the dictates of tradition and function and should also submit himself to the Zen discipline of repetition. The object should exist in itself without reference to external factors such as age, the name of the maker, fashion and so on. In other words, it should exist in a limbo of anonymous purity, the main inspiration for this being the anonymity of Sung and T'ang ceramics, those of the Koryŏ dynasty of Korea (which Leach values above all other Oriental ceramics), and the stoneware and earthenware of Japan and medieval England. There was, in addition, the strong belief in the doctrines of 'Fitness for Purpose' which made Leach and the *Mingei* movement as a whole natural successors to the nineteenth-century English ideas propounded by Henry Cole, William Morris and many other leading designers. Leach was nine years old when Morris died, and later a pupil of Sir Frank Brangwyn, one of the leading members of the Arts and Crafts movement and a collaborator with Morris in the 1880s. Thus Leach, both historically and practically, was the last link with a great English art movement. However, his influence was not total in the 1920s and 1930s, nor was the inspiration of early Chinese ceramics and Japanese folk pottery new in Europe. Several French potters in the 1880s were producing work which attempted to synthesise Japanese forms and glazes with traditional European methods. The most famous was Jean Carriès, who settled in the village of St Amand-en-Puisaye in the Nièvre, a centre for the manufacture of traditional peasant earthenware. In the late 1890s, and especially after a visit to the Exposition Universelle in Paris in 1900, the English potter Edwin Bruce Martin began producing gourd vases with ribbing, incising and abstract glaze effects.

In the early twentieth century, before the St Ives pottery had opened, certain English potters, notably Reginald Wells and George Cox of the Mortlake Pottery, were producing rough-hewn pots with splashed monochrome glazes. Of Leach's own pupils, Michael Cardew has always shown more interest in the techniques of English slip-decoration, having studied under W. Fishley Holland at Fremington, one of the last English country potteries. In the 1920s, the principal alternative to Leach's ideas was to be found in the work of William Staite-Murray. Unlike Leach he was concerned with making his pottery react to the artistic ideas of his time. During the First World War, he had worked with the Vorticist painter, Cuthbert Hamilton, at the Yeoman Pottery, where simple dishes with abstract or semi-abstract painted decoration were produced. Subsequently Staite-Murray became a close friend of many of the leading painters, including Christopher Wood and Ben Nicholson, and exhibited his pottery at the Lefevre, then as now one of the leading modern art galleries in London. According to Maurice Collis, in the preface to the potter's last exhibition at the Leicester Gallery in 1958, he believed that a pot 'was an abstract work of art'. Unquestionably, he was impressed, and to a certain extent influenced by the St Ives potters, especially Hamada, but his attitude towards ceramics remained uncompromised. For him, a pot was the expression of an individual artistic temperament. As head of the ceramics department at the Royal College of Art from 1925, he taught a distinguished group of potters, including T. S. Haile, Henry Hammond and Reginald Marlow, of whom only Henry Hammond is working today.

Quite different from the work of either Leach or Staite-Murray is the pottery of Charles and Nell Vyse. Although they were deeply influenced by early Chinese wares, their approach may more properly be compared to the English art potters of the late nineteenth/early twentieth centuries, such as William de Morgan, Bernard Moore, Charles Noke and William Howson Taylor. They were attempting to understand, refine and ultimately perfect glaze techniques derived from Oriental sources; in the Vyses' case with wood-ash glaze. The Vyses were not philosophers like Leach, or artists like Staite-Murray, although their best work is worthy of considerable admiration.

ORIENTAL CERAMICS AND ENGLISH STUDIO POTTERY 407

Right
A Bernard Leach stoneware vase, impressed *BL* monogram and St Ives mark, *circa* 1930, height 8in
London £320($576). 1.IV.76

Below
A Kawai stoneware *chawan* with signed *kiri*-wood box, height 3¾in
London £120($216). 18.II.76

Left
A Shoji Hamada stoneware vase, height 8¼in
London £420. 17.X.73

Below
An early Shoji Hamada stoneware vase, impressed mark *Sho*, St Ives pottery stamp, *Bernard Leach Pottery 1923*, height 5in
London £500($900). 18.II.76

A large Vienna porcelain and gilt-metal-mounted clockcase, painted with scenes of children and putti, one panel signed *Reme*, shield in underglaze blue, *circa* 1860, height 1ft 7in
London £1,700($3,060). 15.IV.76

Furniture, Decorations and Textiles

A Louis XV giltwood fire-screen with tapestry panels, 3ft 3in by 4ft 7in
Monte Carlo Fr60,000 (£7,143:$12,857). 23.VI.76

410 FURNITURE, DECORATIONS AND TEXTILES

Left
George Washington's mahogany campaign stool, *circa* 1775, with Mount Vernon label, 1ft 5in by 1ft 9¾in
New York $12,500(£6,250). 8.XI.75

Below
A pair of beaded and embroidered mauve silk wedding slippers worn by Martha Washington, *circa* 1758, with Mount Vernon label and the number 53, length 9in
New York $4,100(£2,050). 8.XI.75

These two items come from the collection of Mrs Walter Gibson Peter, Jnr. They were part of an important group which belonged to George and Martha Washington and were passed down in Mrs Washington's family

A Pilgrim-century carved oak Hadley chest, Hadley, Massachusetts, *circa* 1685, attributed to John Allis, 3ft 5in by 4ft
New York
$24,000(£13,333). 31.I.76

FURNITURE, DECORATIONS AND TEXTILES 411

A copper Columbia weathervane, probably by Cushing and White, Waltham, Massachusetts, *circa* 1865, 3ft 2in by 2ft 2in
New York $6,500(£3,611). 1.V.76

A Queen Anne maple sidechair, labelled *William Savery, Philadelphia, circa* 1750
New York $9,500(£5,277). 31.I.76

A Chippendale carved mahogany block-front chest of drawers, Massachusetts, 1760-80, 2ft 8½in by 3ft 2¾in
New York $27,000(£15,000). 1.V.76
From the collection of Marietta Peabody Tree

412 FURNITURE, DECORATIONS AND TEXTILES

The Fitzsimons family Chippendale carved mahogany chest-on-chest, attributed to Thomas Affleck, Philadelphia, 1765-75, 8ft 1½in by 3ft 11½in
New York $31,000(£17,222).
1.V.76

A late Ming hardstone and padoukwood *huang-hua-li-kuei*, inlaid with mother-of-pearl, stained ivory, jade and other hardstone with brass hinges and escutcheons, 7ft 10in by 5ft 2in London £6,600($11,880). 30.IV.76

FURNITURE, DECORATIONS AND TEXTILES

1. One of a set of six mid eighteenth-century Portuguese rosewood side chairs $4,700(£2,611). 27.III.76. **2.** One of a pair of Chinese horseshoe-back *huang-hua-li* armchairs, late Ming $10,000(£5,555). 15.V.76. **3.** One of ten fine George II mahogany dining chairs $17,000(£8,500). 20.IX.75. **4.** One of a set of twenty George III mahogany dining chairs £6,500($11,700). 23.I.76. **5.** One of a pair of George III mahogany wheel-back armchairs $2,900(£1,611). 7.II.76. **6.** One of a pair of early George III mahogany library armchairs £9,500($17,100). 26.III.76. **7.** One of a pair of Regency mahogany caned *bergères* $2,600(£1,444). 15.V.76. **8.** An early George III mahogany stool £1,400($2,520). 20.II.76. **9.** A small Queen Anne walnut settee £1,540($3,080). 26.IX.75.

FURNITURE, DECORATIONS AND TEXTILES 415

A small Queen Anne walnut bureau,
3ft by 2ft 2in
London £3,000($6,000). 26.IX.75

A George III mahogany *bonheur-du-jour*,
3ft 8in by 2ft 6in
London £2,400($4,320). 20.II.76

A mid eighteenth-century
Anglo-Indian ivory-inlaid
kneehole pedestal desk, 2ft 9in
by 3ft 5½in
London £2,400($4,800). 14.XI.75
From the collection of
Mr and Mrs Henry Cotton

416 FURNITURE, DECORATIONS AND TEXTILES

A George III mahogany Carlton House desk, 3ft 5in by 5ft 4in
New York $36,000(£18,000). 20.IX.75

Opposite page
A Queen Anne walnut bureau bookcase, 7ft 9in by 3ft 4in
New York $28,000(£14,000). 20.IX.75

An early eighteenth-century Italian walnut bureau cabinet inlaid with bone and pewter, 8ft 6in by 4ft 5in
London £9,800($19,600). 12.XII.75

A Dutch eighteenth-century walnut marquetry *armoire*, 8ft 1in by 6ft 10in
London £4,000($8,000). 31.X.75
From the collection of the Rt Hon Lord Swansea

420 FURNITURE, DECORATIONS AND TEXTILES

A Lenzburg faience stove by Johann Jacob Frey, with original metal radiators, *circa* 1785, 6ft 3in by 4ft 7in
Monte Carlo Fr80,000(£9,548:$17,186). 23.VI.76

A mid eighteenth-century Lombardy writing-cabinet inlaid with burr-walnut and palisanderwood, 4ft by 4ft 6in
Florence L15,000,000(£10,000:$20,000). 18.XII.75

FURNITURE, DECORATIONS AND TEXTILES

An eighteenth-century Flemish walnut commode, 2ft 11in by 4ft 6in
London £2,100($4,200). 5.XII.75

A late seventeenth-century Italian side table with moulded top, painted to simulate *griotte* marble, 2ft 9in by 4ft 7in
London £2,400($4,800). 12.XII.75

An eighteenth-century Danish burr-walnut commode with gilt mouldings, 2ft 7in by 2ft 10in
London £2,475($4,950). 19.IX.75

A mid eighteenth-century Chinese export table, painted and gilded and mounted with Canton enamel plaques, 2ft 7in by 3ft
New York $16,000(£8,000). 20.IX.75

A Brussels Renaissance tapestry of Aeneas and the Sibyl descending into the Underworld as told in Virgil's *Aeneid, circa* 1525, 14ft 8in by 19ft 9in
London £9,000($18,000). 12.XII.75
Formerly in the collection of Princess Maria Christina of Bourbon, daughter of Francis I, King of the Two Sicilies

FURNITURE, DECORATIONS AND TEXTILES 425

A French or Flemish mille-fleurs tapestry, late fifteenth/early sixteenth century, 7ft 2in by 8ft 3in
New York $80,000(£44,444). 18.VI.76
From the collection of Mme M. Blondin-Walter

A pair of late Louis XIV 'Marine' barometers in ormolu and tortoiseshell, attributed to André-Charles Boulle, height 5ft
London £46,000($82,800). 30.IV.76

FURNITURE, DECORATIONS AND TEXTILES 427

A mid eighteenth-century *surtout de table* in gilt-bronze, French or Italian, height 1ft 6in
Monte Carlo Fr90,000 (£10,714:$19,285). 24.VI.76

A coffer inlaid with ebony, mother-of-pearl, copper and pewter, attributed to André-Charles Boulle, *circa* 1700, 10in by 1ft 2in
Monte Carlo Fr95,000 (£11,310:$20,357). 23.VI.76

A Régence gilt-wood table with agate top, *circa* 1720, 2ft 3in by 2ft 4in
Monte Carlo Fr110,000(£13,095:$23,571). 23.VI.76

A Louis XV *coffre de voyage* and stand in satinwood veneer and marquetry with ormolu decorations, signed with the letters *BVRB*, 3ft 6in by 3ft 3in
Monte Carlo Fr200,000(£23,809:$42,856). 23.VI.76

A Louis XV gilt-bronze console table with marble top, *circa* 1766, 1ft 5in by 4ft 6in Monte Carlo Fr200,000(£23,809:$42,856). 24.VI.76

A Louis XVI ormolu-mounted mahogany, amboyna and thuyawood cabinet with marble top, attributed to Adam Weisweiler, 3ft 1in by 5ft 3½in New York $78,000(£39,000). 1.XI.75 From the collection of the late Mrs Randolph Hearst Snr

A Louis XVI ormolu-mounted marquetry *secrétaire à abattant*, attributed to Pierre-Antoine Foullet,
4ft 10½in by 3ft 5in
New York $110,000(£55,000). 1.XI.75

An almost identical piece, signed *foulet*, is in the Wallace Collection

A Louis XVI *secrétaire* stamped *A. Weisweiler*, decorated with Sèvres porcelain plaques and ormolu, the rectangular plaques carrying the mark of Chauveaux-ainé
Monte Carlo Fr1,500,000(£178,574:$321,433). 24.VI.76

This piece was in the boudoir of the Grand Duchess Maria Feodorovna, wife of the future Tsar Paul I, at the palace of Pavlovsk in St Petersburg. She probably bought it from the dealer, Daguerre, while she and her husband were visiting Paris incognito in 1784

A French amboyna and purple-heart commode with painted door, signed in the bronze *Henry Dasson* and dated 1878
London £5,500($11,000). 26.XI.75

A Louis XV/XVI style ormolu-mounted marquetry *bureau à cylindre* with jasperware plaques, signed *F. Linke*, late nineteenth century, 4ft 11in by 6ft 2in
New York $41,000(£22,777). 21.II.76

F. Linke was a Parisian cabinet-maker during the last quarter of the nineteenth century. This piece is a copy of the desk begun by Oeben and completed and delivered to Louis XV by Riesener in 1769

An ivory-inlaid Gothic Revival high-backed settee with needlework panels of Byzantine figures and silk-covered cushions, English or Italian, *circa* 1850, 6ft 8½in by 5ft 11in
London £2,300($4,600). 12.XI.75

FURNITURE, DECORATIONS AND TEXTILES 437

An ebonised-wood oval tea table by Charles Rennie Mackintosh, the underside bearing two exhibition labels for the Scottish Arts Council Mackintosh Centenary Exhibition 1968, cat. no. 246, 2ft by 3ft
London £1,000($2,000). 27.XI.75

This table was designed by Mackintosh for Hill House, Helensburgh

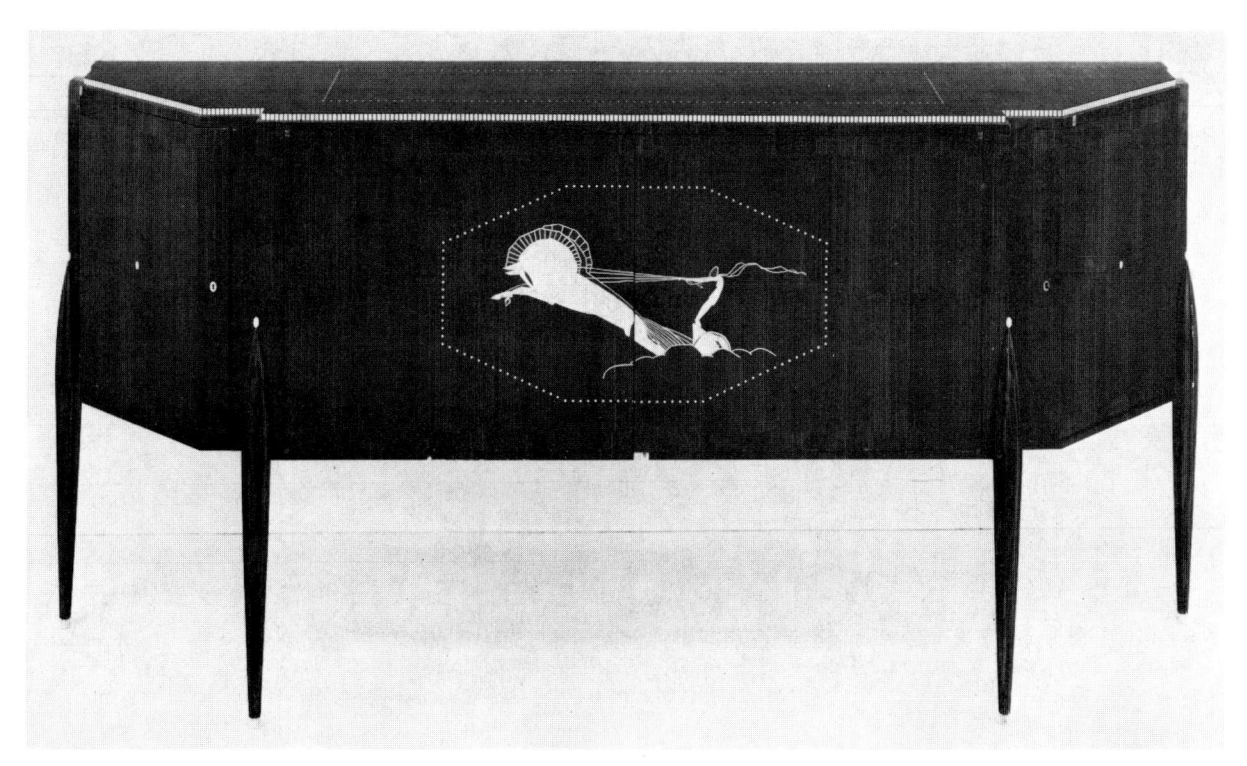

A Ruhlmann ivory-inlaid ebony carving table, *circa* 1925, 3ft 7¾in by 7ft 4in
Los Angeles $7,000(£3,888). 9.VI.76

FORD MADOX BROWN
The marriage of St Editha to Sigtrig, King of Northumbria
Stained glass panel, circa 1873 610mm by 510mm
London £850($1,530). 5.V.76

SIR EDWARD COLEY BURNE-JONES, Bt, ARA
St Peter sinking in the Sea of Tiberias
Stained glass panel, 1857, 1,085mm by 375mm
London £2,100($3,780). 23.III.76
From the collection of Whitefriars Glass Ltd

PHILIP WEBB
The birds and the fishes
Design for a roundel in brown and black ink and coloured wash, inscribed with colour directions, diameter 650mm
London £320($576). 23.III.76
From the collection of Whitefriars Glass Ltd, formerly known as James Powell and Sons

Victorian stained glass and decorative design

Martin Harrison

The casual visitor who stops in a church to admire a stained glass window is in all probability looking at a window which dates from after 1840, and indeed most likely from the period of Victoria's reign. The Anglo-Catholic movement, and the 'Gothic Revival' in architecture, resulted in a phenomenal demand for new stained glass; concerned architects wanted to modulate, along medieval lines, the light entering their churches, and the stained glass window all but replaced the sculptured monument as the most acceptable way of commemorating a loved one.

Such were the implications of this rise in demand that, while in 1836 London could boast fewer than a score of stained glass artists, by 1901 the 'Trades' section of the 'Post Office London Directory' carried advertisements for as many as 107 firms and artists in London alone, with many others not listed; there was considerable activity in the provinces too, and a realistic figure for the combined total of people engaged in stained glass production at the turn of the century would certainly be in excess of 2,000 in England. Several of the most prolific firms are recorded as having employed over one hundred artists and craftsmen at a given time; William Wailes of Newcastle did so at the height of his popularity around 1860, and at a later date so did the London-based firms Heaton, Butler & Bayne, and C. E. Kempe. Even a relatively unknown provincial business such as that run by William Holland at Warwick is reported to have employed more than eighty men in its heyday, 'all of whom went to work in top hats'!

The prodigious number of windows produced in the Victorian era has, perhaps not surprisingly, proved something of a deterrent to the would-be researcher. The majority of examples are unsigned, especially those from the 'High Victorian' period (*circa* 1850-70), when, often under the close supervision of the best architects of the day such as Street or Butterfield, a number of firms produced a consistently high standard of work, combining a respect for archaeological accuracy modified by a modern attitude to design which often showed the strong influence of the early Pre-Raphaelites. Unfortunately firms which had, as it were, grown up with the Gothic Revival, were usually played out as creative forces by the 1880s (exactly the point at which they began to sign their windows), and it follows that while their finest work languishes in obscurity, their reputation has to rest on the reactionary and feeble examples of their decline. On the other side of the coin though, for a growing band of enthusiasts this has meant a profound pleasure in rescuing from oblivion 'discoveries' such as Clayton & Bell's masterful *Last Judgement* at Hanley Castle Church, Worcestershire, their apse windows at Denstone Church, Staffs, and whole series by them in the large group of churches built by Sir Tatton Sykes in the East Riding of Yorkshire. In the same category are Heaton, Butler & Bayne's great windows at East Dereham Church, Norfolk, and All Saints, Clapham Park, those by Lavers & Barraud at Cookham Dene, Berks, and Higher Walton, Lancs, and by James Powell & Sons at Thursford, Norfolk, and Mere, Wilts. All of these examples date from the early 1860s.

James Powell & Sons is a firm of particular topical interest, having been the subject of a recent major auction at the showrooms of Sotheby's Belgravia. The first stage in the making of a stained glass window is for the artist to make a small watercolour design of the whole window, usually at a scale of one inch to one foot. If this design is approved by the architect or client the next step is to make full-sized cartoons for the whole window. After this the glass is chosen, cut, painted if necessary, fired in a kiln, and subsequently leaded up. At the recent sale, besides several highly important windows, there were numerous examples of the two early stages in the stained glass-making process: the scale design and full-sized cartoon. As the popularity of Victorian stained glass gathers momentum increasing numbers of cartoons and designs are coming to light: both the finely-wrought inch scale designs – on which the artist often appears to have lavished an amount of attention akin to a medieval illuminator – and the large, often strong and surprisingly well-drawn, cartoons are attractive propositions for the connoisseur and student.

James Powell & Sons and William Morris's firm share an important position in the history of the nineteenth-century revival of the stained glass art. While both had their early roots in the Gothic Revival, their chief significance lies in the fact that, largely due to Burne-Jones within Morris & Co and Henry Holiday within Powell's, a genuinely nineteenth-century tradition in stained glass was founded, classical rather than gothic in inspiration. Both of these artists were well represented at Sotheby's Belgravia, as was a most interesting protégé of theirs, Henry Ellis Wooldridge, another 'neo-Classicist' whose designs showed strong affinities with the work of Albert Moore. Particularly outstanding, and perhaps a surprise to some, were the early Henry Holiday designs, made in the 1860s when he was still under the stylistic spell of Rossetti; the *Wise and foolish virgins* series, dated 1864, were as good as anything Holiday ever did and the reader may like to see these designs translated into glass at Avington Church, Berks.

By providing an alternative in stained glass to the historicism of the Gothic Revival, Burne-Jones, Holiday, and their followers showed the way to the Arts and Crafts movement of the next generation: Christopher Whall, Selwyn Image, and Robert Anning Bell. These artists and their pupils were responsible for a fresh approach to stained glass, and the Arts and Crafts style held sway until the outbreak of World War One. In practice this still meant a strong reliance on the 'elder statesmen' such as Burne-Jones so far as *design* was concerned, but now it was demanded that the designer himself had a more intimate relationship with every stage of the production of a window – that he became a *craftsman* too. After 1918 England, which had led the world in stained glass for a hundred years, fell behind; as with architecture the muse had left for Europe. While most English work became genteel Gothicism, strong, direct and vital work was done by two Irish ladies, Wilhelmina Geddes and Evie Hone; it was not until 1955, and John Piper's windows for Oundle School Chapel, that the art was resurrected in England.

SIR EDWARD COLEY BURNE-JONES, Bt, ARA
The Ascension
Pencil design for a window in the south transept of Jesus College chapel, Cambridge, 527mm by 426mm
London £900($1,620). 23.III.76

Both these designs are from the collection of Whitefriars Glass Ltd, formerly known as James Powell and Sons

HENRY G. HOLIDAY
The wise and foolish virgins
One of three ink and coloured wash cartoons for stained glass, 990mm by 460mm
London £160($288). 23.III.76

An interesting postscript occurred whilst this article was in progress, and is again an example of how important items, which help to complete our picture of the progress in Victorian design, are constantly turning up. In 1873 Ford Madox Brown designed, and William Morris executed, a window of four lights for the south chancel clerestory of St Editha's Church, Tamworth, Staffs, depicting the Marriage of St Editha to Sitrig, King of Northumbria. The following year saw the re-formation of the Morris firm with Morris in sole charge and Burne-Jones as the only designer of figures for stained glass; this brought about the famous breach with Rossetti and Madox Brown, never to be healed in Rossetti's case, and only many years later by Brown. So serious was the dispute that naturally, had Madox Brown received a commission for a stained glass window to be made from one of his existing designs, he would not have taken it to Morris's firm to be executed. All the more intriguing then that such a panel has recently come to light in a recent auction of Arts and Crafts furniture and works of art at Sotheby's Belgravia. This so far unique example utilises the cartoons for the two

A Merton Abbey tapestry entitled *Flora*, designed by Sir Edward Coley Burne-Jones, with background by J. H. Dearle, *circa* 1900, 5ft 4¾in by 3ft 1¼in London £3,000($5,400). 5.V.76

central lights of the Tamworth window and, being set in a rectangular border, appears to have been adapted for secular use – for which it was clearly well suited. It appears to have been most sympathetically executed and it is fascinating to speculate just how much supervision Madox Brown may have had over the making of the panel – certainly it would seem far more than had Morris made the panel. The same sale included a Merton Abbey tapestry of *Flora*, designed by Burne-Jones and a large quantity of late nineteenth-century furniture which provides an instructive link with the Arts and Crafts stained glass designers mentioned earlier.

Clocks, Watches and Scientific Instruments

A boulle bracket clock by Thomas Tompion, *circa* 1700, height 10½in
New York $22,000(£11,000). 6.XII.75
From the collection of the late Mrs Charles E. Dunlap

From left to right
A walnut marquetry longcase clock signed *Stephen Rayner, London, circa* 1695, height 6ft 10in
London £2,000($3,600). 10.V.76

A burr-walnut month longcase clock by Daniel Quare, *circa* 1700, height 7ft 6in
New York $9,000(£4,500). 6.XII.75
From the collection of the late Mrs Charles E. Dunlap

An eighteenth-century Dutch walnut alarum longcase clock signed *Jan Henkels Amsteldam*, height 9ft 4in
London £2,400($4,800). 20.X.75

A George III mahogany longcase clock signed *Vulliamy London*, height 7ft 1in
London £2,000($3,600). 2.II.76

A walnut longcase clock, the $9\frac{1}{2}$-inch dial signed *Joseph Knibb Londini fecit, circa* 1690, height 6ft 5in
London £8,500($17,000). 20.X.75

1. A Louis XVI ormolu *grande sonnerie* alarum *pendule d'officier* signed *Musy Père & Fils Hgers de S. A. Sme*, 8in £1,500($2,700). 30.IV.76. 2. A French gilt-bronze and porcelain repeating carriage clock, inscribed *Lund, London, c.* 1870, 7¼in £850($1,700). 26.XI.75. 3. An enamel-mounted *grande sonnerie* carriage clock, the backplate numbered 2129, 7in £1,500($2,700). 2.II.76. From the collection of Colonel Maxwell. 4. An English quarter-striking carriage clock signed *James McCabe, Royal Exchange, London 3157*, 8½in £3,200($5,760). 21.VI.76. 5. A Louis XVI ormolu mantel clock Amsterdam Fl10,200(£2,082:$3,747). 26.III.76. 6. A skeletonised orrery clock, early nineteenth century, 15¼in £3,400($6,120). 22.III.76. 7. A George III tortoiseshell alarum bracket clock, 18½in £1,000($2,000). 20.X.75. 8. A French gilt-bronze mantel clock with the figure of Washington, by Dubuc, Paris, *c.* 1805, 20in $6,500(£3,611). 31.I.76. 9. A veneered ebony quarter-repeating bracket clock, the 7-inch dial signed *Thomas Tompion Londini fecit*, no. 203, 15in £10,000($20,000). 20.X.75. 10. An ebony bracket clock signed *Joseph Knibb Londini fecit*, 13½in £7,200($12,960). 10.V.76. 11. A silver-mounted quarter-repeating bracket clock, the 5½-inch dial signed *Geo: Graham London, c.* 1720, 14in £9,000($16,200). 10.V.76.

Left
A chiming skeleton clock signed *Jas. Condliff Liverpool*, dated 1860, height 25in
London £3,000($5,400). 2.II.76
From the collection of B. H. Fish

Right
A brass lantern clock signed *Jonathan Chambers Fecit*, circa 1690, height 17in
London £950($1,710). 10.V.76
From the collection of the late Mrs Eila Smith

Left
THOMAS TOMPION
NO. 85
A quarter-repeating month alarum timepiece, *circa* 1680, height 13in
New York $28,000(£14,000). 6.XII.75
From the collection of the late Mrs Charles E. Dunlap

Right
A small yew-wood bracket clock, signed *John Hallifax London*, circa 1740, height 11¾in
London £3,400($6,120). 2.II.76

An ormolu-mounted microscope by Alexis Magny, with original gold-stamped, fitted case with drawer containing accessories, *circa* 1750, height of microscope 49cm, case 62cm
Monte Carlo Fr350,000(£41,667:$75,000). 23.VI.76

The microscope is said to have been presented by Louis XV to the Marquise de Pompadour. Made by Alexis Magny about 1751-54, it is one of a group of related instruments of which five or six similar examples are known. Employed by the Duc de Chaulnes, Magny specialised in richly decorated ormolu-mounted microscopes, and listed among his clients Louis XV, the King of Poland, Réaumur and the Austrian Ambassador. The ormolu mounts were most probably provided by the bronze worker Caffieri

448 WATCHES

Left
A gold watch key, the centre with four-draw spy glass, *circa* 1810, length overall 45mm
London £400($720).
10.V.76

Above left
CHARLES FRODSHAM NO. 06989
A gold hunting cased keyless lever minute repeating clockwatch with perpetual calendar and split seconds, hallmarked 1884, diameter 69mm
London £12,000($21,600). 10.V.76

Far left
CHARLES FRODSHAM
NO. 010295
A gold cased fusee keyless lever tourbillon signed *Chas. Frodsham London*, 1824, diameter 59mm
London £8,000($14,400).
22.III.76

Left
An eighteenth-century gold and enamel outer case, signed indistinctly *Moser*, diameter 47mm
London £1,000($1,800).
22.III.76

Far left
A gold pair cased quarter striking clockwatch by Brockbanks, no. 2879, 1811, diameter 64mm
London £1,400($2,520). 22.III.76

Left
A gold cased pocket chronometer by Parkinson and Frodsham, no. 1801, 1827, diameter 58mm
London £1,100($1,980).
22.III.76

WATCHES 449

A Swiss gold and enamel quarter repeating erotic automaton watch, *circa* 1820, diameter 58mm
New York $19,000(£10,555). 11.II.76

A Swiss gold and enamel musical automaton clockwatch, *circa* 1820, diameter 83mm
New York $17,000(£8,500). 12.XI.75

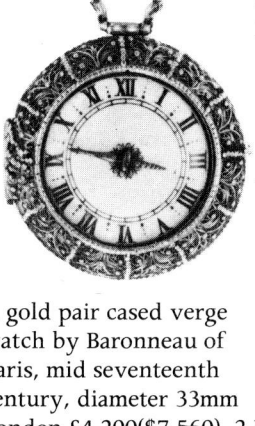

A gold pair cased verge watch by Baronneau of Paris, mid seventeenth century, diameter 33mm
London £4,200($7,560). 2.II.76

A gold verge watch, no. 396 by Augustin Bourdillon of Stockholm, mid eighteenth century, diameter 49mm
London £1,500($3,000). 1.XII.75

A Swiss gold and enamel duplex watch by Vaucher of Fleurier, *circa* 1820, diameter 54mm
New York $9,000(£4,500). 12.XI.75

Left
A gilt-metal striking table clock with alarum signed *Rellahes London*, mid eighteenth century, 90mm
London £1,320($2,376). 2.II.76

450 SCIENTIFIC INSTRUMENTS

A small eight-day marine chronometer, by Barrauds and numbered $\frac{2}{607}$, diameter 100mm
London £1,600($2,880). 10.V.76

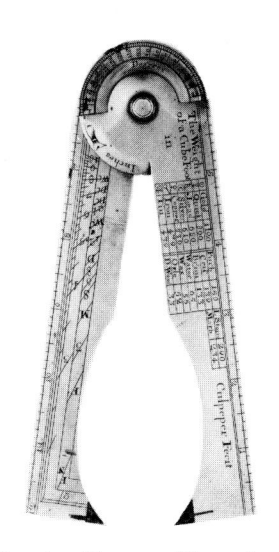

A pair of brass callipers by Culpeper, early eighteenth century, length 177mm
London £700($1,260). 29.VII.76

A Persian brass astrolabe, late seventeenth century, signed: *Made by Qâsim 'Alî Qâ'Inî*, diameter 152mm
Los Angeles $6,500(£3,611). 10.VI.76

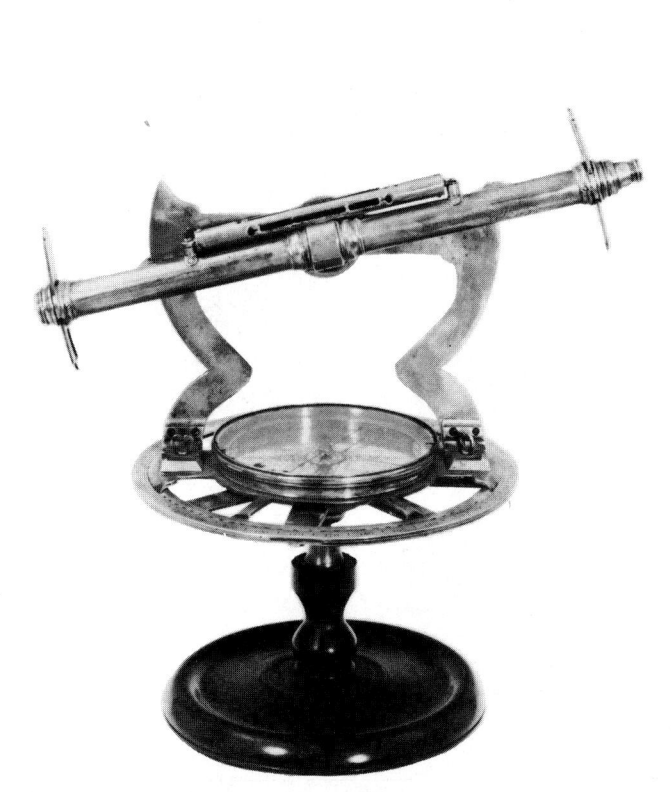

A brass theodolite by Thomas Heath of London, mid eighteenth-century, length of tube 390mm
London £900($1,620). 10.V.76

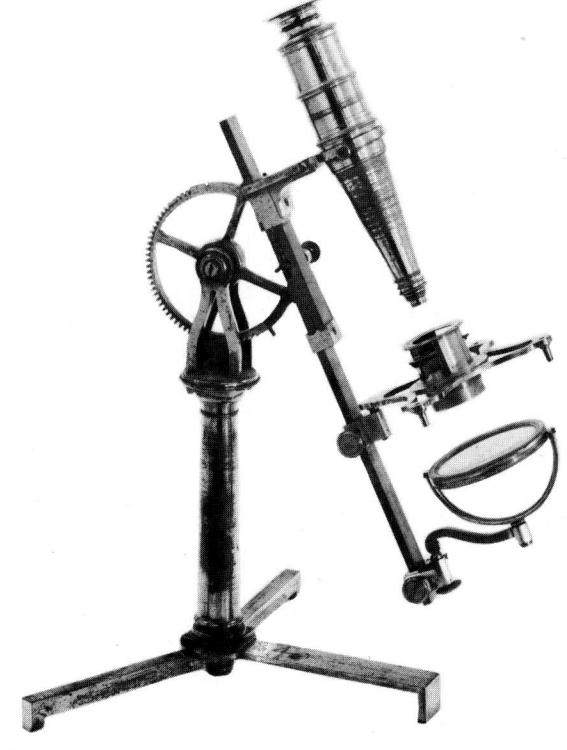

A brass variable microscope by George Adams, of no. 60 Fleet Street, London, 1770, average height 420mm
London £1,700($3,400). 20.X.75

Musical Instruments

A composite violin labelled *Antonius Stradivarius Cremonenfis faciebat Anno 1713*, length of back 14in
London £7,800($14,040). 12.II.76

Whilst the table of this violin is by Antonio Stradivari, the back and ribs are probably the work of Nicholas Lupot of Paris and the head is the work of Peter Guarneri of Mantua. The certificates which accompanied this instrument were lost during the Second World War. It is traditionally believed to have been given by a Polish nobleman to the celebrated violinist Bronislav Hubermann during the early part of his career

452   MUSICAL INSTRUMENTS

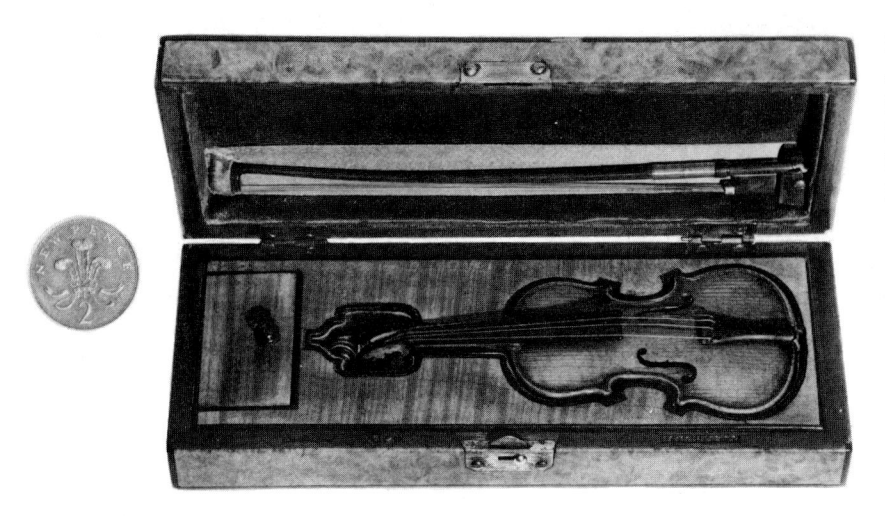

Left
A miniature violin by John Shaw, labelled *J. Shaw, Manchester 1905*, length of back 2$\frac{11}{16}$in
London £1,600($2,880). 6.V.76

A Norwegian Hardanger fiddle by Ellef J. Stenkjondalen, labelled *Fabrikeret af Ellef J. Stenkjondalen, 1864*, length of back 14$\frac{1}{8}$in
London £1,400($2,800). 27.XI.75

A Swiss sackbut engraved on the garland *Jacob Steimer in Zoffingen macht* and with the arms of Bern, early eighteenth century, length of tube without mouthpiece 105$\frac{1}{2}$in
London £2,800($5,040). 6.V.76

MUSICAL INSTRUMENTS 453

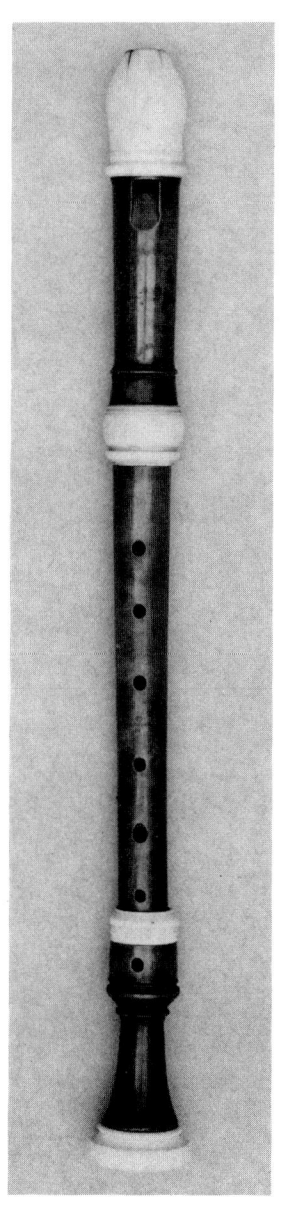

A treble (alto) recorder by Joseph Bradbury, stamped *Jo. Bradbury*, late seventeenth century, length 20½in
London £2,900($5,220). 12.II.76

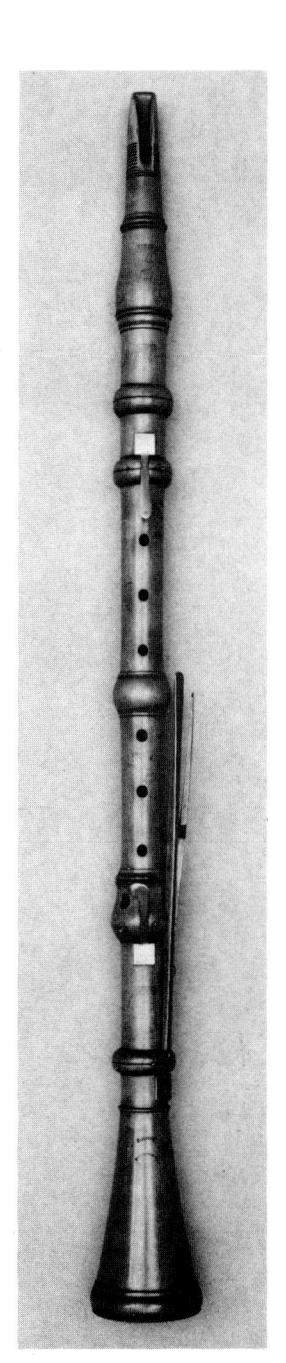

A five-keyed boxwood clarinet by Henry Kusder, stamped *Kusder, London*, and *Simpson, Royal Exchange*, the brass keys by John Hale, stamped *I.H.*, circa 1865, length 26¼in
London £2,600($4,680). 6.V.76

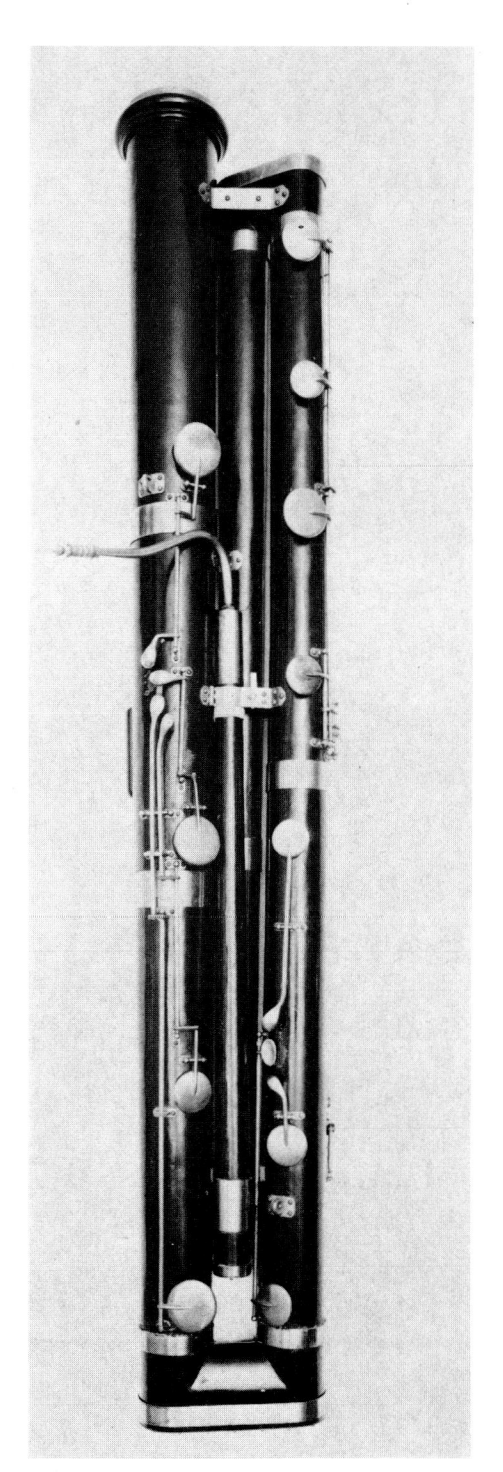

A contrabassophon, keywork probably by Alfred Morton, mid nineteenth century, length 50in
London £850($1,700). 27.XI.75
The contrabassophon was originally devised by Heinrich J. Hasenier of Coblenz. It was adopted in England by Dr W. H. Stone, one of the only players of this instrument in the country before 1900

A violoncello by Antonius and Hieronymus Amati, labelled *Antonio & Hieronymus Fr. Amati Cremonen Andreae fil F. 1614*, length of back 30¼in London £15,000($30,000). 27.XI.75

The Jansen, a violoncello by Antonio Stradivari, labelled *Antonius Stradivarius Cremonenfis Faciebat Anno 1721*, length of back 29½in London £50,000($100,000). 27.XI.75

Art Nouveau and Art Deco

A silver-mounted green glass decanter by the Guild of Handicraft Ltd under the direction of Charles Robert Ashbee, maker's mark of the Guild of Handicraft Ltd, London 1901, 20.5cm
London £1,500($3,000). 27.XI.75

An Art Nouveau brooch by René Lalique, stamped *Lalique*, *circa* 1900, 7.25cm
London £4,200($7,560). 2.VII.76

René Lalique is perhaps best known for his glassware, produced in such large quantities between the wars that he became a household name. The high point of his career, however, was reached around 1900 when he still showed a deep concern for craftsmanship and had not been tempted to design for mass production. He trained with some of the foremost jewellers in Paris and first became known in the 1880s. By 1900 his style had matured and he was internationally celebrated as one of the leading exponents of the highly fashionable Art Nouveau style, of which this piece of jewellery is a perfect example

From left to right
A pair of enamel-on-copper covered urns, both inscribed *Louis C. Tiffany*, heights 28cm $14,000(£7,000)
Green iridescent Favrile glass vase with alabaster, blue and amber decoration, inscribed *L.C.T.*, circa 1904, height 20.4cm $1,400(£700)
Amber and pink iridescent Favrile glass jack-in-the-pulpit vase, inscribed *L.C. Tiffany Favrile*, circa 1916, height 39.4cm $5,600(£2,800)
Green and brown cypriote vase with amber iridescent latticework decoration, inscribed *L.C.T.*, circa 1900, height 15.2cm $1,900(£950)
Copper and blue iridescent Favrile glass vase with blue collar and foot and green and copper decoration, inscribed *L.C. Tiffany Favrile*, circa 1916, height 15.2cm $2,600(£1,300)

The Tiffany glass illustrated on this page is from the collection of Marion S. Riseman sold in New York on 30 October 1975

458 ART NOUVEAU AND ART DECO

The Scottish Musical Review
Lithographic poster, signed and dated in the block *Chas. R. Mackintosh inv. delt. 1896*, 226cm by 995cm
London £1,700($3,060). 31.III.76
From the Mackintosh Collection, University of Glasgow

Left An unsigned Tiffany Favrile glass and bronze ball lamp, base impressed *Tiffany Studios, New York, 3051, circa* 1899, diameter of shade 26cm, height of base 59cm
Los Angeles $22,000(£12,222). 10.III.76

Jewellery

An emerald and diamond necklace by Meister, the largest emerald weighing 8.50 carats
St Moritz SF300,000(£58,027:$120,000). 20.II.76

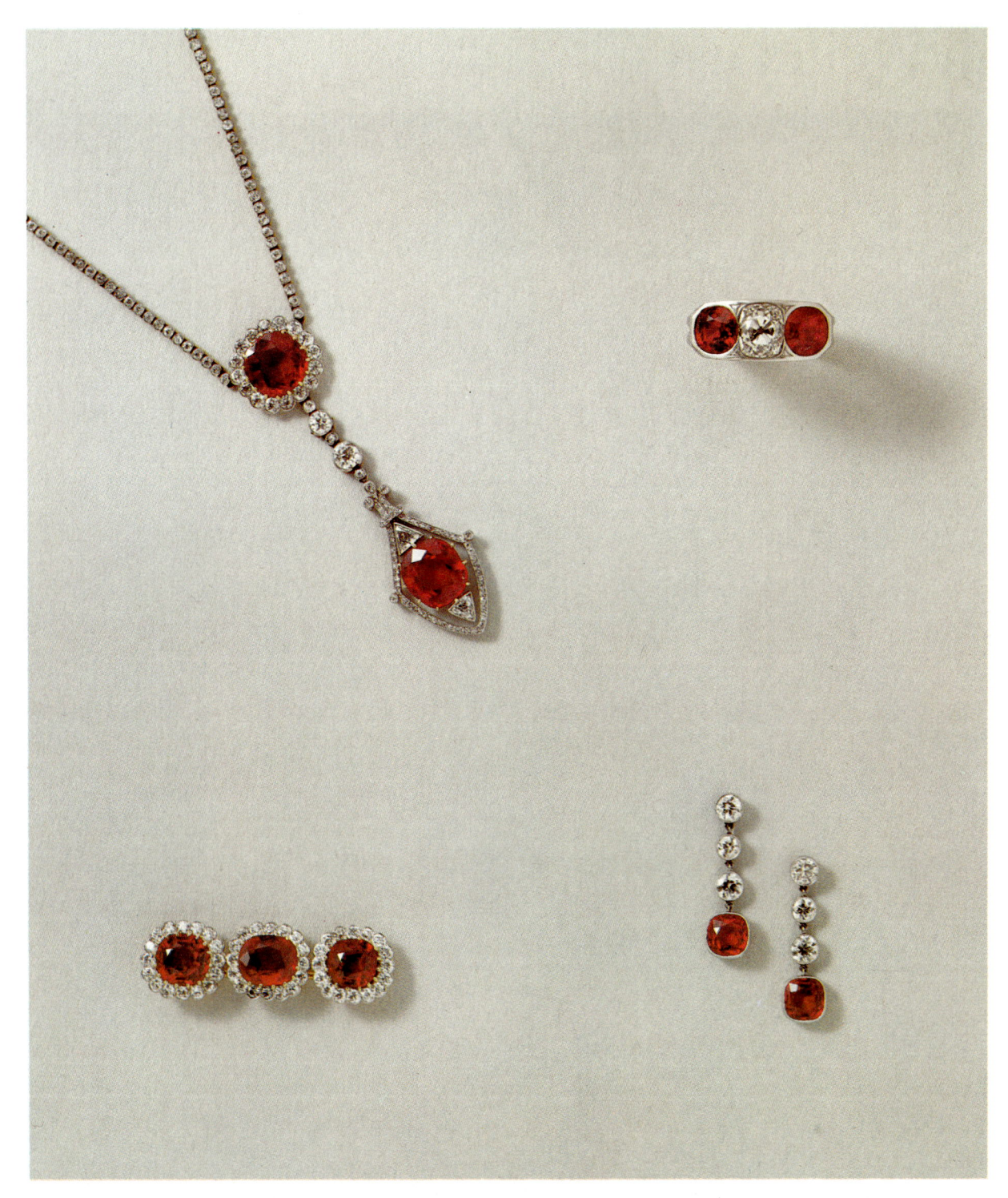

Above left A ruby and diamond necklace set in gold and platinum, the two rubies weighing 12 carats
$330,000(£165,000)
Above right A ruby and diamond ring by Gillot & Co, the two rubies weighing 4.50 carats
$67,500(£33,750)
Below left A ruby and diamond brooch by Gillot & Co, the three rubies weighing 12 carats
$210,000(£105,000)
Below right A pair of ruby and diamond earrings, the mounts set with old-mine diamonds, the rubies weighing 3.75 carats
$82,500(£41,250)

The jewellery illustrated on this page is from the collection of the late Geraldine Rockefeller Dodge sold in New York on 15 October 1975 for a total of $690,000

JEWELLERY 461

Above left A diamond ring by Gillot & Co, the round diamond weighing 3.90 carats $21,000(£10,500)
Above right A diamond ring by Gillot & Co, centring on an old-mine diamond weighing 2.15 carats $11,000(£5,500)
Centre A natural black pearl and diamond pendant by Gillot & Co, the pearl measuring 12mm by 15.3mm $80,000(£40,000)
Below left A pair of diamond earrings $37,000(£18,500)
Below right A diamond pendant, the pear-shaped diamond weighing 26.60 carats $475,000(£237,500)

The jewellery illustrated on this page is from the collection of the late Geraldine Rockefeller Dodge sold in New York on 15 October 1975

462 JEWELLERY

From left to right
A sapphire and diamond ring by J. E. Caldwell & Co, the cushion-shaped sapphire weighing 9.20 carats $36,000(£18,000)
An emerald and diamond bracelet by J. E. Caldwell & Co $28,000(£14,000)
A diamond ring by J. E. Caldwell & Co, the emerald-cut diamond weighing 8.15 carats $105,000(£52,500)
An emerald and diamond ring by J. E. Caldwell & Co, the emerald weighing 4.70 carats $32,000(£16,000)
A ruby and diamond bracelet by J. E. Caldwell & Co $34,000(£17,000)
A ruby and diamond ring, the cushion-shaped ruby weighing 7.90 carats $23,000(£11,500)

The jewellery illustrated on this page is from the collection of the late Ellen Biedlingmaier sold in New York on 10 December 1975

JEWELLERY

Above left A sapphire pendant/necklace, the cushion-shaped sapphire weighing 27 carats on a platinum chain set at intervals with 10 old-mine diamonds weighing 1.50 carats $40,000(£20,000)
Above right A sapphire and diamond ring by Gillot & Co, the cushion-shaped sapphire weighing 2.50 carats, the 2 old-mine diamonds weighing 2.25 carats $13,000(£6,500)
Centre A sapphire and diamond pendant, the cushion-shaped sapphire weighing 40 carats, surrounded by 8 old-mine diamonds weighing 10 carats $300,000(£150,000)
Below left A sapphire ring by Gillot & Co, the round sapphire weighing 12 carats $25,000(£12,500)
Below right A sapphire and diamond ring, the oval cabochon sapphire weighing 18.65 carats $39,000(£19,500)

The jewellery illustrated on this page is from the collection of the late Geraldine Rockefeller Dodge sold in New York on 15 October 1975

An antique sapphire and diamond necklace, the three oval-faceted sapphires weighing a total of 138 carats
New York $210,000(£105,000). 16.X.75

JEWELLERY 465

From left to right
A sapphire ring, the cushion-shaped sapphire weighing 14 carats $36,000(£18,000)
A sapphire and diamond ring, the emerald-cut sapphire weighing 13.80 carats $60,000(£30,000)
A sapphire and diamond ring, the cushion-shaped sapphire weighing 10.70 carats $56,000(£28,000)
A sapphire and diamond brooch, the emerald-cut sapphire weighing 82.65 carats $230,000(£115,000)

The jewellery illustrated on this page was sold in New York on 16 October 1975

Above
An Edwardian black opal and diamond crescent brooch £1,500($2,700)
Centre from left to right
A Victorian diamond brooch/pendant £12,000($21,600). From the collection of Mrs Victor Sassoon
An emerald and diamond clip brooch £10,500($18,900)
A Victorian turquoise and diamond oval cluster brooch £2,800($5,040)
From the collection of Mrs A. E. Dennis
Below from left to right
An Edwardian black opal brooch £2,200($3,960)
A cushion-shaped sapphire of mixed cutting weighing 14.08 carats £7,000($12,600)
An Edwardian ruby and diamond brooch £2,300($4,140)

The jewellery illustrated on this page was sold in London on 20 May 1976

JEWELLERY 467

A ruby and diamond necklace £8,000($14,400)
A black opal and diamond brooch £4,200($7,560)
A step-cut emerald weighing 5.63 carats £22,000($39,600)
A step-cut diamond weighing 11.63 carats set solitaire as a ring £28,000($50,400)

The jewellery illustrated on this page was sold in London on 22 January 1976

468 JEWELLERY

From left to right
A cat's eye ring, the oval cat's eye weighing 25.80 carats SF110,000(£20,183:$42,307)
An Art Deco bracelet with carved rubies, emeralds and sapphires and round and baguette diamonds mounted in platinum and gold SF18,000(£3,302:$6,923)
An alexandrite ring, the cushion-cut alexandrite weighing 5.12 carats SF42,000(£7,706:$16,154)

The jewellery illustrated on this page was sold in Zürich on 7 November 1975

JEWELLERY 469

A diamond necklace by Cartier, the centre diamond weighing 6.09 carats SF160,000(£29,357:$61,538)
A diamond ring, the oval cushion-cut diamond weighing 14.25 carats SF340,000(£62,385:$130,769)
A diamond ring, the round diamond weighing 11.51 carats SF95,000(£17,431:$36,538)

The jewellery illustrated on this page was sold in Zürich on 6 November 1975

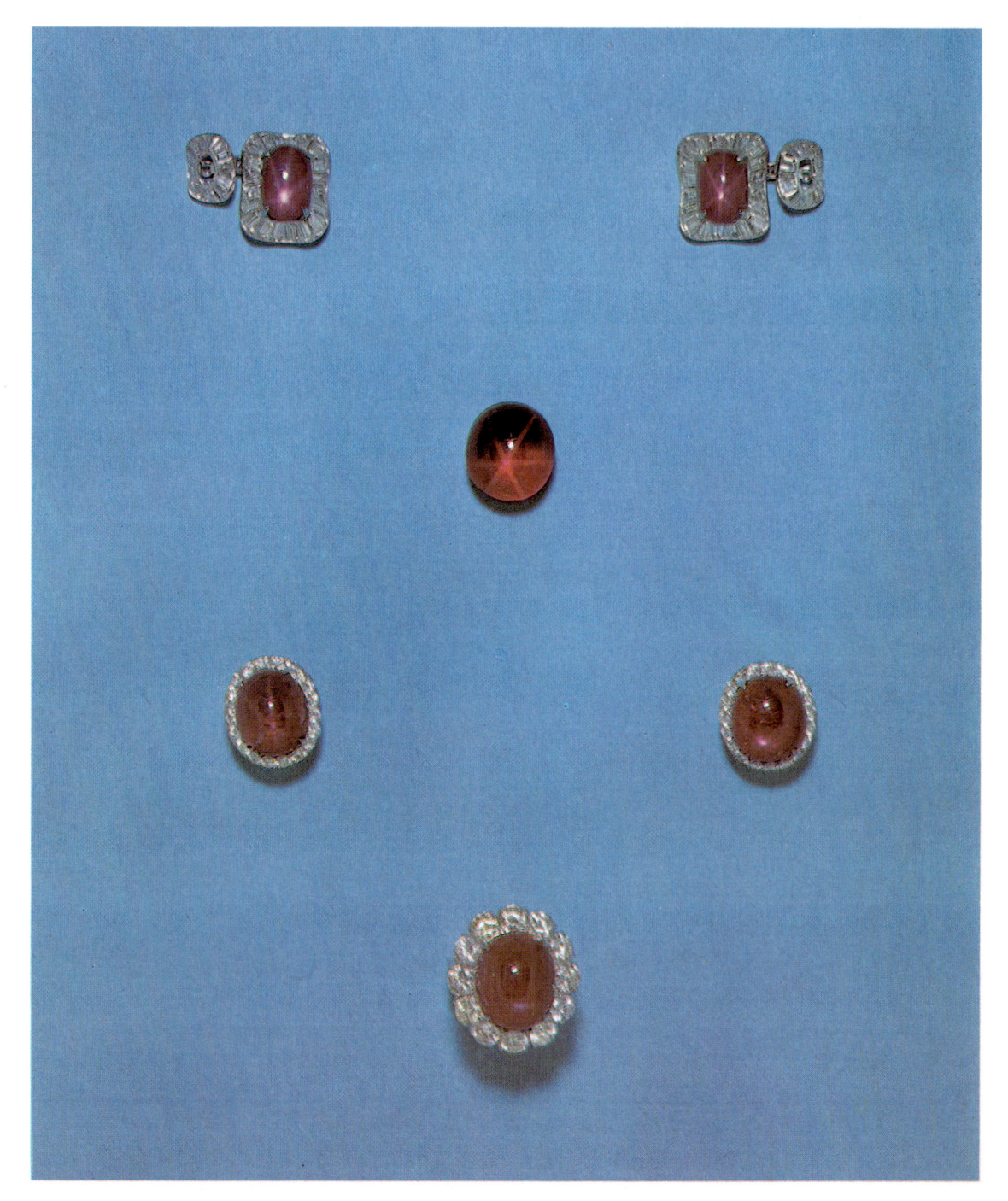

From top to bottom
A pair of ruby and diamond cuff links, the rubies weighing 14 carats £4,500($9,000)
A star ruby weighing 26.66 carats £46,000($92,000)
A cabochon ruby and diamond cluster ring, the ruby weighing 15 carats and a pair of star ruby and diamond earrings, the rubies weighing 22 carats £7,200($14,400)

The jewellery illustrated on this page was sold in Hong Kong on 18 November 1975

JEWELLERY

1. An emerald and diamond ring, the emerald weighing 25 carats, New York $36,000(£18,000). 15.X.75. **2.** An emerald ring, the emerald weighing 7.49 carats, Hong Kong £53,000($106,000). 18.XI.75. **3.** An emerald ring, the emerald weighing 10.65 carats, New York $110,000(£61,111). 28.IV.76. **4.** A late Victorian emerald and diamond ring, London £4,300($7,740). 25.III.76. **5.** A cabochon ruby and diamond ring, the ruby weighing 5.75 carats, Hong Kong £4,500($9,000). 18.XI.75. **6.** A sapphire ring, the sapphire weighing 16 carats, New York $62,000(£34,444). 28.IV.76. **7.** A ruby ring, the ruby weighing 26.40 carats, Hong Kong £26,000($52,000). 18.XI.75. **8.** A ruby ring, the ruby weighing 7.25 carats, New York $230,000(£127,777). 28.IV.76. **9.** A lilac pink step-cut diamond weighing 24.44 carats, Zurich SF2,700,000(£600,000:$1,088,710). 6.V.76. **10.** A diamond ring by Trabert & Hoeffer, Mauboussin, the diamond weighing 24.25 carats, New York $210,000(£105,000). 16.X.75. **11.** A late nineteenth-century Russian sapphire and diamond brooch, London £6,000($12,000). 16.X.75. **12.** The Jonker diamond, number four, mounted as a ring by Harry Winston, the diamond weighing 30.70 carats, New York $570,000(£285,000). 16.X.75

472 JEWELLERY

A ruby and diamond collar
London £52,000($104,000). 11.XII.75
From the collection of Miss M. Benton

Glass and Paperweights

A Clichy flat bouquet weight, $3\frac{1}{4}$in
London £1,700($3,400).
24.XI.75

A Clichy bouquet weight, $2\frac{7}{8}$in
London £3,000($5,400). 12.VII.76

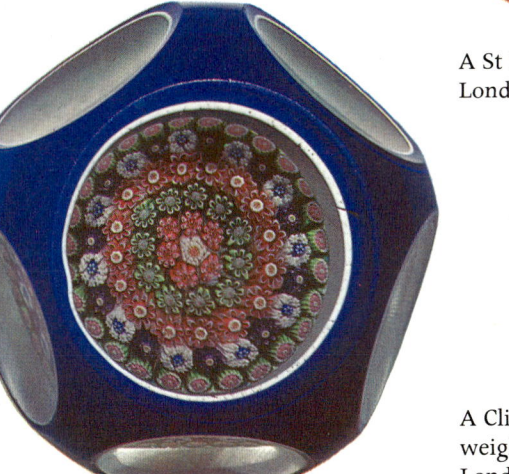

A St Louis pom-pom weight, $2\frac{5}{8}$in
London £2,250($4,050). 12.VII.76

A Clichy dark-blue overlay weight, $2\frac{7}{8}$in
London £1,200($2,160). 12.VII.76

GLASS

A Bohemian wheel-engraved royal portrait beaker by the 'Master of the Koula beaker', Riesengebirge, circa 1690, height 4⅜in
London £3,100($6,200). 15.XII.75

A Venetian enamelled armorial bowl, bearing the coat-of-arms of a Medici Pope, 1513-34, height 6½in
London £4,800($8,640). 23.II.76

A Venetian 'Calcedonio' flask, seventeenth century, height 9⅜in
London £720($1,440). 15.XII.75

A Silesian wheel-engraved goblet, attributed to Christian Gottfried Schneider, Warmbrunn, circa 1755, height 9in
London £1,700($3,060). 12.VII.76
From the collection of Miss Elisabeth Bergner

A Mughal enamelled hookah base, early eighteenth century, height 6¾in
London £700($1,260). 3.V.76

A *façon de Venise* serpent-stem flute, Low Countries, seventeenth century, height 11⅜in
London £1,100($1,980). 23.II.76

GLASS 475

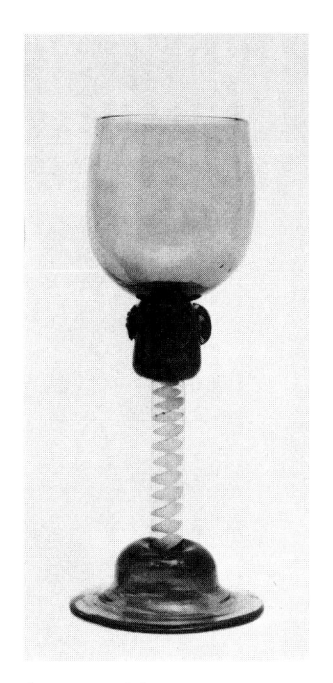

A composite-stem green-bowled wine glass, *circa* 1750, height 6¼in
London £350($700).
24.XI.75

A goblet inscribed with *Prosperity to Fox Hunting, circa* 1760, height 8in
London £540($972). 3.V.76
From the collection of
Mrs C. M. E. Hornsby

A wine glass set on a hollow four-sided Silesian stem, *circa* 1715, height 6in
London £800($1,600). 15.XII.75

A portrait goblet of James, 20th Earl of Kildare and 1st Duke of Leinster, *circa* 1760, height 7⅛in
London £850($1,530). 3.V.76

A blue-glass Masonic decanter and stopper, *circa* 1765, height 11⅜in
London £850($1,700). 24.XI.75
From the collection of
Mrs E. A. Essex

A 'Ravenscroft' silver-mounted engraved decanter jug, the silver marked The Hague, 1681, height 10⅝in
London £2,200($3,960). 3.V.76

A Woodall three-colour cameo-glass vase signed *Geo Woodall, circa* 1885, height 10in
London £12,000($21,600). 8.VII.76

A Webb cameo-glass vase entitled *The Muses*, by Thomas and George Woodall, *circa* 1885, height 8in
New York $38,500(£19,250). 9.XII.75
From the collection of Louis Winer

A Venetian enamelled armorial ewer, bearing the coat-of-arms of a Medici Pope, 1513-34, height 8in
London £2,100($4,200). 15.XII.75

Wine Sales

The Wine Department in London has completed its most successful season since it began in 1970, holding eighteen sales in the United Kingdom and three overseas. Net sales reached £1,093,864. In October 1975 and May 1976 sales at Sotheby Mak van Waay in Amsterdam were very well attended and their total value was Fl757,311(£144,794). In February 1976 a sale of some of the finest wines that South Africa produces was conducted on behalf of Stellenbosch Wine Farmers near Paarl, with a turnover of R174,655(£105,851).

Generally the market for fine wines, especially those now considered rare, has risen. Prices at London auctions are now about 30 per cent to 40 per cent above those attained last season for similar wines. Younger vintages of Bordeaux, Burgundy, the Rhine, Moselle and Port are obtaining better prices, but the upward trend has been relatively slow. Until international demand for fine wine improves or their

From left to right
A rare sealed wine bottle, the shoulder applied with a dolphin seal, early nineteenth century London £200($360). 21.V.76
Château Montrose 1870 (three bottles) London £155($279). 21.V.76
Renault Cognac 1910 (three bottles) London £40($72). 21.V.76
Waterloo Port 1815 (one bottle) London £40($72). 21.V.76
Château Pétrus 1920 (three bottles) London £160($288). 21.V.76

production is decreased, the present surpluses of red, white and rosé wine of adequate quality will inhibit further price increases at auction for the younger vintages. This advantage to buyers will continue for some time.

Paradoxically, it will not pay growers to improve quality for a future market, because the return on their investment is barely adequate. Recent price increases at the vineyard, in the order of 50 per cent, will not effect the consumer for two years.

During the season, some of the more interesting items to have come under the hammer were one bottle Ch. d'Yquem 1847, £130($234); three bottles Ch. Pétrus 1961, £92($165); one bottle Ch. Lafite 1868, £130($234); two magnums Ch. Latour 1929, £265($477); six magnums Bollinger 1934, disgorged April 1976, £205($369); one bottle Waterloo Port 1815, £40($72); and a bottle Terrantez Vintage Madeira 1795, £72($130).

Collectors' items, including corkscrews, cellar equipment, bottles and books, continued to attract enthusiastic buyers. An auction record was broken when a Royal Club single lever corkscrew, patented by Charles Hull of Birmingham in 1864, reached a price of £185($370). Other interesting corkscrews included a late eighteenth-century Dutch folding silver corkscrew at £140($252); an example of Robert Jones' first registered design from 1840, £150($270); and an Eclipse brass bar corkscrew, £155($279).

Brass single lever corkscrew, marked J.B. & Sons
London £165($330). 1.X.75

Left
Charles Hull's Royal Club patent single lever corkscrew
London £185($370). 1.X.75

Photographs

JOSEPH CUNDALL and ROBERT HOWLETT
Trumpeter Gritten and Trumpeter Lang at Woolwich
Albumen print, early 1856, 254mm by 207mm
London £900($1,620). 19.III.76

The photograph was taken on the occasion of the visit to Woolwich by Queen Victoria and Prince Albert to witness the arrival of troops of the Royal Artillery from the Crimea

ROGER FENTON
Rivaulx Abbey, looking north
Salt print from a waxed paper negative, mounted on folio card, titled in ink and with the embossed stamp *R. Fenton*, 1854–55, 346mm by 297mm
London £1,000($1,800). 19.III.76

BARON DE MEYER
Self portrait
Circa 1902, 240mm by 190mm
New York $1,050(£583). 4.V.76

EDWARD S. CURTIS
The North American Indian
20 volumes of text illustrated with 1500 full-page photogravures, approximately 40 in colour, each volume supplemented by an elephant folio with at least 36 photogravures
New York $60,000(£33,353). 4.V.76

Collectors' Sales

An Edison Amberola 1A
phonograph, serial no. 1923,
American, *circa* 1909-11,
height 4ft 1in
London £1,100($2,200). 2.XII.75

From left to right
A flower-girl automaton, German, early twentieth century, height 1ft 8in
London £650($1,170). 14.VII.76

A cymbalist automata, the bisque-headed doll impressed on the back *Vte Jumeau S.G.D.G., 4.*, French, late nineteenth century, height 1ft 7in
London £850($1,530). 14.VII.76

A dancing-girl automaton, French, early twentieth century, height 1ft 10in
London £800($1,440). 14.VII.76

From left to right
A gilt-metal clock automaton, the two-train movement stamped on the back plate *H.L.*, French, *circa* 1900, height 2ft 2in
London £1,100($1,980). 14.VII.76

A magician's 'cups and balls' clock automaton, the two-train movement signed *P. Garnier, Paris*, French, late nineteenth century, height 1ft 9in
London £1,500($2,700). 14.VII.76

Index

Aarne, Johann Victor 258
Achenbach, Andreas 88
Adams, George 450
Affleck, Thomas 412
Aghaphir 192
Albertinelli, Mariotto 21
Albertszenn, Jost 282
Alexander, William 48–53
Alken, Henry, Snr 63
Amati, Antonius and Hieronymous 454
Angarano 392, 394
Angas, George French 98, 101
Annigoni, Pietro 84
Ashbee, Charles Robert 455
Aspertini, Amico 39
Astbury-Whieldon 378
Atkinson, Robert 290
Augustin, Jean-Baptiste 277
Avelli, Francesco Xanto 392
Avercamp, Hendrick 24
Azima, Muhammad 193

Bacon, Francis 167
Baines, Thomas 99
Bakst, Léon 146, 149, 151
Balzac, Edmé Pierre 284
Barlach, Ernst 403
Baronneau 449
Barraud, Charles Decimus 99
Barrauds 450
Barye, Antoine-Louis 113, 251
Baudesson, Daniel 261
Beccafumi, Domenico 46
Beckmann, Max 182
Benton, Thomas Hart 125
Besche, Lucien 267
Beyard, Nicholas 223
Bierstadt, Albert 121
Bilston enamel 266
Bloemaert, Abraham 41
Böcklin, Arnold 94
Bol, Hans 25
Boldini, Giovanni 142
Bonheur, Isadore-Jules 251
Bonheur, Rosa 66, 70–72
Bonnard, Pierre 231
Bouguereau, William Adolphe 94
Boulle, André-Charles 426, 427
Boullemier, A. 402
Bourdillon, Augustin 449
Bourgoin, François Jules 103

Bow porcelain 388
Bradbury, Joseph 453
Breitner, George Hendrik 96
Breton, Jean-François 262
Bristol porcelain 388, 389
Brockbanks 448
Brome, Richard 224
Brookshaw, G. 210
Browning, Elizabeth Barrett 223
Brueghal, Jan the Elder 24
Brueghel, Pieter Pietersz. 10
Brunfels, O. 202
Brussels tapestry 424
Bugiardini, Giuliano 21
Buonarroti, Michelangelo 43
Burne-Jones, Sir Edward 78, 438, 441, 442
Buron, Pierre-Etienne 263
Bustelli, Franz Anton 398
Byron, Lord 217

Caffiéri, Philippe 447
Caldwell, J. E. & Co. 462
Canton enamel 423
Capodimonte porcelain 396, 397
Cardew, Michael 404
Carlevaris, Luca 33
Carpeaux, Jean-Baptiste 249
Carr, Alwyn 291
Cartier 469
Castelli 394
Cézanne, Paul 140
Chagall, Marc 144
Chalon, John James 186
Chambers, Jonathan 446
Chantilly porcelain 399
Chantrey, Sir Francis 299
Chao Tso 364
Charlier, Jacques 263
Chelsea porcelain 389, 390
Ch'êng Hua 359
Ch'ên Shun 364
Chia Ching 354, 357, 360
Chippendale 411, 412
Chlebnikov, Ivan 257
Choki, Eishosai 375
Chün-yao 348
Churchill, John Spencer 85
Claesz, Pieter 28
Clichy 473
Cocteau, Jean 150
Colt revolver 305

Condliff, James 446
Cooper, Alexander 276
Corradini, Antonio 242
Cotterill, Edmund 299
Crespel, Sebastian and James 281
Crichton, Alexander 290
Crosse, Lawrence 278
Crowe, Eyre 77
Culpeper 450
Cundall, Joseph 481
Curtis, Edward S. 482
Cushing and White 411

da Bologna, Giovanni 244
Dali, Salvador 161
Dallin, Cyrus Edwin 119
da Mariano, Pellegrino 20
Dasson, Henry 434
d'Autel, Amelie d'Aubigny, née 278
Dearle, J. H. 442
Debèche, Gérard 265
de Brailes, William 197
Dee, Henry William and Louis 267
Degas, Edgar 136
de Lamerie, Paul 281
Delft 394
de Meyer, Baron 482
De Morgan, William 404
Denby and Condor Park 403
Diaz de la Peña, Narcisse-Virgile 129
di Fruosino, Bartolomeo 19
Doomer, Lambert 44
Drais, Pierre-François 265
Drouais, François-Hubert 29
Dubuc 445
Dubufe, Edouard Louis 64
Dubuffet, Jean 162
Ducrollay, Jean 263
Dupré, Louis 232
Dürer, Albrecht 43

Edison 483
Ehret 226
Ekels, Jan the Elder 86
Elizabeth I, Queen of England 216
Engleheart, George 278
Ernst, Max 181, 229

Fabergé 256, 258, 259
Faust, Isaac 302
Fenton, Roger 482
Ferneley, John, Snr 62

Ferogio 207
Firdausi 290
Fitzgerald, Edward 230
Flaxman, John 280
Flinck, Govaert 42
Fogelberg, Andrew 280
Forrest, Charles Ramus 98
Foullet, Pierre-Antoine 432
Fournié, Johann George Daniel 283
Fragonard, Jean-Honoré 46
Francis, Sam 172
Fraser, James Earl 116
French, Daniel Chester 108
Freud, Lucian 80
Frey, Johann Jacob 420
Fritzsche, Georg 400
Frodsham, Charles 448
Fryers, Sir John, Bt 302

Gabriël, Paul Joseph Constantin 96
Gainsborough, Thomas 58, 59
Ganbun 370
Garneray, Ambrose Louis 187
Garnier, P. 485
Garrard, R. & S. & Co. 299, 301
Garrard, Robert 301
Gauguin, Paul 135, 138, 140, 184
Gerome, L. 248
Giacometti, Alberto 165
Gilbert, Stephen 280
Giles, James 391
Gillot & Co. 460, 461
Gleizes, Albert 157
Goltzius, Hendrick 42
Gorky, Arshile 170
Goya y Lucientes, Francisco José de 176, 177
Graham, George 445
Grant, Charles 292
Gricci, Giuseppe 396, 397
Guardi, Francesco 34

Hadley, James 402
Hakuryu, Unsho 370
Hallifax, John 446
Hamada, Shoji 407
Harris, Lawren Stewart 105
Haydn, Joseph 219
Heath, George 300
Heath, Thomas 450
Helmhack, Abraham 394
Helmcke, Hinrich 302
Henkels, Jan 444
Henry, Edward Lamson 112
Herat carpets 332, 333
Herez carpets 331, 336, 337
Herring, John Frederick, Snr 62
Hilliard, Nicholas 276
Hiroshige, Ando 375
Höchst 399
Hockney, David 169
Hodgkins, Frances 81
Holiday, Henry G. 441
Hollming, August 259
Holmström, August 258
Horenbout, Gerard ii, 194, 196
Houdon, Jean-Antoine 109
Howlett, Robert 481

Hsüan Tê 350, 351, 352, 356
Hull, Charles 480
Hunt & Roskell 291
Hunt, John S. 291
Hurd, Jacob 287

Il Parmigianino, Francesco Maria Mazzola, called 38
Il Salviati, Giuseppe Porta, called 37
Israëls, Isaäc Lazarus 97

Jackson, Alexander Young 104
Jackson, Orlando 294
Jihei, Sugimura 376
Jones, Thomas 55
Jongkind, Johan Barthold 17
Joren, Hokutei 376
Josephus 215

Kaendler, J. J. 398, 401
Kajikawa 371
Kakiemon 365, 366, 367, 368, 369
K'ang Hsi 361
Kauba, Carl 127
Kaulbach, Hermann 93
Kibel, Wolf 100
Kipling, Rudyard 230
Klee, Paul 180, 184
Knibb, Joseph 444, 445
Kobel, Johan 227
Koekkoek, Barend Cornelis 92
Ko-Kutani 369
Kowalski, Alfred von Wierus 91
Kuba carpets 335
Kusder, Henry 453
Kyusai, Tetsugendo 370

Lalique, René 456
Lambeth delft 378
Lanceray, Eugène 250
Landseer, Sir Edwin 69, 73
Leach, Bernard 407
Léger, Fernand 155, 159
le Guay, Etienne-Charles 277
Leigh, William Robinson 122
Leighton, Frederick, Lord 75
Lenzburg faience 420
Lévy-Dhurmer, Lucien 94
Lewis, H. & Co. 300
Lewis, John Frederick 56
L'Heritier de Brutelle 205
Lichtenstein, Roy 168
Limoges enamel 247
Lindley, J. 212
Linke, F. 435
Linthorst, Jacobus 28
Lipchitz, Jacques 165
Lodowick, Charles 223
London delft 378
London enamel 266
Longus 231
Lorenzi, Battista 245
Lory, Gabriel Ludwig 187
Lo Schiavone, Andrea Meldolla called 39
Louis, Jean-Jacob 400
Louis, Morris 173

Lowry, Laurence Stephen 85
Lück, Johann Friedrich 399
Ludwigsburg porcelain 400
Lund 445

McCabe, James 445
Mackintosh, Charles Rennie 437, 458
Maclise, Daniel 77
Madox Brown, Ford 438
Magny, Alexis 447
Maimonides, Moses 214
Malnazar 192
Manet, Edouard 130
Manetti, S. 189
Mantegna, Andrea 36
Marieschi, Michele 35
Maris, Jacob Hendricus 97
Marshall, Ben 63
Masanao ʃ 371
Masateru, Kaigyokudo 371
Master of the Koula beaker 474
Master of the Magdalen Legend 20
Matisse, Henri 149
Mauboussin 471
Meissen porcelain 398, 399, 400, 401
Meister 459
Mennecy porcelain 396, 398
Meryon, Charles 181
Mesdag, Hendrik Willem 88
Meyer, Jeremiah 278
Millet, Jean-François 128
Ming Dynasty 350, 351, 356, 357, 358, 359, 413
Minton porcelain 402
Miró, Joan 161
Monamy, Peter 58
Mondrian, Piet 158
Monet, Claude 132
Moore, Henry 81, 82
Morandi, Giorgio 180
Morgan, John 76
Morrice, James Wilson 105
Mortimer & Hunt 299
Morton, Alfred 453
Moser, George Michael 260, 448
Mount, William Sidney 124
Muhammad 'Ali Ashraf 342
Munch, Edvard 175, 185
Murdoch, Jo. 305
Murray, John Fairfax 78
Murray, William Staite- 404
Musy père et fils 445

Nabeshima ware 368
Nagayoshi, Bishu 372
Nash, Paul 80
Nasr Allah Imami 342
Neuber, Johann Christian 265
Nichols and Plinke 290
Nicholson, Ben 83
Noland, Kenneth 173
North, Dudley 218
Northcote, James 226
Northern Ch'i Dynasty 344
Nuremberg faience 394
Nuyen, Wijnand Jan Joseph 89
Nymphenburg porcelain 398

Oliver, Isaac 276
Ortega, Martin Rico y 92
Otoman 370
Otto, Jacob Hinrich 302
Ouderogge, Cornelis 306
Ouwater, Isaak 86

Palizzi, Filippo 93
Palmer, Samuel 55
Panini, Giovanni Paolo 33
Parkinson and Frodsham 448
Passenger, Fred 404
Payne, Claude 286
Peale, Rembrandt 120
Perchin, Michael 259
Persian carpets 329, 330
Peter I, Emperor of Russia 216
Picasso, Pablo 163, 183
Pleyard, Pierre-Nicolas 262
Podie, Peter 287
Portal, Abraham 295
Post, Frans 26
Prattware 378
Proctor, A. Phimister 117, 126

Qâsim 'Ali Qâ'Inî 450
Quare, Daniel 444

Rackham, Arthur 234
Ramsden, Omar 291
Ravenscroft glass 475
Rayner, Stephen 444
Redouté, P. J. 207, 209
Reimers, Harmen Antoni 287
Rellahes 449
Rembrandt, Harmensz. van Rijn 179
Reme 408
Remington, Frederic 123
Remond, Jean-George 264
Renoir, Pierre-Auguste 131, 134
Revere, Paul Jnr 280
Ricci, Marco 178
Richmond, George 59, 188
Riopelle, Jean-Paul 170
Rivers, Larry 171
Rodin, Auguste 164
Rothenstein, Sir William 80
Rothko, Mark 166
Rouault, Georges 152
Rousseau, Etienne-Pierre-Théodore 95, 129
Royal Doulton 404
Rubens, Sir Peter Paul 40
Rugendas, Johann Mauritz 102
Ruhlmann 437
Ruskin pottery 404

Saftleven, Cornelis 43
St Jerome 221
St Louis 473
Salmon, Robert 58
Saverij, Roelant Jacobsz. 16
Schlemmer, Oskar 154
Schneider, Christian Gottfried 474
Schouten, Hubert Pieter 45
Seba, A. 208
Seymour, James 60
Shakespeare, William 222, 224
Shang Dynasty 345
Shaw, John 452
Shaw, John Byam Liston 79
Shepherd, David 84
Shepherd, Henry 294
Shermann, Welby 188
Shiraz carpets 326
Shoyo 371
Sibthorp, J. 212
Signac, Paul 141
Sisley, Alfred 133
Smart, John 277
Smith, Benjamin III 292
Smith, J. E. 212
Soko, Morita 370
Solon, Marc Louis 402
Springer, Cornelius 87
Staffordshire porcelain 403
Steimer, Jacob 452
Stenkjondalen, Ellef J. 452
Stephan, Pierre 388
Stradivari, Antonio 451, 454
Stubbs, George 61, 186
Studio, Hendrik van Lint called 32, 35
Sung Dynasty 348
Sweert, E. 200

T'ang Dynasty 347
Telford, Thomas 217
Teniers, David the Younger 25
Theobalds, William 290
Thomson, Tom 104
Tiepolo, Giovanni Domenico 30, 31, 46, 47
Tiffany & Co. 290
Tiffany Studios 457, 458
Tissot, James Joseph 74
Titian, Tiziano Vecello called 22
Tobey, Mark 174
Tokoku 370
Tomokazu 370
Tomoyoshi, Hitotsuyanagi 372
Tompion, Thomas 443, 445, 446
Toulouse-Lautrec, Henri de 137, 181
Toun, Ikkosai 370
Toyamasa 370

Trabert & Hoeffer 471
Treffler, Johann Christoph 283
Troubetskoy, Prince Paul 250
Turner, Joseph William Mallord 57

Urbino 392
Utrillo, Maurice 153

van den Hecken, Abraham 14
van de Velde, Adriaen 42
van der Heyden, Jan Jansz. 10
van Dongen, Kees 143, 145
van Everdingen, Allaert 42
van Gogh, Vincent 139
van Mieris, Frans the Elder 27
van Ostade, Adriaen 11, 283
Vassadel, Charles 286
Vaucher 449
Verlaine, Paul 231
Verschuur, Wouterus 90
Vesalius, Andreas 227
Vienna porcelain 408
Villon, Jacques 156
von Geer, Maximilian 268–275
von Jacquin, N. J. 213
von Kaiserberg, Johann Geiler 234
Vulliamy, Justin 444
Vyse, Charles 404

Wan Li 358
Warhol, Andy 172
Washington, George 218
Watteau, Jean-Antoine 178
Webb, Philip 438
Webb glass 477
Wedgwood & Bentley 280, 380–387
Wedgwood 379–387
Weissenbruch, Johannes 89
Weisweiler, Adam 431, 433
Western Chou Dynasty 345
Westley Richards 306
Wigström, Henrik 259
Wimar, Carl 103
Winston, Harry 471
Wood, Ralph 377
Woodall, George 476, 477
Woodall, Thomas 477
Woolf, Virginia 219
Worcester porcelain 389, 391, 402, 403

Young, James 294
Ysenbrandt, Adriaen 23
Yüan Dynasty 355
Yung Chêng 362, 363

Zuccarelli, Francesco 32